CURRENCY INTERVENTIONS, FLUCTUATIONS AND ECONOMIC ISSUES

CURRENCY INTERVENTIONS, FLUCTUATIONS AND ECONOMIC ISSUES

L. C. HILBERT
EDITOR

Nova Science Publishers, Inc.
New York

For permission to use material from this book please contact us:
Telephone 631-231-7269; Fax 631-231-8175
Web Site: http://www.novapublishers.com

Library of Congress Cataloging-in-Publication Data

Currency interventions, fluctuations and economic issues / Lawrence C. Hilbert (editor)
p. cm.
ISBN: 978-1-60456-078-7 (hardcover)
1. foreign exchange. 2. Money. 3 International economic relations. 4. Monetary policy. I. Hilbert, Lawrence C.
HG3851.C774 2007
332.4'5--dc22

2007040370

Published by Nova Science Publishers, Inc. ✣ New York

CONTENTS

PREFACE

A currency is a unit of exchange, facilitating the transfer of goods and services. It is one form of money, where money is anything that serves as a medium of exchange, a store of value, and a standard of value. A currency zone is a country or region in which a specific currency is the dominant medium of exchange. To facilitate trade between currency zones, there are exchange rates, which are the prices at which currencies (and the goods and services of individual currency zones) can be exchanged against each other. Currencies can be classified as either floating currencies or fixed currencies based on their exchange rate regime. In common usage, currency sometimes refers to only paper money, as in coins and currency, but this is misleading. Coins and paper money are both forms of currency.

In most cases, each country has monopoly control over the supply and production of its own currency. Member countries of the European Union's Economic and Monetary Union are a notable exception to this rule, as they have ceded control of monetary policy to the European Central Bank.

This new book presents the latest developments in this crucial field of international relations.

Chapter 1 - The continued rise in China's trade surplus with the United States and the world, and complaints from U.S. manufacturing firms and workers over the competitive challenges posed by Chinese imports have led several Members to call for a more aggressive U.S. stance against certain Chinese trade policies they deem to be unfair. Among these is the value of the Chinese yuan relative to the dollar. From 1994 to July 2005, China pegged its currency to the U.S. dollar at about 8.28 yuan to the dollar. On July 21, 2005, China announced it would let its currency immediately appreciate by 2.1% (to 8.11 yuan per dollar) and link its currency to a basket of currencies (rather than just to the dollar). Many Members complain that the yuan has only appreciated only modestly (about 7%) since these reforms were implemented and that China continues to "manipulate" its currency in order to give its exporters an unfair trade advantage, and that this policy has led to U.S. job losses. Numerous bills were introduced in the 109th Congress to address China's currency policy, and these efforts have continued in the 110th session.

If the yuan is undervalued against the dollar (as many analysts believe), there are likely to be both benefits and costs to the U.S. economy. It would mean that imported Chinese goods are cheaper than they would be if the yuan were market determined. This lowers prices for U.S. consumers and dampens inflationary pressures. It also lowers prices for U.S. firms that use imported inputs (such as parts) in their production, making such firms more competitive.

When the U.S. runs a trade deficit with the Chinese, this requires a capital inflow from China to the United States. This, in turn, lowers U.S. interest rates and increases U.S. investment spending. On the negative side, lower priced goods from China may hurt U.S. industries that compete with those products, reducing their production and employment. In addition, an undervalued yuan makes U.S. exports to China more expensive, thus reducing the level of U.S. exports to China and job opportunities for U.S. workers in those sectors. However, in the long run, trade can affect only the composition of employment, not its overall level. Thus, inducing China to appreciate its currency would likely benefit some U.S. economic sectors, but would harm others.

Critics of China's currency policy point to the large and growing U.S. trade deficit ($233 billion in 2006) with China as evidence that the yuan is undervalued and harmful to the U.S. economy. The relationship is more complex, for a number of reasons. First, an increasing level of Chinese exports are from foreign-invested companies in China that have shifted production there to take advantage of China's abundant low cost labor. Second, the deficit masks the fact that China has become one of the fastest growing markets for U.S. exports. Finally, the trade deficit with China accounted for 26% of the sum of total U.S. bilateral trade deficits in 2006, indicating that the overall U.S. trade deficit is not caused by the exchange rate policy of one country, but rather the shortfall between U.S. saving and investment. That being said, there are a number of valid economic arguments why China should adopt a more flexible currency policy. For a brief summary of this report, see CRS Report RS21625, *China's Currency: A Summary of the Economic Issues*, by Wayne M. Morrison and Marc Labonte. This report will be updated as events warrant.

Chapter 2 - Japan's intervention to slow the upward appreciation of the yen has raised concerns in the United States and brought charges that Tokyo is manipulating its exchange rate in order to gain unfair advantage in world trade. This coincides with similar charges being made with respect to the currencies of the People's Republic of China and South Korea. In the 110th Congress, H.R. 2886 (Knollenberg)/S. 1021(Stabenow) (Japan Currency Manipulation Act), H.R. 782 (Tim Ryan)/S. 796 (Bunning) (Fair Currency Act of 2007), S. 1677 (Dodd) (Currency Reform and Financial Markets Access Act of 2007), and S. 1607 (Baucus) (Currency Exchange Rate Oversight Reform Act of 2007) address currency misalignment in general or by Japan in particular.

In the past, Japan has intervened (bought dollars and sold yen) extensively to counter the yen's appreciation, but since March 2004, the Japanese government has not intervened significantly, although some claim that Tokyo continues to "talk down the value of the yen." This heavy buying of dollars has resulted in an accumulation of official foreign exchange reserves that exceeded a record $893 billion (June 2007) by Japan. The intervention, however, seems to have had little lasting effect. It may only have slowed the rise in value of the yen rather than reverse its direction of change. For the past few years, the yen has been depreciating and is now at a 20-year low. Estimates on the cumulative effect of the interventions range from an undervaluation of the yen of about 3 or 4 yen to as much as 20 yen per dollar. Private company estimates of the misalignment of the yen range from an overvaluation of 1.8% to an underevaluation of 29%. The median value of these estimates is that the yen is about 15% undervalued, but it is not known how much of the undervaluation resulted from market forces and how much from intervention.

In 2006, the U.S. Secretary of the Treasury indicated that it had not found currency manipulation by any country, including by Japan. An April 2005 report by the Government Accountability Office reported that Treasury had not found currency manipulation because it viewed "Japan's exchange rate interventions as part of a macroeconomic policy aimed at combating deflation..." In its May 2006 report on consultations with Japan, the International Monetary Fund (IMF), likewise, did not find currency manipulation by Japan. The criteria for finding currency manipulation, however, allows for considerable leeway by Treasury and the IMF.

One problem with the focus on currency intervention to correct balance of trade deficits is that only about half of the increase in the value of a foreign currency is reflected in prices of imports into the United States. Periods of heaviest intervention also coincided with slower (not faster) economic growth rates for Japan.

Major policy options for Congress include (1) let the market adjust ; (2) clarify the definition of currency manipulation; (3) require negotiations and reports; (4) require the President to certify which countries are manipulating their currencies and take remedial action if the manipulation is not halted; (5) take the case to the World Trade Organization or appeal to the IMF; or (6) oppose any change in governance in the IMF benefitting Japan. This report will be updated as circumstances require.

Chapter 3 - The United States has accused the Democratic People's Republic of Korea (DPRK or North Korea) of counterfeiting U.S. $100 Federal Reserve notes (supernotes) and passing them off in various countries. This is one of several illicit activities by North Korea apparently done to generate foreign exchange that is used to purchase imports or finance government activities abroad.

Although Pyongyang denies complicity in any counterfeiting operation, at least $45 million in such supernotes of North Korean origin have been detected in circulation, and estimates are that the country has earned from $15 to $25 million per year from counterfeiting. The illegal nature of any counterfeiting activity makes open-source information on the scope and scale of DPRK counterfeiting and distribution operations incomplete. South Korean intelligence has corroborated information on North Korean production of forged currency prior to 1998, and certain individuals have been indicted in U.S. courts for distributing such forged currency. Media reports in January 2006 state that Chinese investigators have independently confirmed allegations of DPRK counterfeiting.

For the United States, North Korean counterfeiting represents a direct attack on a protected national asset; might undermine confidence in the U.S. dollar and depress its value; and, if done extensively enough, potentially damage the U.S. economy. The earnings from counterfeiting also could be significant to Pyongyang and may be used to purchase weapons technology, fund travel abroad, meet "slush fund" purchases of luxury foreign goods, or even help fund the DPRK's nuclear program.

U.S. policy toward the alleged counterfeiting is split between law enforcement efforts and political and diplomatic pressures. On the law enforcement side, individuals have been indicted and the Banco Delta Asia bank in Macao (a territory of China) has been named as a primary money laundering concern under the Patriot Act. This started a financial chain reaction under which banks, not only from the United States but from other nations, have declined to deal with even some legitimate North Korea traders. North Koreans appear to be moving their international bank accounts to Chinese and other banks. In December 2006, North Korea agreed to return to the six-party talks on its nuclear weapons program, but during the talks Pyongyang refused to discuss denuclearization officially until the Banco Delta financial sanctions were lifted. It is not known whether North Korea currently is engaged in supernote production, but such notes suspected to be from earlier production runs reportedly are readily available in a Chinese town just north of the DPRK border.

The political/security track attempts to stop the alleged counterfeiting activity though diplomatic pressures, the Illicit Activities Initiative, and direct talks with North Korea through a working group on U.S. financial sanctions that in December 2006 first met alongside the six-party talks. In these talks, the U.S. side stated that U.S. sanctions on Banco Delta could be resolved if North Korea punishes the counterfeiters and destroys their equipment. This report will be updated as circumstances warrant.

Chapter 4 - Since 2002, the dollar has depreciated against a broad basket of currencies and against the euro. This depreciation has prompted some observers to question whether the "cheap" dollar is leading to a "fire sale" of U.S. firms, especially of those firms that can be identified as part of the Nation's defense industrial base. Congress has displayed a long and continuing interest in foreign direct investment and its impact on the U.S. economy. Since September 11, 2001, Congress has demonstrated a heightened level of concern about the impact of foreign direct investment in critical industries or in sectors that are vital to homeland security. In the 110th Congress, Members are considering H.R. 556, the National Security Foreign Investment Reform and Strengthened Transparency Act of 2007, which was adopted by the full House on February 28, 2007. The measure reflects a heightened level of concern about the presence of foreign investors in the economy by increasing Congressional oversight over federal reviews of foreign direct investment and by expanding the current areas of review to include homeland security and critical infrastructure.

Academic research and analysis has been relatively limited on the topic of the relationship between a depreciated dollar and any impact on foreign purchases of U.S. firms. There is also a relatively limited amount of information on this topic. Nevertheless, direct investment transactions as a whole seem to be tied more directly to the relative rates of economic growth between economies, as well as expected long-run rates of return and other economic factors, than to relatively short-term movements in the exchange rate of the dollar. Actual and expected movements in the exchange rate may influence the timing and the magnitude of foreign investors' decisions, but little research has been done on this issue.

Firms also engage in a variety of tactics to nullify or mitigate the effects of movements in the exchange rate, which would weaken the linkage between movements in the exchange rate and direct investment transactions. U.S. and foreign multinational firms have come to raise a significant part of their investment funds in the capital markets in which they are investing, which also lessens the impact of movements in the exchange rate. Furthermore, U.S. and foreign multinational firms have become skilled at using various techniques to hedge the risks of changes in exchange rates. This report assesses the current state of knowledge concerning the role of exchange rate movements in direct investment transactions, presents data on some of the major factors that influence direct investment, and provides an overview of some of the factors that influence the way in which firms finance their investments.

This report will be updated as events warrant.

Chapter 5 - The Single European Payments Area (SEPA) is a planned electronic payments system that upon completion in 2010 would allow individuals, small- and medium-sized businesses, and corporations to make electronic payments throughout the European

Union as efficiently and safely as such payments are being made on the national level today. However, the implementation process has been plagued with delays. The most recent delay occurred on December 12, 2006, when a vote on the Payment Services Directive was scheduled to be taken. But unresolved regulatory policy issues among member states prevented it from happening. One reason for the delay is pressure from European bankers who are uncertain about their ability to profitably recoup their costs once the system is constructed. The legislative status of the directive is that the President of the European Council is re-drafting it and between July 12 and September 12, 2007, a vote should be taken in the Plenary Committee of the European Parliament.

Congress is interested in SEPA because it has been monitoring the European Union's effort to unify its 27 member countries' financial markets. Congress recognizes that upon implementation of these efforts, such as the EU Financial Services Action Plan (FSAP), the Financial Conglomerate Directive (FCD), and now the Payment Services Directive (PSD), American firms doing business with the European Union could be significantly impacted.

The European payments systems are extremely fragmented. There are 27 national systems governed by national and local laws and practices. On average, the cost of making payments in the EU remains relatively expensive, even though more less-expensive electronic payments are being made, replacing the more costly cash and paper-check payments. European payment services costs include the inefficiencies caused by the use of non-standard customer interface, incompatible formats between foreign and domestic banks, and a low degree of automation in banks' internal systems. By one measure, these inefficiencies and others are estimated to cost the EU between 2% to 3% of its gross domestic product (GDP) (the EU GDP was $13.4 trillion in 2005 which would mean between $268 and $402 billion).

This report presents a brief background on the efforts to create SEPA by the European government and the banking industry. It assesses the current electronic payments systems from the wholesale (large value) level and the retail (small value) level of payments. The report then examines the attempts to develop the pan-European automated clearinghouse system (PEACH). It summarizes the provisions of the Payment Services Directive that establishes the legal and regulatory basis for SEPA. The last two sections examine the implications of SEPA for U.S. international banks and conclude with an outline of the potential advantages and disadvantages of SEPA for European and American financial services providers.

This report will be updated as developments warrant.

Chapter 6 - Globally, central bank holdings of reserve currency assets have risen sharply in recent years. These "official holdings" have nearly tripled since 1999 to reach $5 trillion by the end of 2006. Nearly $3 trillion has been amassed by developing Asia and Japan. China, in particular, now has official reserves that exceed $1 trillion. In addition, the oil-exporting countries have increased their official reserves by about $700 billion. The dollar's status as the dominant international currency has meant that as much 70% of this large accumulation of official reserves are of some form of dollar asset.

There are significant advantages for the United States in having the dominant reserve currency. These advantages include reduced exchange rate risk and lower borrowing costs. However, these large accumulations of dollar assets in foreign official holdings also means that foreign central banks have become important participants in and influences on U.S. financial markets and the wider U.S. economy.

Four factors — share of world output and trade, macroeconomic stability, degree of financial market development, and network externalities — combine to influence the choice of a reserve currency. The euro has improved its standing in all four areas but the dollar retains significant advantages. Available data show only modest diversification from dollar assets by foreign central banks from the time of the euro's introduction in 1999 through the end of 2006. The dollar's share of total official reserves rose through the 1990s, reaching a peak value of about 72% global reserves in 2001. By 2003 that share fell to about 66% and remained near that level through 2006. The euro's share of global official reserves rose from about 18% in 1999 to 25% in 2003, but has remained near this level through 2006.

Looking to the future, the dollar's status as the dominant reserve currency may be challenged by the euro because it increasingly offers many of the advantages of the dollar but fewer of the risks. The dollar's most important advantage is the size, quality, and stability of dollar asset markets, particularly the short-term government securities market where central banks tend to be most active. The high liquidity of these financial markets makes the dollar an excellent medium of exchange. A further advantage is the power of "incumbency" conferred by the "network-externalities" that accrue to the currency that is dominant. Together these factors make it unlikely there will be a large or abrupt change in the dollar's reserve currency status.

However, the euro is seen by some as poised to challenge the dollar in the store of value function of a reserve currency. The sheer magnitude of dollar assets in the official reserves of foreign central banks and the realistic prospect of continued, and perhaps disorderly, depreciation of the dollar against most currencies, place central banks at considerable risk of incurring large capital losses on their dollar asset holding. With more than enough dollar reserves to meet liquidity needs, prudent asset management would seem to dictate some diversification away from the dollar and toward the euro. This report will be updated as events warrant.

Chapter 7 - The International Monetary Fund (IMF) and World Trade Organization (WTO) approach the issue of currency manipulation differently. The IMF Articles of Agreement prohibit countries from manipulating their currency for the purpose of gaining unfair trade advantage, but the IMF lacks effective means for enforcing that rule. The WTO has rules against export subsidies, but these are very narrow and specific and do not seem to encompass currency manipulation. Several options might be considered for addressing this matter in the future, if policymakers deem this a wise course of action. This report will be updated as conditions require.

This report describes how the International Monetary Fund (IMF) and World Trade Organization (WTO) deal with the issue of currency manipulation. It identifies possible venues for the discussion of currency manipulation. It also discusses apparent discrepancies in their charters and ways those differences might be addressed.

Chapter 8 - Many Members of Congress charge that China's policy of accumulating foreign reserves (especially U.S. dollars) to influence the value of its currency constitutes a form of currency manipulation intended to make its exports cheaper and imports into China more expensive than they would be under free market conditions. They further contend that this policy has caused a surge in the U.S. trade deficit with China and has been a major factor in the loss of U.S. manufacturing jobs. Threats of possible congressional action led China to make changes to its currency policy in 2005, which has since resulted in a modest appreciation of the yuan. However, many Members have expressed dissatisfaction with the pace of China's currency reforms and have warned of potential legislative action. This report summarizes the main findings CRS Report RL32165, *China's Currency: Economic Issues and Options for U.S. Trade Policy*, by Wayne M. Morrison and Marc Labonte and will be updated as events warrant.

From 1994 until July 21, 2005, China maintained a policy of pegging its currency (the renminbi or yuan), to the U.S. dollar at an exchange rate of roughly 8.28 yuan to the dollar. The Chinese central bank maintained this peg by buying (or selling) as many dollar-denominated assets in exchange for newly printed yuan as needed to eliminate excess demand (supply) for the yuan. As a result, the exchange rate between the yuan and the dollar basically stayed the same, despite changing economic factors which could have otherwise caused the yuan to either appreciate or depreciate relative to the dollar. Under a floating exchange rate system, the relative demand for the two countries' goods and assets would determine the exchange rate of the yuan to the dollar. Many economists contend that for the first several years of the peg, the fixed value was likely close to the market value. But in the past few years, economic conditions have changed such that the yuan would likely have appreciated if it had been floating. The sharp increase in China's foreign exchange reserves (which grew from \$403 billion at the end of 2003 to \$1.2 trillion at the end of March 2007) and China's large merchandise trade surplus (which totaled \$178 billion in 2006) are indicators that the yuan is significantly undervalued.

In: Currency Interventions, Fluctuations... ISBN: 978-1-60456-078-7
Editor: L. C. Hilbert, pp. 1-48

Chapter 1

CHINA'S CURRENCY: ECONOMIC ISSUES AND OPTIONS FOR U.S. TRADE POLICY*

***Wayne M. Morrison*[1] *and Marc Labonte*[2]**

[1] Specialist in International Trade and Finance Foreign Affairs, Defense, and Trade Division

[2] Specialist in Macroeconomics Government and Finance Division

ABSTRACT

The continued rise in China's trade surplus with the United States and the world, and complaints from U.S. manufacturing firms and workers over the competitive challenges posed by Chinese imports have led several Members to call for a more aggressive U.S. stance against certain Chinese trade policies they deem to be unfair. Among these is the value of the Chinese yuan relative to the dollar. From 1994 to July 2005, China pegged its currency to the U.S. dollar at about 8.28 yuan to the dollar. On July 21, 2005, China announced it would let its currency immediately appreciate by 2.1% (to 8.11 yuan per dollar) and link its currency to a basket of currencies (rather than just to the dollar). Many Members complain that the yuan has only appreciated only modestly (about 7%) since these reforms were implemented and that China continues to "manipulate" its currency in order to give its exporters an unfair trade advantage, and that this policy has led to U.S. job losses. Numerous bills were introduced in the 109th Congress to address China's currency policy, and these efforts have continued in the 110th session.

If the yuan is undervalued against the dollar (as many analysts believe), there are likely to be both benefits and costs to the U.S. economy. It would mean that imported Chinese goods are cheaper than they would be if the yuan were market determined. This lowers prices for U.S. consumers and dampens inflationary pressures. It also lowers prices for U.S. firms that use imported inputs (such as parts) in their production, making such firms more competitive. When the U.S. runs a trade deficit with the Chinese, this requires a capital inflow from China to the United States. This, in turn, lowers U.S. interest rates and increases U.S. investment spending. On the negative side, lower priced goods from China may hurt U.S. industries that compete with those products, reducing their production and employment. In addition, an undervalued yuan makes U.S. exports

* Excerpted from CRS Report RL32165, dated July 15, 2007.

to China more expensive, thus reducing the level of U.S. exports to China and job opportunities for U.S. workers in those sectors. However, in the long run, trade can affect only the composition of employment, not its overall level. Thus, inducing China to appreciate its currency would likely benefit some U.S. economic sectors, but would harm others.

Critics of China's currency policy point to the large and growing U.S. trade deficit ($233 billion in 2006) with China as evidence that the yuan is undervalued and harmful to the U.S. economy. The relationship is more complex, for a number of reasons. First, an increasing level of Chinese exports are from foreign-invested companies in China that have shifted production there to take advantage of China's abundant low cost labor. Second, the deficit masks the fact that China has become one of the fastest growing markets for U.S. exports. Finally, the trade deficit with China accounted for 26% of the sum of total U.S. bilateral trade deficits in 2006, indicating that the overall U.S. trade deficit is not caused by the exchange rate policy of one country, but rather the shortfall between U.S. saving and investment. That being said, there are a number of valid economic arguments why China should adopt a more flexible currency policy. For a brief summary of this report, see CRS Report RS21625, *China's Currency: A Summary of the Economic Issues*, by Wayne M. Morrison and Marc Labonte. This report will be updated as events warrant.

INTRODUCTION

From 1994 until July 21, 2005, China maintained a policy of pegging its currency (the renminbi or yuan) to the U.S. dollar at an exchange rate of roughly 8.28 yuan to the dollar. The Chinese central bank maintained this peg by buying (or selling) as many dollar-denominated assets in exchange for newly printed yuan as needed to eliminate excess demand (supply) for the yuan. As a result, the exchange rate between the yuan and the dollar basically stayed the same, despite changing economic factors which could have otherwise caused the yuan to either appreciate or depreciate relative to the dollar. Under a floating exchange rate system, the relative demand for the two countries' goods and assets would determine the exchange rate of the yuan to the dollar. Many economists contend that for the first several years of the peg, the fixed value was likely close to the market value. But in the past few years, economic conditions have changed such that the yuan would likely have appreciated if it had been floating. The sharp increase in China's foreign exchange reserves (which grew from $403 billion at the end of 2003 to $1.3 trillion at the end of June 2007) and China's large trade surplus (which totaled $178 billion in 2006) are indicators that the yuan is significantly undervalued. Because its currency is not fully convertible in international markets, and because it maintains tight restrictions and controls over capital transactions, China can maintain the exchange rate policy and still use monetary policy to pursue domestic goals (such as full employment).[1]

The Chinese government modified its currency policy on July 21, 2005. It announced that the yuan's exchange rate would become "adjustable, based on market supply and demand with reference to exchange rate movements of currencies in a basket," (it was later announced that the composition of the basket includes the dollar, the yen, the euro, and a few other currencies), and that the exchange rate of the U.S. dollar against the yuan would be immediately adjusted from 8.28 to 8.11, an appreciation of about 2.1%. Unlike a true floating exchange rate, the yuan would (according to the Chinese government) be allowed to fluctuate by 0.3% on a daily basis against the basket. Since July 2005, China has allowed the yuan to appreciate steadily, but slowly. It has continued to accumulate foreign reserves at a rapid pace, which suggests that if the yuan were allowed to freely float it would appreciate much more rapidly. The current situation might be best described as a "managed float" — market forces are determining the general direction of the yuan's movement, but the government is retarding its rate of appreciation through market intervention.

The modest increase in the value of the yuan to date has done little to ease concerns raised in the United States, but the Chinese, with concerns about their own economy, have been reluctant to make significant changes to their currency. This paper reviews the various economic issues raised by China's present currency policy.[2] Major topics surveyed include

- The economic concerns raised by the United States over China's currency policy and China's concerns over changing that policy.
- How China's fixed exchange rate regime works and the various economic studies that have attempted to determine China's real, or market, exchange rate.
- Trends and factors in the U.S.-China trade imbalance. (What is causing it? Is China's currency policy to blame?)
- Economic consequences of China's currency policy for both China and the United States.
- Policy options on how the United States might induce China to reform its present currency policy, including current legislation introduced in Congress.

U.S. Concerns over China's Currency Policy and Recent Action

Many U.S. policymakers, business people, and labor representatives have charged that China's currency is significantly undervalued vis-a-vis the U.S. dollar by as much as 40%, making Chinese exports to the United States cheaper, and U.S. exports to China more expensive, than they would be if exchange rates were determined by market forces. They further argue that the undervalued currency has contributed to the burgeoning U.S. trade deficit with China, which has risen from $30 billion in 1994 to an estimated $232 billion in 2006, and has hurt U.S. production and employment in several U.S. manufacturing sectors (such as textiles and apparel and furniture) that are forced to compete domestically and internationally against "artificially" low-cost goods from China. Furthermore, many analysts contend that China's currency policy induces other East Asian countries to intervene in currency markets in order to keep their currencies weak against the dollar to remain competitive with Chinese goods.[3] Several groups are pressing the Bush Administration to pressure China either to revalue its currency or to allow it to float freely in international markets.[4] These issues are addressed in more detail later in the report.

President Bush and Administration officials have criticized China's currency policy on a number of occasions, stating that exchange rates should be determined by market forces. Initially, the Bush Administration rejected calls from several Members of Congress to apply direct pressure on China to force it to abandon its currency peg. Instead, the Administration sought to encourage China to reform its financial system — under the auspices of a joint technical cooperation program agreed to on October 14, 2003, for example — and take other measures that would pave the way toward adopting a more flexible currency policy.

The Administration's position on China's currency peg appears to have toughened beginning around April 2005 when then-U.S. Treasury Secretary John Snow asserted at a G-7 meeting (on April 16, 2005) that "China is ready now to adopt a more flexible exchange rate." This was likely driven in part by growing complaints from Members over China's currency policy and the introduction of numerous currency bills.

During the 109th congressional session, the Senate on April 6, 2005, failed (by a vote of 33 to 67) to reject an amendment (S.Amdt. 309) attached by Senator Schumer to S. 600 (a foreign relations authorization bill), which would have imposed a 27.5% tariff on Chinese goods if China failed to substantially appreciate its currency to market levels.[5] In response to the outcome of the vote, the Senate Republican leadership negotiated an agreement with the supporters of the bill to allow a vote on S. 295 (which was sponsored by Senator Schumer and which has same language as S.Amdt. 309) at a later date as long as the sponsors of the amendment agreed not to offer similar amendments to other bills for the duration of the 109th Congress. Supporters of S. 295 threatened to bring the bill up a vote on the bill on two separate occasions in 2006, but were convinced not to by Administration and Chinese officials.

Most Recent Events

Over the past year, some of the most significant events concerning China's currency policy have including the following:

- On December 14 and 15, 2006, the United States and China held high level talks under the newly-created "Strategic Economic Forum" (SED), designed to be a forum to meet on "bilateral and global strategic economic issues of common interests and concerns." China's currency policy was a major item of discussion. According to Treasury Secretary Henry Paulson, the two sides agreed on the need for balanced, sustainable growth in China, without large trade imbalances, with more exchange rate flexibility and greater emphasis on domestic consumption.[6]
- On May 15, 2007, the Chinese government announced it would increase the daily band in which the yuan is allowed to fluctuate against the dollar from 0.3% to 0.5%.[7]
- On May 17, 2007, 42 House Members filed a Section 301 petition with the U.S. Trade Representative's office over China's currency practices and requested that a trade dispute case be brought to the World Trade Organization (WTO). On June 13, 2007, the USTR's office announced that it had declined the petition.
- On May 22-23, 2007, the second round of SED meetings was held. Although China reiterated its commitments to greater reform and flexibility, it did not agree to any new major changes to its currency policy.
- On July 11, 2007, the Bank of China reported the yuan/dollar exchange rate at 7.57, an appreciation of 6.7% since July 21, 2005 (after the currency was reformed).[8]

Treasury Department Reports on Exchange Rates

The 1988 Omnibus Trade and Competitiveness Act requires the Treasury Department to annually report on the exchange rate policies of foreign countries that have large global current account surpluses and large trade surpluses with the United States and to determine if they "manipulate" their currencies against the dollar in order to prevent "effective balance of payment adjustments" or to gain an "unfair competitive advantage in international trade." If currency manipulation is found, Treasury is required to negotiate an end to such practices. Over the past several years, Treasury has issued a *Report on International Economic and Exchange Rate Policies* on a semi-annual basis, focused mainly on major U.S. trading partners. China was cited under this report for manipulating its currency five times from May 1992 to July 1994, largely because of its use of a dual exchange rate system (which it unified in early 1994) and restrictions that were imposed on access to foreign exchange by domestic firms. Neither China nor any other country has been designated as a currency manipulator since 1994.[9] However, over the past few years, the Treasury Department reports have increased their focus on China and have stepped up criticism of China's currency policy and the pace of its reforms. For example:

- In its May 17, 2005 report on exchange rate policies, the Treasury Department stated that China's currency peg policy was a substantial market distortion and posed a risk to its economy, its trading partners, and to global economic growth, and that "China is now ready to move to a more flexible exchange rate and should move now." The report noted that China had "committed to push ahead firmly and steadily to a market-based exchange rate and is taking concrete steps to bring about exchange rate flexibility," but warned that Treasury would monitor progress on China's foreign exchange market developments "very closely" over the next six months in advance of the preparation of the fall report.
- The Treasury Department's November 28, 2005 report praised China's July 2005 currency reforms, but stated that it had failed to fully implement its commitment to make its new exchange rate mechanism more flexible and to increase the role of market forces to determine the yuan's value. The report further stated that China's new managed float exchange rate regime, which Chinese officials described as "based on market supply and demand with reference to a basket of currencies," did not appear to play a significant role in determining the daily closing level of the yuan, and that trading behavior since the reforms strongly suggested that "the new mechanism remains, in practice, a tightly managed currency peg against the dollar."[10] However, Treasury stated that it decided not to cite China as a currency manipulator under U.S. trade law because of assurances it had received from Chinese officials that China was committed to "enhanced, market-determined currency flexibility" and that it would put greater emphasis on promoting domestic sources of growth, including financial reform.[11]
- The May 2006 Treasury report stated that the Chinese government has recognized the need to lessen its reliance on net exports for economic growth (and pledged to reduce the current account surplus) and to increase the role of domestic consumption. The report emphasized ongoing bilateral and multilateral discussions that were being

held with China to induce it to adopt a more flexible currency policy and noted that a Treasury Department Financial Attache had been posted to Beijing in April.

- The Treasury Department's December 2006 report on exchange rate policies called China's currency policy "a core issue" in the U.S.China relationship. The report noted that China had made progress in 2006 in making its currency more flexible, but stated that such reforms were cautious and "considerably less than needed."[12]
- The Treasury Department's June 2007 report stated that although China's central bank continued to heavily intervene in currency markets and that China's currency was significantly undervalued, it did not meet the technical requirements under U.S. law regarding currency manipulation. However, the report stated that "Treasury forcefully raises the Chinese exchange rate regime with Chinese officials at every available opportunity and will continue to do so."[13]

Many Members have been critical of Treasury's decision (since 1994) not to cite China as a currency manipulator, despite its large scale currency interventions to control the exchange rate with the dollar, its large global current account surpluses, and large and growing trade surpluses with the United States. Many Members have called for enactment of legislation to revise the criteria Treasury uses to make its currency manipulation determination or to require it to estimate the level of the yuan's misalignment against the dollar (see section on legislation in the 110th Congress).

China's Concerns over Changing Its Currency Policy

Chinese officials argue that its currency policy is not meant to promote exports or discourage imports. They claim that China adopted its currency peg to the dollar in order to foster economic stability and investor confidence, a policy that is practiced by a variety of developing countries. Chinese officials have expressed concern that abandoning the current currency policy could spark an economic crisis in China and would especially be damaging to its export industries at a time when painful economic reforms (such as closing down inefficient state-owned enterprises and laying off millions of workers) are being implemented.[14] In addition, Chinese officials also appear to be worried about the rising level of unrest in the rural areas, where incomes have failed to keep up with those in urban areas and public anger has spread over government land seizures and corruption. Chinese officials contend that appreciating the currency could reduce domestic food prices (because of increased imports) and agricultural exports (by raising prices in overseas markets), thus lowering the income of farmers and further raising tensions. They further contend that the Chinese banking system is too underdeveloped and burdened with heavy debt to be able to deal effectively with possible speculative pressures that could occur with a fully convertible currency, which typically accompanies a floating exchange rate.[15]

The combination of a convertible currency and poorly regulated financial system is seen to be one of the causes of the 1997-1998 Asian financial crisis.[16] Prior to the crisis, Chinese officials were reportedly considering moving towards reforming their currency policy, but the severe negative economic impact among several East Asian countries that had a floating currency appears to have convinced officials that China's currency peg was one of the main reasons why China's economy was relatively immune from crisis, and that gradually implementing reforms to make the currency more flexible is the best way to maintain stable economic growth.

U.S. officials counter that they are not asking China to immediately adopt a floating currency system, but to move more quickly to reform the financial sector and to make the currency more flexible (including allowing faster appreciation of the yuan, widening the band, and decreasing the level of intervention in international currency markets). The economics of a fixed exchange regime is examined in the next section.

THE ECONOMICS OF FIXED EXCHANGE RATES

Fixed exchange rates have a long history of use, including the Bretton Woods system linking the major currencies of the world from the 1940s to the 1960s and the international gold standard before then. To understand how China's currency policy works, it is easiest to start with an explanation of how a fixed exchange rate works, which China operated until July 2005. Under the fixed exchange rate, the Chinese central bank bought or sold as much currency as was needed to keep the yuan-dollar exchange rate constant at level (formerly about 8.28 yuan per dollar).[17] The primary alternative to this arrangement would be a floating exchange rate, as the U.S. maintains with economies like the Euro area, in which supply and demand in the marketplace causes the euro-dollar exchange rate to continually fluctuate. Under a floating exchange rate system, the relative demand for the two countries' goods and assets determines the exchange rate of the euro to the dollar. If the demand for Euro area goods or assets increased, more euro would be demanded to purchase those goods and assets, and the euro would rise in value (if the central bank kept the supply of euro constant) to restore equilibrium.

When a fixed exchange rate is equal in value to the rate that would prevail in the market if it were floating, the central bank does not need to take any action to maintain the peg. However, over time economic circumstances change, and with them change the relative demand for a country's currency. If the Chinese had maintained a floating exchange rate, appreciation would likely have occurred in the past few years for a number of reasons. For instance, productivity and quality improvements in China may have increased the relative demand for Chinese goods and foreign direct investment in China. For the exchange rate peg to be maintained when economic circumstances have changed requires the central bank to supply or remove as much currency as is needed to bring supply back in line with market demand, which it does by increasing or decreasing foreign exchange reserves. This is shown in the following accounting identity, used to record a country's international balance of payments:

Current Account Balance = Capital Account Balance

[(Exports-Imports) + Net Investment = [(Private Capital Outflow-Inflow) + Income+ Net Unilateral Transfers]Change in Foreign Exchange Reserves]

Net investment income and net unilateral transfers between the United States and China are relatively small, so the current account balance is close to the trade balance (exports less imports). Thus, anytime net exports (exports less imports) or net private capital inflows (private capital inflows less outflows) increase, foreign exchange reserves must increase by an equivalent amount to maintain the exchange rate peg.

For the past several years, there has been excess demand for yuan (equivalently, excess supply of dollars) at the prevailing exchange rate peg. For the central bank to maintain the peg, it must increase its foreign reserves by buying dollars from the public in exchange for newly printed yuan. As seen in table 1, foreign reserves grew from $75 billion in 1995 to $168 billion in 2000 to $1,066 billion in 2006.[18]

A significant level of China's reserves are believed to be in U.S. assets.[19] From 2004 to 2006, China's foreign exchange holdings rose by $456 billion, or 75%. China overtook Japan in 2006 to become the world's largest holder of foreign exchange reserves.

China's accumulation of foreign exchange reserves has continued to boom in 2007. From January-March 2007, those reserves increased by $136 billion to $1,202 billion. As long as the Chinese are willing to accumulate dollar reserves, they can continue to maintain the peg.[20] Rather than hold U.S. dollars, which earn no interest, the Chinese central bank mostly holds U.S. financial securities — primarily U.S. Treasury securities, but also likely U.S. Agency securities (e.g., the obligations of Fannie Mae and Freddie Mac).[21]

Table 1. China's Foreign Exchange Reserves and Overall Current Account Surplus: 1995-2006

	Cumulative Foreign Exchange Reserves			Current Account Balance	
Year	Billions of $	% of GDP	% of Imports	% of GDP	Billions of $
1995	75.4	10.8	57.1	0.2	1.3
1996	107.0	13.1	77.1	0.8	5.6
1997	142.8	15.9	100.4	3.6	32.5
1998	149.2	15.8	106.4	3.1	31.2
1999	157.7	15.9	95.1	1.4	21.1
2000	168.3	15.6	74.8	1.7	20.5
2001	215.6	18.1	88.5	1.3	17.5
2002	291.1	22.1	98.6	2.4	35.4
2003	403.3	28.1	97.7	2.8	31.4
2004	609.9	31.5	108.6	3.5	58.7
2005	818.9	35.5	124.1	7.1	116.1
2006	1,066.3	39.8	134.7	7.8	207.9

Source: Economist Intelligence Unit, International Monetary Fund, and People's Bank of China. Note: 2006 data for GDP, imports, and current account balance are estimates.

Since July 2005, China has continued to accumulate foreign reserves at a rapid pace, but, unlike a fixed exchange rate regime, it has no longer purchased enough foreign reserves to entirely prevent the yuan from appreciating against the dollar. After an initial revaluation of 2% in July 2005, the yuan has appreciated steadily but very slowly by another 4.6% through the end of January 2007 (see figure 1).[22] The current situation might be best described as a "managed float" — market forces are determining the general direction of the yuan's movement, but the government is retarding its rate of appreciation through market intervention (and thus, to some extent, is still pegging the yuan to the dollar).[23] Many of

China's neighbors also maintain managed floats, including Japan, whose foreign reserves increased by more than $30 billion from the third quarter of 2005 to the third quarter of 2006. The continued rapid accumulation of foreign reserves suggests that if the yuan were allowed to freely float, it would appreciate much more rapidly. In dollar terms, China's foreign reserves increased faster in 2006 than any other year despite the move to a managed float.

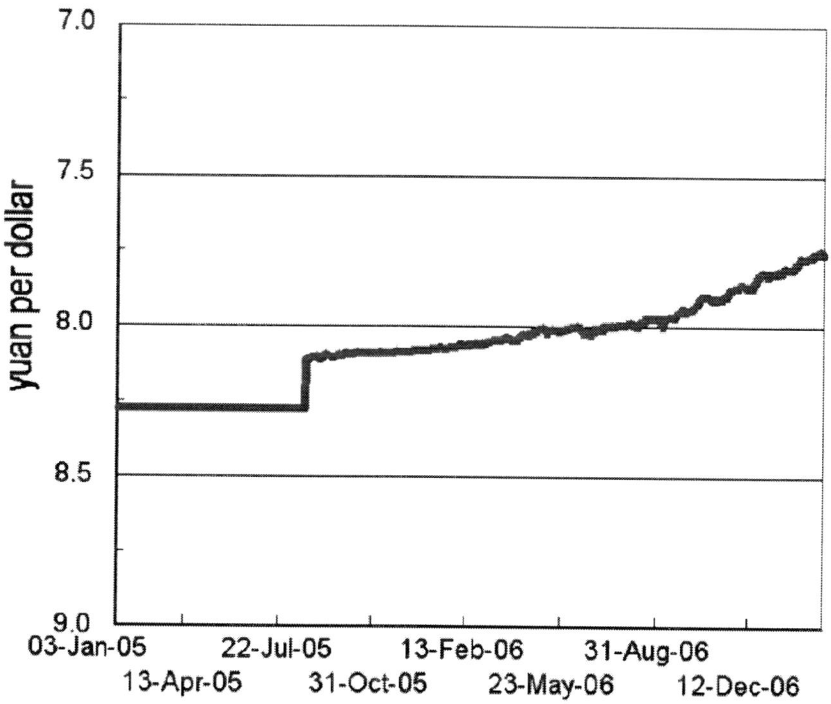

Source: Federal Reserve.
Note: Exchange rates plotted in the chart are daily values.

Figure 1. Yuan-Dollar Exchange Rate Before and After the July 2005 Announcement.

Preventing the yuan from appreciating is not the only reason the Chinese government could be accumulating foreign exchange reserves. Foreign exchange reserves are necessary to finance international trade (in the presence of capital controls) and to fend off speculation against one's currency. A country would be expected to increase its foreign reserves for these purposes as its economy and trade grew. However, table 1 illustrates that the increase in foreign exchange reserves in China has significantly outpaced the growth of GDP or imports in the last few years.

Ironically, speculation that the yuan would be revalued may have forced the Chinese central bank to accumulate even more reserves than they otherwise would have in the past few years. If investors believed that a revaluation of the yuan would soon occur, then they could profit by purchasing Chinese assets (popularly referred to as "hot money"), since those assets would be worth more in the investor's home currency after a revaluation. As shown in the equation on page 8, for any given trade balance, if private capital flows increase (putting upward pressure on the yuan), then official foreign reserves must also increase to keep the exchange rate constant. Since there are capital controls limiting private capital flows in China, it is not clear how well such a phenomenon could be measured. In any case, there is no way to differentiate between "speculative" and "non-speculative" capital flows. Nevertheless, data from the IMF provide evidence that is supportive of the hypothesis. In 2001, $3 billion of private portfolio capital flowed out of China, while in 2004 $82 billion flowed into China. To place that data in perspective, foreign reserves increased by $207 billion in 2004, so 40% of reserve accumulation offset capital inflows rather than the trade surplus. In 2005, inflows fell to $38 billion, perhaps because speculation subsided following the July revaluation.[24]

Economic activity, including the level of imports and exports, is not determined by the nominal exchange rate, but by the real (inflation-adjusted) exchange rate. Because the United States and China have had roughly similar increases in the overall price levels since 1994 (39% in China vs. 31% in the United States), the difference between the real and nominal rate has been small between 1994 and 2003. However, China had much higher inflation than the United States from 1994 to 1997, so the real and nominal exchange rates diverged considerably during that time. The real exchange rate appreciated from China's perspective, making their exports more expensive and U.S. imports cheaper. Since then, the real and nominal exchange rates have converged because China's inflation rate has been lower than U.S. inflation in the past few years. This can be seen in figure 2. In 2003, the Chinese exchange rate reached its lowest level since 1994 in real terms, from the Chinese perspective, making their exports progressively less expensive since 1997. The yuan has risen slightly in real terms since 2004, so that there was virtually no difference between the nominal and real exchange rate in 2006.[25]

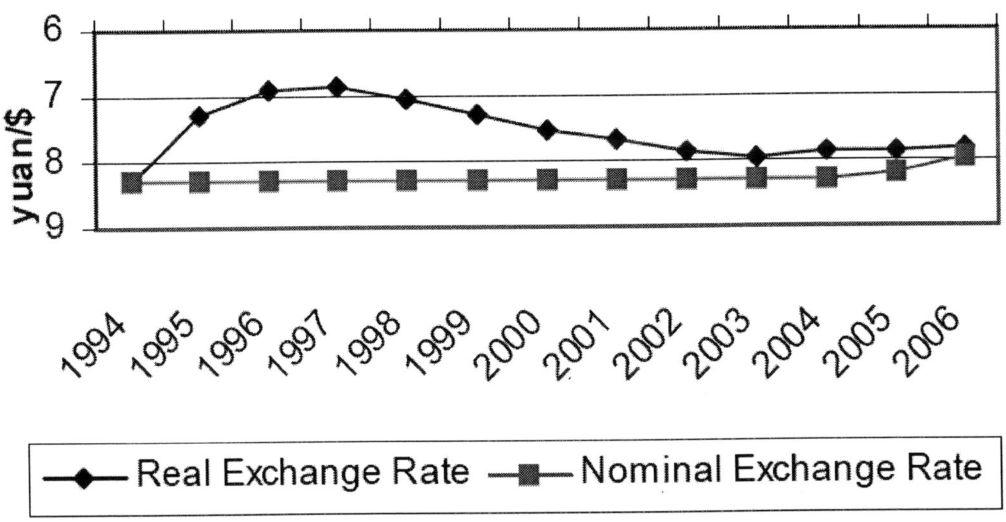

Source: CRS calculations based on IMF data.

Note: Real exchange adjusted for inflation using the consumer price index. Charted is inverted for illustrative purposes.

Figure 2. Nominal and Real Yuan-Dollar Exchange Rate, 1994-2006.

In the long run, real (inflation-adjusted) exchange rates return to their market value whether they are (nominally) fixed or floating. Imagine that the demand for Chinese goods and services were to increase. If the yuan were floating, it would appreciate, as more yuan were acquired to purchase Chinese goods. It would continue to appreciate until the excess demand for Chinese goods was exhausted (since they are now more expensive in terms of foreign currency), at which point the trade balance would return to its equilibrium level. With a fixed exchange rate, the real exchange rate returns to its market value through price adjustment instead, which takes time. If the exchange rate were fixed below the level that would prevail in the market, Chinese exports would be relatively inexpensive and U.S. imports would be relatively expensive. As long as this situation prevailed, the trade surplus with the United States would persist. The trade surplus (plus net remittances) is equal to the capital flowing from China to the United States. Part of this capital consists of the purchase of U.S. assets by private Chinese citizens. The other portion consists of the accumulation of dollar reserves by the Chinese central bank. By increasing its dollar reserves, the central bank is also increasing the supply of yuan. This causes the inflation rate in China to rise, all else equal.[26] Over time, as prices rise, exports will become more costly abroad and imports less costly. At that point, the trade surplus will return to its equilibrium value. Although the nominal exchange rate never changed, because of the rise in prices, the real exchange rate would now equal the market rate that would prevail if the exchange rate had been floating. Thus, undervaluing a fixed exchange rate does not confer any permanent competitive advantage for a country's exporters and import-competing industries. However, because price adjustment takes time, floating exchange rates return to the equilibrium value much more quickly than fixed exchange rates.

Thus, when a country uses its monetary policy to influence the value of it currency, it can no longer use its monetary and fiscal policy to counteract changes in the business cycle (the U.S. loses no policy flexibility from China's peg). For example, a peg would prevent a country from lowering its interest rates to offset an economic downturn. If it did, capital would flow out of the country to assets with higher interest rates in the rest of the world, and the country would find its currency peg under pressure (since investors would sell the country's currency and buy foreign currency to transfer their capital abroad) until it raised its interest rates.

This loss of monetary autonomy is relatively unimportant for small countries that fix their exchange rate to large neighbors that share the same business cycle, since the large neighbor would also likely be affected by the downturn and lower its interest rates. But the loss in autonomy is costly when a country is tied to a partner to whom it is not closely linked and does not experience similar business cycles, as is arguably the case between the United States and China.

However, China loses less monetary autonomy than most countries with a fixed exchange rate through its use of capital controls (legal barriers restricting access to foreign currency). The currency is convertible on a current account basis (such as for trade transactions), but not on a capital account basis (for various types of financial flows, such as portfolio investment). In addition, nearly all Chinese enterprises are required to turn over their foreign currency holdings to China's state bank in exchange for yuan, and purchases of foreign exchange by individuals and firms in China are closely regulated. Because capital cannot easily leave China when interest rates are lowered, China retains some flexibility over its monetary and fiscal policy despite the fixed exchange rate.

A Critique of Various Estimates of the Yuan's Undervaluation

Although it is certain that the yuan would appreciate if the central bank were not increasing its foreign reserves, since the value of the yuan has changed little since 1994, there is no direct way to determine how much it would appreciate — even if there was a consensus about what China's current account balance should be, there are no observations until June 2005 to estimate how sensitive its imports and exports would be to changes in the exchange rate. Estimates of the extent of the yuan's undervaluation have been cited in many articles and interviews. This report attempts to evaluate only those estimates in which the author explains how the estimate was derived. It should be noted that many of the estimates were made some time ago, so the yuan may be more or less undervalued at this point than when the estimates were made. The estimates are grouped below into two broad methodological categories: the "fundamental equilibrium exchange rate" method and the "purchasing power parity" method.

Estimates Based on Fundamental Equilibrium Exchange Rates

One method for estimating misalignments in exchange rates is referred to as the fundamental equilibrium exchange rate (FEER) method. It is based on the belief that current account balances at the present are temporarily out of line with their "fundamental" value, either because of unsustainable forces in the economy or government intervention. Once an estimate has been made of what the fundamental current account balance should be, one can calculate how much the exchange rate must change in value to achieve that current account adjustment. As will be discussed below, this is not an uncontroversial method. Many economists would reject the notion that current account balances worldwide are misaligned, or that economists can predictably determine how much they must be adjusted to come back into alignment. Thus, the following estimates are only valid if one accepts the assumptions underlying them.

Ernest Preeg, senior fellow at the Manufacturers' Alliance, estimated that the yuan was undervalued by 40% in 2003.[27] While this claim is not based on any formal analysis, he uses several rule-of-thumb estimates to reach this conclusion. His first observation is that the increase in Chinese foreign exchange reserves equaled 100% of the Chinese trade surplus less net foreign direct investment (FDI) flows in the first six months of 2002. He concludes that the entire trade surplus less net foreign direct investment would be zero in the absence of the increase in foreign exchange reserves. His second observation is a rule-of-thumb estimate that a 1% decline in the dollar leads to a $10 billion decline in the trade deficit in the United States He then observes that the dollar would need to decline by 40% according to that rule of thumb to eliminate the trade deficit since the U.S. trade deficit equaled about $400 billion in 2002. Since the Chinese trade surplus plus net FDI flows equaled 100% of the increase in foreign exchange reserves, he concludes that if the central bank no longer increased its foreign exchange reserves by letting the yuan float, the surplus less FDI would be zero and the yuan would appreciate by 40%, based on the U.S. ratio.[28]

The Institute for International Economics (IIE) estimates that the yuan was 1525% undervalued in 2003. It argues that the "underlying" current account surplus was 2.5-3% of GDP in 2003, larger than the actual surplus (1.5%) (it does not explain why).[29] It then argues that the surplus should be reduced by $50 billion (or 4% of GDP) to return to equilibrium, which would leave China with a deficit of 1-1.5% of GDP in equilibrium. It believes that the revaluation required to achieve this reduction in the current account surplus is unusually large because of the extensive use of imports in the production of Chinese exports. IIE Fellow Morris Goldstein testified that

> These estimates of [yuan] misalignment can be obtained either by solving a trade model for the appreciation of the RMB that would produce equilibrium in China's overall balance of payments, or by gauging the appreciation of the RMB that make a fair contribution to the reduction in global payment imbalances, especially the reduction of the U.S. current-account deficit to a more sustainable level.[30]

Goldman Sachs Economic Research Group has estimated that the yuan was 9.515% undervalued in 2003.[31] They argue that the current account less FDI should be zero in equilibrium (which means that China would have a current account deficit equal to FDI), which could be accomplished with a 9.5-15% revaluation. This is based on their elasticity (i.e., the degree to which demand changes due to price changes) estimates that exports would fall 0.2% and imports would rise 0.5% when the exchange rate rose 1%.

Virginie Coudert and Cecile Couharde use the most sophisticated analysis to estimate their parameters. They argue that China has an underlying current account deficit of between 1.5% and 2.8% of GDP. The smaller number comes from a cross-country regression of the current account balance based on variables such as per-capita income, demographics, and the budget deficit; the larger number is an estimate of the largest current account deficit that would stabilize China's debt-to-GDP ratio. They estimate that the yuan was 44%-54% undervalued against the dollar in 2003.[32]

All of these estimates are based on a similar logic, so a few general observations can be made about all of them. First, none of the estimates are the product of theoretically grounded, econometrically estimated economic models. Rather, they are "back of the envelope" estimates based on a few simple "rule of thumb" assumptions. "Rules of thumb" such as the Preeg 10%-$1 billion estimate or the Goldman Sachs import and export elasticities may not be accurate over time or over large changes in the exchange rate.

The main source of contention in all of the estimates of the yuan's undervaluation is the definition of an "equilibrium" current account balance. All of the estimates are based on the appreciation that would be required for China to attain "equilibrium" in the current account balance. But there is no consensus based on theory or evidence to determine what equilibrium would be; rather, the authors base equilibrium on their own personal opinion, with some using arbitrary assumptions and others more sophisticated ones.[33] Yet this assumption is crucial — Dunaway et al. demonstrate that changing the assumed equilibrium current account balance by 2 percentage points of GDP changes the estimated undervaluation by as much as 25 percentage points.[34] Some economists argue that the current account balance would always be close to zero in equilibrium, but this neglects the fact that countries with different saving and investment rates may willingly lend to and borrow from one another for long periods of time.

In fact, the Preeg, IIE, and Goldman Sachs estimates use an assumption of equilibrium less favorable to China than the current account balance. These studies actually call for balance only in official and portfolio borrowing. They still allow for foreign direct investment (FDI) inflows, which means their estimate of China's overall "equilibrium" current account position is actually a deficit. If they had chosen balance (the traditional "equilibrium" measure with a fixed exchange rate) instead of a deficit as their equilibrium benchmark, their estimates of the yuan's undervaluation would have been smaller. Even if portfolio flows are essentially limited by capital controls at present, it is not clear why requiring the Chinese to borrow from the rest of the world is any less unsustainable than the current arrangement where China is lending to the rest of the world. With capital controls and net FDI inflows, increasing foreign reserves is the only way that China can keep its net foreign indebtedness from increasing. And all measures rule out any accumulation of foreign official reserves for reasons other than to influence the exchange rate.

It is particularly difficult to determine the equilibrium current account balance in China because of the presence of capital controls. If China were to maintain capital controls after currency reform (if, for example, they revalued the peg rather than let the yuan float), current account balance may be a reasonable assumption. But if capital controls were eliminated, as is typically the case with a floating exchange rate, the economic situation would change entirely — "equilibrium" could now involve persistent borrowing from or lending to the rest of the world by private Chinese citizens, which would result in a corresponding persistent trade deficit or surplus, respectively. If private citizens lent as much to the United States in equilibrium as the Chinese central bank is currently lending (and U.S. lending to China remained unchanged), then the equilibrium market exchange rate would be equal to the current fixed rate, and the trade deficit would remain unchanged. If private capital outflows exceeded the current increase in foreign reserves, the yuan would depreciate. Since China is a country with both a high national saving rate and a high investment rate, it is not clear whether China would be a net borrower (in which case it would run a current account deficit) or lender (current account surplus) if their currency floated and capital controls wereabolished. This issue is particularly relevant when the equilibrium exchange rate is defined as "market determined," since capital controls currently prevent portfolio investment flows from being market determined. Bosworth argues that China's high internal saving rate is more than sufficient to finance its investment, so it makes sense for China to offset FDI inflows with official outflows in the form of foreign reserve accumulation rather than run a current account deficit. Therefore, he argues, foreign reserve accumulation should not be considered proof of undervaluation.[35] Wang argues that, based on estimates derived from other developing economies, China's equilibrium current account surplus may be even larger than the actual surplus, so the yuan is overvalued.[36]

The FEER approach is also based on a belief that the overall U.S. trade deficit is unsustainable, and revaluing the yuan would reduce it. This goes beyond an argument that China has fixed the yuan at an artificially low level, and argues that the dollar, which is market determined against most of its trading partners, is incorrectly valued. For example, the Coudert and Couharde estimate that the yuan is 54% undervalued is based on a corresponding estimate that the dollar was 35% overvalued, the yen 37% undervalued, and the euro 27% undervalued in 2003. If trade and financial markets are rational over the medium run, then the value of the dollar and the size of the trade deficit are never unsustainable — if they were, investors would be unwilling to hold U.S. assets and would sell the dollar, and the trade deficit would decline. There is no widely accepted theoretical approach to determining trade deficit sustainability, and *prima facie* evidence does not suggest the U.S. trade deficit is unsustainable over the next few years — it has lasted several years, it did not prevent the U.S. economy from achieving record growth and low unemployment in the late 1990s, U.S. investment income paid to foreigners is not large, and there have not been any unusually large or sudden declines in the dollar since the trade deficit emerged.[37]

Further, if the Chinese central bank stopped buying U.S. assets, and hence reduced its bilateral trade deficit with the United States, it is unlikely that the overall U.S. trade deficit would fall by a corresponding amount. Other foreigners would still be free to lend to the United States, which could cause its other bilateral trade deficits to widen. Thus, it is not clear that a "fair share" of a reduction in the U.S. trade deficit can be apportioned to China. And even if China's overall trade surplus were eliminated, it might still run a bilateral trade surplus with the United States. Even countries with overall trade deficits, including the United States, have some trading partners with whom they run surpluses and some with whom they run deficits.

Does international experience suggest what the Chinese current account balance would be in equilibrium? The closest comparison is probably to other East Asian countries, which also grew rapidly and maintained high saving rates in recent decades. The experience of these countries is mixed. From 1980 to 1997, Korea, Malaysia, Philippines, Indonesia, and Thailand typically ran current account deficits, while Hong Kong, Singapore, Taiwan, and Japan (which had already industrialized) typically ran current account surpluses. Since the Asian financial crisis in 1997, all of these countries have run large current account surpluses. This may suggest that the current economic environment is not conducive to developing world borrowing.

As seen in table 2, the same combination of large foreign exchange reserves and a large current account surplus can be seen in several other countries in the region, even though these countries range in their exchange rate regimes from a float (Japan and South Korea) to a currency board (Hong Kong). Compared with its neighbors, China's current account balance does not look unusual.

Table 2. Foreign Exchange Reserves and Current Account Balance in Selected Asian Countries, 2006

	Foreign Exchange Reserves		Current Account Surplus	
	Billions of $	% of GDP	Billions of $	% of GDP
Japan	895.3	20.5%	185.8	4.3%
China	1,066.3	39.8%	207.9	7.8%
Taiwan	266.2	75.2%	21.3	6.0%
South Korea	237.0	26.4%	3.4	0.4%
Hong Kong	134.0	71.7%	18.6	9.9%

Source: Economist Intelligence Unit estimates.

Sensible rules of thumb for long-term sustainability, such as estimating the current account deficit that would keep U.S. assets a constant share of foreign investment portfolios, need not hold in the short run. For instance, after a change in fundamentals, current account deficits may persist for several years as the United States transitions to a new steady state.

Estimates Based on Purchasing Power Parity

There are other estimates of the yuan's undervaluation based on the theory of purchasing power parity (PPP) — the theory that the same good should have the same price in two different countries. If it did not, then arbitrageurs could buy it in the cheaper country and sell it in the more expensive country until the price disparity disappeared.

One of the simplest estimates based on PPP is the *Economist* magazine's Big Mac Index, which estimated that China's currency was undervalued by 56% in February 2007.[38] The *Economist* portrays the Big Mac Index as a "light hearted guide" to exchange rates, and there are important drawbacks to relying too heavily on it. The Big Mac Index compares the price of a McDonald's Big Mac in China and the United States. Since a Big Mac in China was 56% cheaper than in the United States, the index concludes that the yuan is undervalued by that much. But purchasing power parity only applies to tradeable goods, and a Big Mac is not tradeable. In fact, Li Ong estimates that 94% of the value of a Big Mac comes not from the hamburger itself, but the services associated with the hamburger.[39] These include the wages of employees serving the Big Mac and the rent of the restaurant in which it is eaten, both of which are determined by local factors. Since the hamburger itself is the only tradeable portion of the Big Mac, only a small fraction of the Big Mac's value should be determined by purchasing power parity. As a result, a Big Mac in New York City is more expensive than a Big Mac purchased in the U.S. rural south. Taken literally, the Big Mac Index would imply that a dollar in the rural south is undervalued compared to a dollar in New York City.

While PPP is a simple idea that is powerful in theory, it has been proven to be unreliable in reality: prices are consistently lower in developing countries than industrialized countries. Some economists have tried to estimate what the yuan's value would be by attempting to control for predictable divergences from PPP. Still, these estimates should be considered with caution — even when sophisticated modifications have been made, PPP has been shown to help predict exchange rates only over the long run. Estimates based on PPP would identify any country's currency as overvalued or undervalued.

Economist Jeffrey Frankel argues that income level can be regressed on the exchange rate using a cross-sample of countries to find a predictable relationship between a country's income level and its equilibrium exchange rate based on PPP. By this measure, he estimates that China's exchange rate was undervalued by 36% in 2000.[40] He speculates that, if anything, the undervaluation has increased since then. Coudert and Couharde make a similar calculation for 2003 and estimate the yuan to be undervalued by 41%-51%, depending on what countries are included in their sample.[41] Frankel acknowledges a number of caveats to this analysis. First, PPP only holds over the long run, at best, and financial flows can cause even market-determined exchange rates to significantly diverge from PPP for several years. Second, the regression does not control for other factors and only explains 57% of the variation in the data. Third, he argues that any adjustment in the exchange rate should be gradual so as not to be economically disruptive. He also warns that "It is not even true that an appreciation of the renminbi against the dollar would have an immediately noticeable effect on the overall U.S. trade deficit or employment..."[42]

There should be some theoretical rationale for linking income levels to exchange rate values; otherwise, the results may represent nothing more than spurious correlation. One rationale is called the "Balassa-Samuelson" effect: as countries get richer, their exchange rates are predicted to appreciate because productivity growth will be more rapid for tradeable goods than non-tradeable goods. Since these differences in productivity growth cannot easily be measured directly, income levels can be used as a proxy. But if the proxy is not an accurate one, then neither will be the results. Another proxy is the ratio of the consumer price index to the producer price index. When Coudert and Couharde used this proxy over time with a smaller sample, they estimated that the yuan was 18% undervalued in 2003. Benassy-Quere et al. regressed this proxy and net foreign assets on a panel of the G20 countries and found the yuan to be undervalued by 47% in 2003.[43] Wang also uses this proxy (for China only), as well as net foreign assets and openness to trade, in a regression, and finds evidence that the yuan was only modestly undervalued in 2003.[44] However, the authors cautioned that the price index proxy could be inaccurate for China since many consumer prices are not market determined. In addition, they observed that restrictions on the mobility of labor and capital in China may interfere with the Balassa-Samuelson effect.[45]

Cheung et al. are able to replicate others' results that the yuan is significantly undervalued, but point out that these estimates do not meet generally accepted standards of statistical inference. Specifically, the undervaluation estimates are not statistically significant, which means that the results are not robust enough to be sure that the yuan is undervalued at all. Moreover, when they adjust their specification to take into account serial correlation (the fact that this year's exchange rate is influenced by last year's), the estimated undervaluation becomes much smaller.[46] Dunaway et al. demonstrate that when additional explanatory variables are added to the PPP model, such as openness to trade, the estimated undervaluation becomes much smaller. They also show that the estimate changes greatly when seemingly insignificant changes are made to the model, such as changing the time period or omitting one country from the sample.[47]

Treasury Department Assessment of Economic Models

The Treasury Department's December 2006 report on exchange rates discusses the use of economic models and methodology to estimate a currency's "misalignment" or what the fair market rate exchange rate should be. The report noted that there is no single model that accurately explains exchange rate movements, that such models rarely, if ever, incorporate financial market flows, and that their conclusions can vary considerably, based on the variables used. However, Treasury stated that examining such models can produce useful information in understanding exchange rate movements if they: focus only on serious misalignments; use real effective, not bilateral, exchange rates; utilize several different models, recognizing that no one model will provide precise answers; focus only on protracted misalignments where currency adjustments are not taking place; supplement judgments about misalignment with analysis of empirical data, indicators, policies and institutional factors; and verify whether there are any market-based reasons for a currency's misalignment. Treasury points out that most models (including the two classes analyzed above) estimate equilibrium exchange rates in terms of trade flows, while in reality trade flows are swamped by financial flows.[48]

TRENDS AND FACTORS IN THE U.S.-CHINA TRADE DEFICIT

Critics of China's currency peg often point to the large and growing U.S.-China trade imbalance as proof that the yuan is significantly undervalued and constitutes an attempt to gain an unfair competitive advantage over the United States in trade. However, bilateral trade balances reflect structural causes as well as exchange rate effects. There are a number of other factors at work that are also important to consider when analyzing the bilateral trade deficit.

First, although China had (according to U.S. statistics) had a $233 billion merchandise trade surplus with the United States in 2006, its overall trade surplus was $178 billion

(Chinese data), indicating that China had a trade deficit of $55 billion in its trade with the world excluding the United States; it had a $100 billion deficit in 2005 (see table 3).[49] If the yuan is undervalued against the dollar, it should also be undervalued against the other currencies, yet China runs trade deficits against some of those countries. For example, according to Chinese data, it had a $66.4 billion trade deficit with Taiwan and a $45.3 billion deficit with South Korea.

Table 3. China's Merchandise Trade Balance: 2002-2006 (+surplus/-deficit) ($billions)

	2002	2003	2004	2005	2006
China's merchandise trade balance (Chinese data)	30.4	25.6	32.0	101.9	177.6
China's merchandise trade balance with the United States (U.S. data)	103.1	124.0	162.0	201.6	232.2
China merchandise trade balance with the rest of the world (U.S. and Chinese data)	-72.7	-98.4	-130.0	-99.7	-54.6

Sources: Global Trade Atlas.

Note: Trade balance with the rest of the world equals Chinese data on global trade balance minus U.S. data on imports from China

Second, the sharp rise in the U.S. trade deficit with China diverts attention from the fact that, while U.S. imports from China have been rising rapidly, U.S. exports to China have been increasing sharply as well. Table 4 lists U.S. exports to its top 10 major export markets in 2006. These data indicate that U.S. exports to China have risen significantly faster than both total U.S. exports to the world and any other top 10 U.S. trading partners. In 2006, total U.S. exports rose by 14.7%, while those to China rose by 32.0%. From 2001 to 2006, total U.S. exports to China rose by 187.5%. China ranked as the 4th largest export market in 2006 and it will likely replace Japan as 3rd in 2007.

Third, productivity gains in Chinese exporting firms have increased rapidly in the past few years, a boost to exports that is unrelated to the fixed exchange rate. For example, Chinese export prices have fallen by a cumulative 27% since 1995 in Chinese prices.

Table 4. U.S. Merchandise Exports to Major Trading Partners in 2001 and 2006

	2001 ($billions)	2006 ($billions)	Percent Change 2005-2006	Percent Change 2001-2006
Canada	163.7	230.3	8.9	40.7
Mexico	101.5	134.2	11.8	32.2
Japan	57.6	59.6	7.7	3.5
China	19.2	55.2	32.0	187.5
United Kingdom	40.8	45.4	17.5	11.3
Germany	30.1	41.3	21.0	37.2
South Korea	22.2	32.5	32.5	46.4
Netherlands	19.5	31.1	17.4	59.5
Singapore	17.7	24.7	19.6	39.5
France	19.9	24.2	8.1	21.6
World	731.0	1,037.3	14.7	41.9

Source: USITC DataWeb. Note: Ranked by top 10 U.S. export markets in 2006.

Finally, there is strong evidence to suggest that a significant share of the growing level of imports (and hence U.S. trade deficit) from China is coming from export-oriented multinational companies, especially from East Asia, that have moved their production facilities to China to take advantage of China's abundant low-cost labor (among other factors). Chinese data indicate that the share of China's exports produced by foreign-invested enterprises (FIEs) in China has risen dramatically over the past several years. As indicated in table 5, in 1986, only 1.9% of China's exports were from FIEs, but by 1996, this share had risen to 40.7%, and by 2006 it had risen to 58.2% A similar pattern can be seen with imports: FIEs accounted for only 5.6% of China's imports in 1986, rose to 47.9% by 2000, and to 59.7% in 2006. FIEs import raw materials and components (much of which come from East Asia) for assembly in China, after which point, much of the final product is exported. As a result, China tends to run trade deficits with East Asian countries and trade surpluses with countries with high consumer demand, such as the United States. These factors have led many analysts to conclude that much of the increase in U.S. imports (and hence, the rising U.S. trade deficit with China) is a result of China becoming a production platform for many foreign companies (who are the largest beneficiaries from this arrangement), rather than unfair Chinese trade policies.[50] The rising importance of FIEs may represent a fundamental change in trade between China and the United States that could affect the bilateral trade deficit independently of the exchange rate regime.

Table 5. Exports and Imports by Foreign-Invested Enterprises in China: 1986-2006

Year	FDI in China	Exports by FIE		Imports by FIEs		U.S. Trade Deficit with China ($ billions)
	$ billions	$ billions	As a % of Total Chinese Exports	$ billions	As a % of Total Chinese Imports	
1986	1.9	$0.6	1.9%	$2.4	5.6%	-1.7
1990	3.5	7.8	12.6	12.3	23.1	-10.4
1995	37.5	46.9	31.5	62.9	47.7	-33.8
2000	40.7	119.4	47.9	117.2	52.1	-83.8
2001	46.9	133.2	50.0	125.8	51.6	-83.1
2002	52.7	169.9	52.2	160.3	54.3	-103.1
2003	53.5	240.3	54.8	231.9	56.0	-124.0
2004	60.6	338.2	57.0	305.6	58.0	-162.0
2005	60.3	444.2	58.3	387.5	57.7	-201.6
2006	63.0	563.8	58.2	472.6	59.7	-232.2

Source: China's Customs Statistics and U.S. International Trade Commission *Dataweb*.

The sharp rise in the share of China's trade by FIEs appears to be strongly linked to the rapid growth in foreign direct investment (FDI) in China, which grew from $1.9 billion in 1986 to $63.0 billion in 2006, much of which went to export-oriented manufacturing, a large share of which was exported to the United States. Table 5 indicates that the U.S. trade deficit with China began to increase rapidly beginning in the early 1990s; a significant rise in FDI and exports by FIEs in China occurred at roughly the same time. By comparing exports and imports in table 5, one can see that FIEs have little effect on China's overall trade balance, since the FIEs import roughly 88% as much as they export.

Table 6 provides an illustration of how foreign multinational companies have shifted a significant level of production from other (mainly) East Asian countries to China in one industry. The table lists data on U.S. imports of computer equipment and parts from its major suppliers for 2000-2006. In 2000, Japan was the largest foreign supplier of U.S. computer equipment (with a 19.6% share of total shipments), while China ranked 4th (with a 12.1% share). In just six years, Japan's ranking fell to 4th , the value of its shipments dropped by over half, and its share of shipments declined to 7.5% (2006). China was by far the largest foreign supplier of computer equipment in 2006 with a 47.8% share of total U.S. imports. While U.S. imports of computer equipment from China rose by 382% over the past six years, the total value of U.S. imports from the world of these commodities rose by only 22%. Many analysts contend that a large share of the increase in Chinese computer production has come from foreign computer companies that have manufacturing facilities in China.

Table 6. Major Foreign Suppliers of U.S. Computer Equipment Imports: 2000-2006 ($ in billions)

	2000	2001	2002	2003	2004	2005	2006	2000-2006 % change
Total	68.5	59.0	62.3	64.0	73.9	78.4	83.8	22.3%
China	8.3	8.2	12.0	18.7	29.5	35.5	40.0	381.9
Malaysia	4.9	5.0	7.1	8.0	8.7	9.9	11.1	126.5
Mexico	6.9	8.5	7.9	7.0	7.4	6.7	6.6	-4.3
Japan	13.4	9.5	8.1	6.3	6.3	6.1	6.3	-53.0
Singapore	8.7	7.1	7.1	6.9	6.6	5.9	5.6	-35.6

Source: U.S. International Trade Commission Trade Data Web.

Note: Ranked according to top 6 suppliers in 2006.

ECONOMIC CONSEQUENCES OF CHINA'S CURRENCY POLICY

If the yuan is undervalued against the dollar, as many critics charge, then there are benefits and costs of this policy for the economies of both China and the United States.

Implications for China's Economy

If the yuan is undervalued, then Chinese exports to the United States are likely cheaper than they would be if the currency were freely traded, providing a boost to China's export industries (which employ millions of workers and are a major source of China's productivity gains). An undervalued currency also increases the attractiveness of China as a destination for foreign investment in export-oriented production facilities, much of which comes from U.S. firms. Foreign investment is an important source of technology transfers, which contribute to economic development. However, an undervalued currency makes imports more expensive, hurting Chinese consumers and Chinese firms that import parts, machinery, and raw materials. Such a policy, in effect, benefits Chinese exporting firms (many of which are owned by foreign multinational corporations) at the expense of non-exporting Chinese firms, especially those that rely on imported goods. This may impede the most efficient allocation of resources in the Chinese economy in the long run.

In the short run, a revaluation of the yuan could reduce aggregate spending in China by raising imports and reducing exports. Whether this would be desirable depends on the current state of the Chinese economy. Some observers argue that the Chinese economy is currently overheating, and revaluation would help place it on a more sustainable path and prevent inflation from rising. Others argue that there is a large pool of underemployed labor in rural China that the undervalued yuan is helping to absorb. In this view, revaluation could be economically and socially disruptive.

Many economists note that China's currency policy essentially denies the government the ability to use monetary policy (such as interest rates) to promote stable economic growth (e.g., fighting inflation). Secondly, they contend that the currency policy has skewed the economy into becoming overly dependent on fixed investment and net exports for economic growth, which, in the long run can not be sustained. Thirdly, they maintain that China's currency policy may actually be undermining the financial viability of the banking system by expanding the level of easy credit, which has made the banks more prone to extend loans to risky and/or speculative ventures, and thus may increase the level of bank-held non-performing loans. In addition, the policy has contributed to an inflow of "hot money" into short-term speculative ventures (such as real estate and the stock market) by investors hoping to cash in on future appreciation of the currency. Banks are restricted from using interest rate policies to better regulate investment decisions because raising interest rates beyond a certain level could increase flows of foreign capital into the country. Keeping interest rates low in a booming economy may prevent the most efficient allocation of capital and could lead to overproduction in some sectors.[51]

The accumulation of large foreign exchange reserves by China may make it easier for Chinese officials to move more quickly toward adopting a fully convertible currency (if the government feels the reserves could defend the currency against speculative pressures). However, the accumulation of large foreign exchange reserves also entails opportunity costs for China: such funds could be used to fund China's massive development needs (such as infrastructure improvements and pollution control), improvements to China's education system and social safety net, and recapitalization of financially shaky banks. These alternatives may have higher rates of return to the economy than U.S. Treasuries or Chinese bonds held by banks to sterilize the effects of exchange rate intervention.[52]

Implications for the U.S. Economy

Effect on Exporters and Import-Competitors

When a foreign reserve accumulation causes the yuan to be less expensive than it would be if it were determined by market forces, it causes Chinese exports to the United States to be relatively inexpensive and U.S. exports to China to be relatively expensive. As a result, U.S. exports and the production of U.S. goods and services that compete with Chinese imports fall, in the short run.[53] Many of the affected firms are in the manufacturing sector, as will be discussed below. This causes the U.S. trade deficit to rise and reduces aggregate demand in the short run, all else equal.

China has become the United States's second largest supplier of imports (2006 data). A large share of China's exports to the United States are labor-intensive consumer goods, such as toys and games, textiles and apparel, shoes, and consumer electronics. Many of these products do not compete directly with U.S. domestic producers — the manufacture of many such products shifted overseas several years ago. However, there are a number of U.S. industries (many of which are small and medium-sized firms), including makers of machine tools, hardware, plastics, furniture, and tool and die that are expressing concern over the growing competitive challenge posed by China.[54] An undervalued Chinese currency may contribute to a reduction in the output of such industries.

On the other hand, U.S. producers also import capital equipment and inputs to final products from China. For example, U.S. computer firms use a significant level of imported computer parts in their production, and China was the largest foreign supplier of computer equipment to the United States in 2006. An undervalued yuan lowers the price of these U.S. products, increasing their output and competitiveness in world markets. And many imports from China are produced by U.S.-invested enterprises (as discussed above), which benefit from an undervalued exchange rate.

Effect on U.S. Borrowers

An undervalued yuan also has an effect on U.S. borrowers. When the United States runs a current account deficit with China, an equivalent amount of capital flows from China to the United States, as can be seen in the U.S. balance of payments accounts. This occurs because the Chinese central bank or private Chinese citizens are investing in U.S. assets, which allows more U.S. capital investment in plant and equipment to take place than would otherwise occur. Capital investment increases because the greater demand for U.S. assets puts downward pressure on U.S. interest rates, and firms are now willing to make investments that were previously unprofitable. This increases aggregate spending in the short run, all else equal, and also increases the size of the economy in the long run by increasing the capital stock.

Private firms are not the only beneficiaries of the lower interest rates caused by the capital inflow (trade deficit) from China. Interest-sensitive household spending, on goods such as consumer durables and housing, is also higher than it would be if capital from China did not flow into the United States. In addition, a large proportion of the U.S. assets bought by the Chinese, particularly by the central bank, are U.S. Treasury securities, which fund U.S. federal budget deficits. According to the U.S. Treasury Department, China held $414 billion in U.S. Treasury securities (as of April 2007), making it the second largest foreign holder of such securities (after Japan).[55] From June 2006 to April 2007, China's Treasury security holdings increased by nearly $42 billion. If the U.S. trade deficit with China were eliminated, Chinese capital would no longer flow into this country on net, and the U.S. government would have to find other buyers of its U.S. Treasuries at higher interest rates. This would increase the government's interest payments, increasing the budget deficit, all else equal.

Effect on U.S. Consumers

A society's economic well-being is usually measured not by how much it can produce, but how much it can consume. An undervalued yuan that lowers the price of imports from China allows the United States to increase its consumption of both imported and domestically produced goods through an improvement in the terms-of-trade. The terms-of-trade measures the terms on which U.S. labor and capital can be exchanged for foreign labor and capital. Since changes in aggregate spending are only temporary, from a long-term perspective the lasting effect of an undervalued yuan is to increase the purchasing power of U.S. consumers.[56]

U.S.-China Trade and Manufacturing Jobs

Critics of China's currency policy argue that the low value of the yuan has had a significant effect on the U.S. manufacturing sector, where 2.7 million factory jobs have been lost since July 2000. While job losses in the U.S. manufacturing sector have been significant in recent years, there is no clear link between job losses and imports from China. First, only some manufacturers export to China or compete with Chinese imports. Second, the economic recession and subsequent "jobless recovery" that ended in August 2003 reduced employment across the entire economy. Since then, manufacturing output has reached an all-time high; manufacturing employment has fallen over this time because of productivity growth, not a decline in output. Third, the growing trade deficit has not been limited to China; the overall trade deficit is still increasing.

Finally, there is a long-run trend that is moving U.S. production away from manufacturing and toward the service sector.[57] U.S. employment in manufacturing as a share of total nonagricultural employment has fallen from 31.8% in 1960 to 22.4% in 1980, to 10.7% in 2005, to 10.5% in 2006.[58] This trend is much larger than the Chinese currency issue, and is caused by changing technology (which requires fewer workers to produce the same number of goods) and comparative advantage. With enhanced globalization, comparative advantage predicts the United States will produce knowledge- and technology-intensive goods that it is best at producing for trade with countries, such as China, who are better at producing labor-intensive goods. Since the production of some manufactured goods is labor-intensive and some services cannot be traded, trade leads to more manufacturing abroad, and less in the United States.[59] Over time, it is likely that the trend shifting manufacturing abroad will continue regardless of China's currency policy.

The decline in manufacturing employment is not unique to the United States. According to a study by Alliance Capital Management, employment in manufacturing among the world's 20 largest economies declined by 22 million jobs between 1995 and 2002. At the same time, the study estimated that total manufacturing production among these economies increased by more than 30% (due largely to increases in productivity). As indicated in table 7, while the number of manufacturing jobs in the United States declined by 1.9 million (or 11.3%) during this period, they declined in many other industrial countries as well, including Japan (2.3 million or 16.1%), Germany (476,000 or 10.1%), the United Kingdom (446,000 or

10.3%), and South Korea (555,000 or 11.6%). The study further estimated employment in manufacturing in China during this period declined by 15 million workers (from 96 million workers in 1995 to 83 million in 2002), a 15.3% reduction.[60] In the United States and United Kingdom, the employment decline began in 1999; in the other countries in table 6, the decline began earlier. In 2004, the industrialized countries experienced a loss of 865,000 more manufacturing jobs, and a cumulative 6.3 million manufacturing job losses over the previous five years.[61]

Table 7. Manufacturing Employment in Selected Countries: 1995 and 2002 (in thousands and percent change)

	Manufacturing Employment (thousands)		Change in Manufacturing Employment: 1995/2002	
	1995	2002	Total Change (thousands)	Percent Change
United States	17,251	15,304	-1,947	-11.3
Japan	14,570	12,230	-2,340	-16.1
Germany	8,439	7,963	-476	-10.1
United Kingdom	4,402	3,956	-446	-10.3
South Korea	4,796	4,241	-555	-11.6
China	98,030	83,080	-14,950	-15.3

Source: Alliance Capital Management L.P., Alliance Bernstein, *Manufacturing Payrolls Declining Globally: The Untold Story*, U.S. Weekly Economic Update, October 10, 2003.

The sharp increases in U.S. imports of manufactured products from China over the past several years do not necessarily correlate with subsequent production and job losses in the manufacturing sector. Alan Greenspan, former Chairman of the Federal Reserve, testified in 2005 that "I am aware of no credible evidence that ... a marked increase in the exchange value of the Chinese renminbi relative to the dollar would significantly increase manufacturing activity and jobs in the United States."[62] A study by the Federal Reserve Bank of Chicago estimated that import penetration by Chinese manufactured products (i.e., the ratio of imported manufactured Chinese goods to total manufactured goods consumed domestically) was only 2.7% in 2001.[63] The study acknowledged that, while China on average is a small-to-moderate player in most manufacturing sector markets in the United States, it has shown a high growth in import penetration over the past few years, growing by nearly 60% between 1997-2001 (from 1.7% to 2.7%). However, the study concluded that "the bulk of the current U.S. manufacturing weakness cannot be attributed to rising imports and outsourcing," but rather is largely the result of the economic slowdown in the United States and among several major U.S. export markets.[64]

Net Effect on the U.S. Economy

In the medium run, an undervalued yuan neither increases nor decreases aggregate demand in the United States. Rather, it leads to a compositional shift in U.S. production, away from U.S. exporters and import-competing firms toward the firms that benefit from the lower interest rates caused by Chinese capital inflows. In particular, capital-intensive firms and firms that produce consumer durables would be expected to benefit from lower interest rates. Thus, it is expected to have no medium- or long-run effect on aggregate U.S.

employment or unemployment. As evidence, one can consider that while the trade deficit with China (and overall) has widened, the overall unemployment rate has fallen from 6.3% in 2003 to 4.5% in February 2007. However, the gains and losses in employment and production caused by the trade deficit will not be dispersed evenly across regions and sectors of the economy: on balance, some areas will gain while others will lose.

Although the compositional shift in output has no negative effect on aggregate U.S. output and employment in the long-run, there may be adverse short-run consequences. If output in the trade sector falls more quickly than the output of U.S. recipients of Chinese capital rises, aggregate spending and employment could temporarily fall. If this occurs, then there is likely to be a decline in the inflation rate as well (which could be beneficial or harmful, depending if inflation is high or low at the time). A fall in aggregate spending is more likely to be a concern if the economy is already sluggish than if it is at full employment. Otherwise, it is likely that government macroeconomic policy adjustment and market forces can quickly compensate for any decline of output in the trade sector by expanding other elements of aggregate demand.

By shifting the composition of U.S. output to a higher capital base, the size of the economy would be larger in the long run as a result of the capital inflow/trade deficit. U.S. citizens would not enjoy the returns to Chinese-owned capital in the United States. U.S. workers employing that Chinese-owned capital would enjoy higher productivity, however, and correspondingly higher wages.

The U.S.-China Trade Deficit in the Context of the Overall U.S. Trade Deficit

While China is a large trading partner, it accounted for only about 15.5% of U.S. imports in 2006 and 26.0% of the sum of the bilateral trade deficits. Over a span of several years, a country with a floating exchange rate can run an ongoing overall trade deficit for only one reason: a domestic imbalance between saving and investment. This has been the case for the United States over the past two decades, where saving as a share of gross domestic product (GDP) has been in gradual decline.[65] On the one hand, the United States has high rates of productivity growth and strong economic fundamentals that are conducive to high rates of capital investment. On the other hand, it has a chronically low household saving rate, and recently a negative government saving rate as a result of the budget deficit. As long as Americans save little, foreigners will use their saving to finance profitable investment opportunities in the United States; the trade deficit is the result.[66] The returns to foreign-owned capital will flow to foreigners instead of Americans, but the returns to U.S. labor utilizing foreign-owned capital will flow to U.S. labor.

China's situation is very different. As table 8 shows, China's gross national saving as a percent of GDP (51.3%) is nearly five times greater than the U.S. level (13.5%).[67] Conversely, the rate of private consumption as a percent of GDP is significantly higher in the United States (70%) than it is in China (36.8%). China maintains a higher rate of gross fixed investment as a percent of GDP than does the United States (42.8% versus 20.0%). Finally, China's gross national saving as a percent of its gross national investment is equal to 118% versus 68% in the United States. Thus, the United States must borrow from abroad to fund its investment needs while China has excess saving that it can invest overseas. The net result of these differences can be seen in the data on current account balances as a percent of GDP: 7.7% for China compared with -6.5% for the United States. These data imply that both China and the United States would need to make fundamental changes to their saving/investment patterns to reduce the overall U.S. trade deficit and China's overall trade surplus in the long run.

Table 8. Comparisons of Savings, Investment, and Consumption as a Percent of GDP Between the United States and China, 2006

	China	United States
Gross savings as a % of GDP	51.3	13.5
Private consumption as a % of GDP	36.8	70.0
Gross fixed investment as a % of GDP	42.8	20.0
Gross national savings as a % of gross national investment	117.8	67.5
Current account balance as a % of GDP	7.7	-6.5

Source: BEA and EIU.

Some analysts contend that China is moving in this direction, based on a number of statements by high level officials that China plans to boost consumer spending. The Treasury Department's November 2005 report on *International Economic and Exchange Rate Policies* stated that a key factor in Treasury's decision not to designate China as a country that manipulates its currency was "China's commitment to put greater emphasis on sustainable domestic sources of growth, including by modernizing the financial sector...." However, others contend that it will take several years for China to switch its reliance on exports and domestic investment to consumption for much of its GDP growth.

Economists generally are more concerned with the overall trade deficit than bilateral trade balances. Because of comparative advantage, it is natural that a country will have some trading partners from which it imports more, and some trading partners to which it exports more. For example, the United States has a trade deficit with Austria and a trade surplus with the Netherlands even though both countries use the euro, which floats against the dollar. Of concern to the United States from an economic perspective is that its low saving rate makes it so reliant on foreigners to finance its investment opportunities, and not the fact that much of the capital comes from China.[68] If the United States did not borrow heavily from China, it would still have to borrow from other countries.[69]

Policy Options for Dealing with China's Currency Policy

The United States could utilize a number of options to try to put more pressure on China to make further reforms to its exchange rate policy if U.S. policymakers desired. Options for currency reform include making the yuan fully convertible, allowing the currency to appreciate by a certain amount (immediately or gradually), lessening China's intervention in currency markets, widening the band in which the currency is allowed to fluctuate, and furthering reforms to the financial sector to enable greater currency flexibility.[70]

Options to induce China to reform its exchange rate regime (including proposed legislation) are listed below (see also section on legislation in the 110th Congress):

Tighten Requirements on Treasury Department's Report on Currency

Several Members of Congress have expressed frustration over the Treasury Department's failure to designate China as a currency manipulator (since 1994) in its semi-annual exchange rate policies report. They contend that such a designation would itself increase pressure on China to reform its currency.[71] According to the Treasury Departments's November 2005 currency report: "Reaching judgments about countries' currency practices and their relationships to the terms of the Act (i.e. currency manipulation) for the purpose of designation is inherently complex, and there is no formulaic procedure that accomplishes this objective." H.R. 782, H.R. 2942, S. 796, and S. 1607 (110th Congress) would require Treasury to identify "fundamentally misaligned currencies" rather than manipulated currencies. S. 1677 would require to Treasury to cite a country for currency manipulation regardless of the "intent" of its currency policy. These bills would increase the likelihood that China would be designated, which, some observers claim, would increase pressure on Treasury to make greater efforts to induce China to reform its currency and might make China more willing to boost reform efforts to avoid being designated.[72]

Intensify Diplomatic Efforts

The U.S. government could attempt to persuade China through direct negotiations to change or reform its exchange rate policy. President Bush and Administration officials have contended that China's currency policy is bad for China's economy, as well as that of its trading partners and world growth as a whole. The United States has attempted to assist China in reforming its financial sector to provide a foundation for further currency reforms. In addition, the United States has sought to utilize high level talks, such as the Strategic Economic Dialogue and the U.S.-China Trade Promotion Coordinating Committee to encourage (and assist) China to adopt policies to promote greater domestic consumption and lessen its dependence on exports and fixed investment.

In recognition of its growing importance as a major world economy, China (since 2004) has been invited to attend G-7 (group of seven largest economies) finance meetings.[73] China's currency policy has been a major topic in these discussions, and the United States has sought to use the forum to bring pressure on China to quicken steps to make the currency more flexible. A February 10, 2007 joint statement of G-7 finance ministers and central bank governors stated that "In emerging economies with large and growing current account surpluses, especially China, it is desirable that their effective exchange rates move so that necessary adjustments will occur."[74] The United States could attempt to build a greater consensus within the G-7 to put more pressure on China to reform its currency policy, including by linking China's possible future membership in the G-7 to such reforms.[75]

Alternatively, the United States could attempt to persuade China to participate in talks with other East Asian economies (that are viewed as intervening in currency markets) in order to reach a consensus on exchange rate policy.[76] Proponents of this approach argue that, because of China's size, other East Asian countries are afraid that their exports would be uncompetitive if they made any unilateral change in their currency's value that was not matched by a similar change by China. Finally, the United States could press the International Monetary Fund to become more active in working with China to help it understand the long-term economic risks of over-relying on exports and domestic investment for much of its growth, and promote the development of policy tools that lead to more balanced economic growth (such as more domestic consumption).[77] A key factor in any negotiations would be to convince China that liberalization of its exchange rate system would serve China's long term economic interests and not lead to economic instability.

Utilize Section 301 or other Trade Sanctions

The U.S. government could attempt to pressure China by threatening to impose unilateral trade sanctions. For example, it could threaten to initiate a *Section 301* case, a provision in U.S. trade law that gives the U.S. Trade Representative authority to respond to foreign trade barriers, including violations of U.S. rights under a trade agreement, and unreasonable or discriminatory practices that burden or restrict U.S. commerce.[78]

U.S. obligations in the WTO would likely require the United States to purse a Section 301 case in the WTO. If the United States failed to use the WTO dispute resolution procedures and instead imposed unilateral trade sanctions under Section 301, China might file a WTO case against the United States. On May 17, 2007, 42 House Members filed a Section 301 petition with the USTR's office over China's currency practices and requested that a trade dispute case be brought to the WTO. However, the USTR declined the petition in June.

Some Members support legislation, such as H.R. 1002, that would impose additional tariffs of 27.5% on imports from China unless it appreciates its currency to fair market levels. Proponents of such legislation contend that congressional threats to sharply increase tariffs on Chinese goods were instrumental in moving China to reform and appreciate its currency policy in July 2005 and hence should be further utilized to press China for greater action to reform and appreciate its currency. Opponents of such legislation contend that imposing sanctions against China would violate WTO rules, and that threats of sanctions may backfire because Chinese officials would be less likely to reform its currency if they felt that such moves were seen as resulting from U.S. political pressure.[79] Some proposals seek to impose sanctions on currency policy that would avoid violating WTO rules. For example, S. 1607 would deny certain designated countries with misaligned policies access to U.S. government procurement, direct U.S. officials to vote against any new multilateral bank loans for such countries, and cut off any new financing by the U.S. Overseas Private Investment Corporation (OPIC).[80]

Utilize the Dispute Resolution Mechanism in the WTO

Some critics have charged that China's currency policy violates WTO rules.[81] The United States could file a case before the WTO's Dispute Settlement Body (DSB) against China's currency peg.[82] If the DSB ruled in favor of the United States, it would direct China to modify its currency policy so that it complies with WTO rules. If China refused to comply, the DSB would likely authorize the United States to impose trade sanctions against China. The advantage of using the WTO to resolve the issue is that it involves a multilateral, rather than unilateral, approach, although there is no guarantee that the WTO would rule in favor of the United States.[83]

In 2004, the Bush Administration rejected two Section 301 petitions on China's exchange rate policy: one by the China Currency Coalition (a group of U.S. industrial, service, agricultural, and labor organizations) and one filed by 30 Members of Congress. Both petitions sought to have the United States bring a case before the WTO against China in the hope that the WTO would rule that China's currency peg violated WTO rules. The Bush Administration has expressed doubts that the United States could win such a case in the WTO and contends that such an approach would be "more damaging than helpful at this time."[84]

H.R. 321, H.R. 782, H.R. 2942, S. 796, S. 1607, and S. 1677 contain provisions that would require U.S. officials (under certain circumstances) to bring a case against China over its currency policy, and H.R. 321 also calls on the United States to work within the WTO to modify and clarify rules regarding currency manipulation for trade advantage to reflect modern day monetary policy not envisioned at the time current rules were adopted in 1947.

Apply U.S. Countervailing Trade Laws to Non-Market Economies

U.S. countervailing laws allow U.S. parties to seek relief (in the form of higher duties) from imported products that have been subsidized by foreign governments. For many years, the Commerce Department contended that countervailing laws could not be applied to non-market economies, such as China, because it would be nearly impossible to identify a government subsidy in an economy that was not market based. However, in November 2006, the Commerce Department decided to pursue a countervailing case against certain imported Chinese coated free sheet paper products. On March 30, 2007, the Commerce Department issued a preliminary ruling to impose countervailing duties (ranging from 11 to 20%) against the products in question. Commerce contends that, while China is still a non-market economy for the purposes of U.S. trade laws, economic reforms in China have made several sectors of the economy relatively market based, and therefore it is possible to identify the level of government subsidies given to the Chinese paper firms in question.

Some Members contend that China's currency policy constitutes a form of export subsidy that should be actionable under U.S. countervailing laws. H.R. 782, H.R. 2942, S. 364, and S. 796 would apply U.S. countervailing laws to non-market economies and would also specify that currency misalignment or manipulation be actionable under those laws. Several Members contend that such legislation would be consistent with WTO rules (which allows countries to utilize countervailing duty procedures). However, critics contend that it would be difficult to determine the subsidy level conveyed by China's currency, and possible U.S. countervailing measures applied against China over its currency could be challenged in the WTO.

Apply Estimates of Currency undervaluation to U.S. Antidumping Measures

U.S. antidumping laws allow U.S. parties to seek relief (in the form of increased duties) from imports that are sold at less than fair value and injure U.S. industries. Many critics of China's currency policy contend that undervaluing the value of the yuan is a major factor affecting the price of Chinese exports to the United States and that this has harmed many U.S. industries. For example, H.R. 2942 and S. 1607 would require the government to factor in the impact of certain fundamentally misaligned currencies on export prices when determining the level of antidumping duties that should be applied. Critics of this approach contend that it would be very difficult to come up with a precise figure on how much a country's currency is undervalued, and it is not clear whether such a method would be compatible with WTO rules on trade remedies.

Utilize Special Safeguard Measures

Another option might be to utilize U.S. trade remedy laws relating to special provisions that were part of China's accession to the WTO. For example, the United States could invoke safeguard provisions (under Sections 421-423 of the 1974 Trade Act, as amended) to impose restrictions on imported Chinese products that have increased in such quantities that they have caused, or threaten to cause, market disruption to U.S. domestic producers.[85] This option could be used to provide temporary relief for U.S. domestic firms that have been negatively affected by a surge in Chinese exports to the United States (regardless of its cause).[86] The sharp increase in textile and apparel imports from China over the past few years led the Bush Administration on a number of occasions to invoke the special China textile and apparel safeguard to restrict imports. Eventually, the Administration sought and obtained (in November 2005) an agreement with China to limit the level of certain textile and apparel exports to the United States through the end of 2008. However, the Bush Administration on six different occasions has chosen not to extend relief to various industries under the China-specific safeguard. H.R. 782 and S.796 would require that exchange rate misalignment by China be considered a factor in making determinations of market disruption under the China-specific safeguard.

Other Bilateral Commercial Considerations

A number of policy analysts have argued against pushing China too hard on its currency policy, either because it would not serve U.S. economic interests, or because U.S. pressure would likely be ineffective as long as the Chinese government believed changing the peg would damage China's economy.[87] Such analysts argue that U.S. policymakers should address China's currency policy as part of a more comprehensive U.S. trade strategy to persuade China to accelerate economic and trade reforms and to address a wide range of U.S. complaints over China's trade practices. This appears to be the Administration's policy in the SED talks. U.S. officials have urged China to boost domestic consumption while making its currency policy more flexible as part of a long-term solution to global trade imbalances.

Some policymakers contend that the more immediate focus of U.S. trade policy should on pressing China to comply with its WTO commitments. Major WTO-related issues of concern to the United States include market access, inadequate protection of U.S. intellectual property rights (IPR), industrial policies that promote domestic content over imports, and indirect subsidization of Chinese state-owned enterprises by China's banking system. Because China's WTO commitments are clear and binding, and there is a legal process within the WTO to seek compliance with trade agreements, the United States is in a stronger position to get China to liberalize its economy and open its markets than it would be if it tried to push China to reform its currency regime (where multilateral rules and options on the issue are less clear). Finally, supporters of this policy argue that China's leaders are more likely to respond to pressures to adhere to international rules of conduct than to perceived direct U.S. pressure.[88]

Changes to the Current Currency Policy and Potential Outcomes

If the Chinese were to allow their currency to float, its value would be determined by private actors in the market based on the supply and demand for Chinese goods and assets relative to U.S. goods and assets. If the relative demand for the Chinese currency has increased since the exchange rate was fixed in 1994, then the floating currency would appreciate.[89] This would boost U.S. exports and the output of U.S. producers who compete with the Chinese. The U.S. bilateral trade deficit would likely decline (but not necessarily disappear). At the same time, the Chinese central bank would no longer purchase U.S. assets to maintain the peg. U.S. borrowers, including the federal government, would now need to find new lenders to finance their borrowing, and interest rates in the United States would rise. This would reduce spending on interest-sensitive purchases, such as capital investment, housing (residential investment), and consumer durables. The reduction in investment spending would reduce the long-run size of the U.S. economy. If the relative demand for Chinese goods and assets were to fall at some point in the future, the floating exchange rate would depreciate, and the effects would be reversed. Floating exchange rates fluctuate in value frequently and significantly.[90]

A move to a floating exchange rate is typically accompanied by the elimination of capital controls that limit a country's private citizens from freely purchasing and selling foreign currency. Capital controls exist in China today, and arguably one of the major reasons China opposes a floating exchange rate is because it fears that the removal of capital controls would lead to a large private capital outflow from China. This might occur because Chinese citizens fear that their deposits in the potentially insolvent state banking system are unsafe. If the capital outflow were large enough, it could cause the floating exchange rate to depreciate rather than appreciate.[91] If this occurred, the output of U.S. exporters and import-competing firms would be reduced below the level prevailing under the current exchange rate regime, and the U.S. bilateral trade deficit would expand. In other words, the United States would still borrow heavily from China, but it would now be private citizens buying U.S. assets instead of the Chinese central bank. China could attempt to float its exchange rate while maintaining its capital controls, at least temporarily. This solution would eliminate the possibility that the currency would depreciate because of a private capital outflow. While this would be unusual, it might be possible. It would likely make it more difficult to impose effective capital controls, however, since the fluctuating currency would offer a much greater profit incentive for evasion.

Another option is to maintain the status quo. Although the nominal exchange rate may change little in this case, over time the real rate would adjust as inflation rates in the two countries diverged. As the central bank exchanged newly printed yuan for U.S. assets, prices in China would rise along with the money supply until the real exchange rate was brought back into line with the market rate. This would cause the U.S. bilateral trade deficit to decline and expand the output of U.S. exporters and import-competing firms. This real exchange rate adjustment would only occur over time, however, and pressures on the U.S. trade sector would persist in the meantime.

None of the solutions guarantee that the bilateral trade deficit will be eliminated. China is a country with a high saving rate, and the United States is a country with a low saving rate; it is natural that their overall trade balances would be in surplus and deficit, respectively. At the bilateral level, it is not unusual for two countries to run persistently imbalanced trade, even with a floating exchange rate. If China can continue its combination of low-cost labor and rapid productivity gains, which have been reducing export prices in yuan terms, its exports to the United States are likely to continue to grow regardless of the exchange rate regime.

Conclusion

The current debate among U.S. policymakers over China's currency policy has been strongly linked to concerns over the growing U.S. trade deficit with China, the sharp decline in U.S. manufacturing employment over the past few years, and the rise of China as a major economic power. Most economists agree that China's currency would likely appreciate against the dollar if allowed to float (barring any disruptive financial crisis). If it did appreciate, there is considerable debate over the net effects this policy would have on the U.S. economy since it may benefit some U.S. economic sectors and harm other sectors, as well as consumers. The trade deficit with China has not prevented the United States from reaching full employment. In addition, U.S. trade with China is only one of a number of factors affecting manufacturing employment, including increased productivity growth, employment shifts to the service sector, and the overall trade deficit. It is also not clear to what extent production in certain industrial sectors has shifted to China from the United States, as opposed to shifting to China from other low-wage countries, such as Mexico, Thailand, and Indonesia.[92] The extensive involvement of foreign multilateral corporations in China's manufactured exports further complicates the issue of who really benefits from China's trade, as well as the implications of a rising U.S. trade deficit with China (since a large share of U.S. imports are coming from foreign firms, including U.S. firms, that have shifted production from one country to China). Thus, there is considerable debate over what policy options would promote U.S. economic interests since changes to the current system would produce both winners and losers in the United States (as well as in China).

Chinese officials have stated they plan to make the currency more flexible in the near term and to eventually adopt a floating currency in the long run, but they insist that reforms should be gradual in order to avoid disruptions to the economy. For example, they claim they need to first implement further reforms to the banking system and to reduce the level of non-performing loans. Yet the present currency policy may be undermining these efforts by expanding the money supply (as a result of contributing to foreign reserves). A rising money supply promotes easy credit policies by the banks — the source of existing non-performing loans in the first place. Efforts to limit bank loans in booming sectors of the economy have mainly been the result of government administrative directives rather than market forces, which may undermine the ability to establish a market-based financial system where monetary policy is used to halt inflation and bank loans are extended to ventures that offer the highest rate of return. In addition, China's currency policy constitutes a de facto subsidy, which, while benefitting some export industries, undermines other sectors, and prevents the most efficient distribution of resources in the economy.

While U.S. officials acknowledge China's concerns over exchange rate reforms, they contend that China's exchange rate reforms are overly cautious. They further contend that China's currency policy is preventing adjustments in global trade imbalances, especially in the United States, and that this could eventually undermine world economic growth. This would hurt China's economy, given its dependence on exports. Both U.S. and Chinese officials publicly agree that China needs to undertake major economic reforms to boost domestic consumption and to obtain more even growth, and that the United States must do more to boost its level of domestic saving. China officials have stated their intention to boost economic development in the hinterland and expand spending on social security, health care, and education. However, this will likely take many years to implement.

CONGRESSIONAL LEGISLATION IN THE 110TH CONGRESS

Currency legislation in the 110th Congress on China's currency policy include the following:

- H.R. 321 (English) would require the Treasury Department to determine if China has manipulated its currency and to estimate the rate of that manipulation (if such a determination were made), which then would require the imposition of additional tariffs on Chinese products (equal to the estimated rate of manipulation). The bill also calls on the United States to file a WTO case against China over its currency policy and to work within the WTO to modify and clarify rules regarding currency manipulation.
- H.R. 782 (Tim Ryan) S. 796 (Bunning) would apply U.S. countervailing laws (dealing with government subsidies) to products imported from non-market economies (such as China) and would establish an alternative methodology for estimating the amount of government subsidy benefit provided if information is not available on the amount of subsidies given to various industries in that country. The bills also make exchange rate misalignment actionable under U.S. countervailing law, require the Treasury Department to determine whether a currency is misaligned in its semi-annual reports to Congress on exchange rates, prohibit the Department of Defense from purchasing certain products imported from China if it is determined that China's currency misalignment has disrupted U.S. defense industries, and would include currency misalignment as a factor in determining (China-specific) safeguard measures on imports of Chinese products that cause market disruption.
- H.R. 1002 (Spratt) would impose 27.5% in additional tariffs on Chinese goods unless the President certifies that China is no longer manipulating its currency.
- H.R. 2942 (Tim Ryan) would apply countervailing laws to nonmarket economies, make an undervalued currency a factor in determining antidumping and countervailing duties, require Treasury to identify fundamentally misaligned currencies and to list those meeting that criteria for priority action. If consultations fail to resolve the currency issues, the USTR would be required to take action in the WTO.
- S. 364 (Rockefeller) would apply U.S. countervailing laws on non-market economies and would make exchange rate manipulation actionable under such laws.

Table 9. Comparison of Major Currency Legislation in the 110th Congress

Major Provisions	S. 1607 (Baucus)	S. 1677 (Dodd)	H.R. 782 (Tim Ryan)/ S. 796 (Bunning)	H.R. 2942 (Tim Ryan)
Official Title	Currency Exchange Rate Oversight Reform Act of 2007	Currency Reform and Financial Markets Access Act of 2007	Fair Currency Act of 2007	Currency Reform for Fair Trade Act of 2007
The Treasury Department's requirement to identify countries that manipulate their currencies in its bi-annual report on international monetary policy and currency exchange rates.	Requires Treasury to identify countries with "fundamentally misaligned currencies" and to designate currencies for "priority action" (based on protracted large-scale intervention, excessive reserve accumulation, restrictions on capital flows, and any other policy or action that would warrant designation). Requires Treasury to seek bilateral negotiations.	Requires Treasury to designate countries that manipulate their currencies regardless of intent, establish an action plan (with specific timetables and benchmarks), and to initiate bilateral negotiations.	Requires Treasury to additionally identify currencies that are in "fundamental misalignment" (defined as a material sustained disparity between the observed levels of an effective exchange rate for a currency and the corresponding levels of an effective exchange rate for that currency that would be consistent with fundamental macroeconomic conditions based on a generally accepted economic rationale); and to seek negotiations.	Requires Treasury to identify countries with "fundamentally misaligned currencies," defined as a situation in which a country's prevailing real effective exchange rate is undervalued relative to the country's equilibrium real effective exchange rate, and the Secretary determines that the amount of the undervaluation exceeds 5% over an 18 month period. Requires Treasury to designate a currency for "priority action" based on protracted large-scale intervention, excessive reserve accumulation, restrictions on capital flows, and any other policy or action that would warrant designation.

Table 9. (Continued).

Major Provisions	S. 1607 (Baucus)	S. 1677 (Dodd)	H.R. 782 (Tim Ryan)/ S. 796 (Bunning)	H.R. 2942 (Tim Ryan)
Countervailing laws	No provision.	No provision.	Applies countervailing laws to non-market economies and establishes alternative methodologies for identifying and measuring subsidies. Includes exchange rate misalignment as a countervailing subsidy.	Applies countervailing laws to non-market economies and establishes alternative methodologies for identifying and measuring subsidies. Includes exchange rate misalignment as a countervailing subsidy if a misaligned currency is found to be undervalued by 5% over an 18month period.
Anti-dumping laws	Would require the Commerce Department to factor in the fundamental misalignment of a currency (identified for priority action) for determining dumping margins on products from such countries.	No provision.	No provision.	Would require the Commerce Department to factor in the fundamental misalignment of a currency (identified for priority action) for determining dumping margins on products from such countries.
Restrictions on federal procurement for designated countries	Would prohibit federal procurement of products from countries designated for priority action unless that country is a member of the WTO's Government Procurement Agreement.	No provision.	Prohibit the Department of Defense from purchasing certain products imported from China (waivable) if it is determined that China's currency misalignment has disrupted U.S. defense industries.	No provision.

Table 9. (Continued).

Major Provisions	S. 1607 (Baucus)	S. 1677 (Dodd)	H.R. 782 (Tim Ryan)/ S. 796 (Bunning)	H.R. 2942 (Tim Ryan)
WTO and IMF provisions	Would require the United States to request the IMF Managing Director to hold consultations with countries whose currencies have been identified for priority action. Would require the USTR to bring a WTO case if there was a persistent failure to adopt appropriate policies after 360 days.	Would require Treasury to request IMF consultations and to bring a WTO case within 300 days if currency manipulation persists (both actions would be waivable).	No provision.	Would require the United States to request the IMF Managing Director to hold consultations with countries whose currencies have been identified for priority action. Would require the USTR to bring a WTO case within 360 days if the currency misalignment persisted.
Financing restrictions	Would ban OPIC financing, instruct U.S. representatives at multilateral banks to oppose the approval of new financing, and require the United States to oppose proposed changes (in the form of increased voting shares or representation) of certain international financial institutions (such as the IMF) for a country whose currency has been designated for priority action.	No provision.	Requires the United States to oppose proposed changes in the governance arrangement (in the form of increased voting shares or representation) of certain international financial institution (such as the IMF) if they are found to benefit countries found to have a currency that is manipulated or in fundamental misalignment and has an adverse impact on the U.S. economy.	Would ban OPIC financing, instruct U.S. representatives at multilateral banks to oppose the approval of new financing, and require the United States to oppose proposed changes (in the form of increased voting shares or representation) of certain international financial institutions (such as the IMF) for a country whose currency has been designated for priority action.

Table 9. (Continued).

Major Provisions	S. 1607 (Baucus)	S. 1677 (Dodd)	H.R. 782 (Tim Ryan)/ S. 796 (Bunning)	H.R. 2942 (Tim Ryan)
Other Major Provisions	Major actions would be waivable, but subject to a possible congressional resolution of disapproval. Treasury would have to consult with the Board of Governors of the Federal Reserve System to consider undertaking remedial intervention in international currency markets in response to the fundamental misalignment of a currency designated for priority action. Would include designations of currencies for priority action as a factor in determining if a country should be treated as a non-market economy country under U.S. anti-dumping law.	Would allow Congress, through enactment of a joint resolution, to disapprove the determination of Treasury relating to its findings over currency manipulation. Would require Treasury to issue annual reports on market access barriers for U.S. financial firms, including (in the first year) progress made on financial services in the U.S.-China Strategic Economic Dialogue.	Makes China's exchange rate misalignment a factor in determining market disruption under the China-specific safeguard provisions of U.S. law. Would include exchange rate misalignment as a factor in determining if a country should be treated as a non-market economy country under U.S. anti-dumping law.	Establishes an Advisory Committee on International Exchange Rate Policy (consisting of six appointees by Congress and one by the President) to advise Treasury, the Congress, and the President.

- S. 1607 (Baucus) would require the Treasury Department to identify currencies that are fundamentally misaligned and to designate such currencies for priority action under certain circumstances in its semiannual reports to Congress on exchange.[93] If after consultations the country maintaining the designated currency policy fails to adopt appropriate policies within 180 days, the U.S. would make currency undervaluation a factor in determining antidumping duties, ban federal procurement of products or services from the designated country, bar financing by the U.S. Overseas Private Investment Corporation (OPIC),[94] and would require U.S. officials to oppose multilateral financing for that country. If the designated country failed to take appropriate measures, the USTR would be required to file a case in the WTO, and the Treasury Department would be directed to consider taking remedial intervention in international currency markets.
- S. 1677 (Dodd) requires the Treasury Department to identify countries that manipulate their currencies regardless of their intent and to submit an action plan for ending the manipulation; and gives Treasury the authority to file a case in the WTO.

A side-by-side comparison of five major currency bills (S. 1607, S. 1677, H.R. 782 and S. 796 (which are identical), and H.R. 2942) is outlined in table 9.

APPENDIX: LEGISLATION IN THE 109TH CONGRESS

Several bills were introduced in the 109th Congress to deal with foreign exchange rate policies. The listed bills provide an overview of the multiple proposals on the issue.

Bills that Saw Legislative Action

- S.Amdt. 309 (Schumer) to S. 600 would impose a 27.5% tariff on Chinese goods if China failed to substantiallyappreciate its currency to market levels. On April 6, 2005, the Senate failed (by a vote of 33 to 67) to reject the amendment, In response to the vote, the Senate leadership moved to allow a vote on S. 295 (which has same language as S.Amdt. 309) no later than July 27, 2005, as long as the sponsors of the amendment agreed not to sponsor similar amendments for the duration of the 109th Congress. However, on June 30, 2005, Senator Schumer and other sponsors of S. 295 agreed to delay consideration of the bill after they received a briefing from Administration officials and were told that China was expected to make significant progress on reforming its currency over the next few months. Disappointment over China's July 2005 currency reforms led Senator Schumer to push for consideration of S. 295 (under the previous compromise). On November 16, 2005, the Senate agreed to consider the bill no later than March 31, 2006. On March 28, 2006, Senators Schumer and Graham stated that they would move to delay taking up S. 295 in the Senate, based on their assessment during a trip to China that the Chinese government was serious about reforming its currency policy. However, on September 14, 2006, Senator Schumer stated that he was disappointed with China's movement to date on currency flexibility, and requested the Senate to take up S. 295. On September 28, 2006, Senators Schumer and Graham announced that they had been persuaded by President Bush not to pursue a vote on S. 295 in order to give Secretary of Treasury Henry Paulson more time to negotiate with China on its currency policy.

- H.R. 3283 (English) would (among other things) apply U.S. countervailing laws (dealing with foreign government subsidies) to non-market economies (such as China); and require the Treasury Department to define "currency manipulation," describe actions that would be considered to constitute manipulation, and report on China's new currency regime. The bill passed (255 to 168) on July 27, 2005. A similar bill was introduced in the Senate, S. 1421 (Collins).

Other Bills

- S. 2467 (Grassley) would require the Treasury Department to engage the International Monetary Fund and other countries to resolve major currency imbalances with the dollar and would take specific action against countries that refuse to promote the fair valuation of their currency; require the Secretary of Treasury to identify "fundamentally misaligned currencies" that adversely affect the U.S. economy; and require the USTR's office to work more closely with Congress in identifying and resolving the most serious trade and investment barriers faced by U.S. firms.
- S. 2317 (Baucus) would require the USTR to identify trade enforcement priorities and to take action with respect to priority foreign country trade practices. It also includes a sense of Congress that the President should instruct the United States Executive Director to the International Monetary Fund to request the Managing Director of the Fund to use more aggressively the Fund's power to request consultations with any member country regarding that country's exchange rate policies.
- S. 14 (Stabenow) and H.R. 1575 (Myrick) direct the Secretary of the Treasury to negotiate with China to accept a market-based system of currency valuation, and would impose an additional duty of 27.5% on Chinese goods imported into the United States unless the President submits a certification to Congress that China is no longer manipulating the rate of exchange and is complying with accepted market-based trading policies.
- H.R. 3004 (English) would require the Treasury Department to determine if China manipulated its currency and to impose additional tariffs on Chinese goods comparable to the rate of currency manipulation.
- H.R. 3157 (Dingell) and S. 377 (Lieberman) direct the President to negotiate with those countries determined to be engaged most egregiously in currency manipulation and to seek an end to such manipulation. If an agreement is not reached, the President is directed to institute proceedings under the relevant U.S. and international trade laws (such as the WTO) and to seek appropriate damages and remedies for the U.S. manufacturers and other affected parties.
- H.R. 2208 (Manzullo), S. 984 (Snowe), and S. 1048 (Schumer) add changes to the criteria that the U.S. Treasury Department is required to consider when making a

determination on currency manipulation (including a protracted large-scale intervention in one direction in the exchange markets) in its bi-annual reports on International Economic and Exchange Rate Policies.

- H.R. 2414 (Rogers, Mike) would require the Treasury Department to make a determination whether China's currency policy interferes with effective balance of payments adjustments or confers a competitive advantage in international trade that would not exist if the currency value were set by market forces. If such a determination were made, the President would be required to bring a WTO case against China to seek across-the-board tariffs on Chinese goods in order to offset the subsidy effects of undervaluation.
- H.R. 1498 (Tim Ryan) would apply U.S. countervailing laws to countries that manipulate their currencies.
- S.Res. 270 (Bayh) expresses the sense of the Senate that the International Monetary Fund should investigate whether China is manipulating its currency.

REFERENCES

[1] The currency is convertible on a current account basis (such as for trade transactions), but not on a capital account basis (for various types of financial flows, such as portfolio investment). In addition, holdings of foreign exchange by Chinese firms and individuals are closely regulated by the government.

[2] A brief summary of this report can be found in CRS Report RS21625, *China's Currency: A Summary of the Economic Issues*, by Wayne Morrison and Marc Labonte.

[3] See Prepared Remarks of Dr. C. Fred Bergsten, President, Institute for International Economics, before the House Small Business Committee, June 25, 2003.

[4] Besides the currency issue, several U.S. interest groups have complained about other Chinese economic policies deemed unfair, including Chinese government subsidies, selling goods below cost (dumping), poor environmental practices, abusive labor practices, and piracy of U.S. intellectual property rights. These issues are discussed in CRS Report RL33536, *China-U.S. Trade Issues*, by Wayne M. Morrison.

[5] Supporters of this legislation cited estimates of the yuan's undervaluation ranging from 15% to 40%; they derived the 27.5% tariff figure in their bill from the average of the low-high estimates.

[6] Treasury Department Press Release, December 15, 2006.

[7] This appears to have been mainly a symbolic gesture since the yuan has never appreciated by the full 0.3% on any day since it was reformed in July 2005.

[8] It has appreciated by 8.0% overall from when the rate was pegged at 8.28 prior to the July reforms.

[9] General Accountability Office, *Treasury Assessments Have Not Found Currency Manipulation, but Concerns about Exchange Rates Continue*, Report GAO-05-351, April 2005 [http://www.gao.gov/new.items/d05351.pdf]. South Korea and Taiwan have also been designated for currency manipulation in the Treasury reports.

[10] U.S. Treasury Department, *Report to Congress on International Economic and Exchange Rate Policies*, November 2005.

[11] The 1988 Omnibus Trade and Competitiveness Act requires the Treasury Department to determine whether countries manipulate the rate of exchange between their currency and the United States dollar for purposes of preventing effective balance of payments adjustment or gaining an unfair competitive advantage in international trade.

[12] U.S. Treasury Department, *Report to Congress on International Economic and Exchange Rate Policies*, December 19, 2006, p. 2.

[13] Treasury Department, *Report to Congress on International Economic and Exchange Rate Policies*, June 2007, p. 2.

[14] China has reportedly eliminated over 60 million jobs in the state sector since 1997; layoffs over the past few years have averaged two million annually. See, Morgan Stanley, Global Economic Forum, *The Coming Rebalancing of the Chinese Economy*, March 27, 2006.

[15] Many analysts counter that China's currency policy may actually be undermining the financial stability of the banking system because, in order to purchase foreign currency to maintain a target exchange rate, the government must boost the money supply. While some of this money may be "sterilized" by government-issued bonds, some of it may enter the economy. Analysts contend that this has made the banks more prone to extend loans to risky ventures and thus may increase the level of bank-held non-performing loans.

[16] Chinese officials contend that during the Asian crisis, when several other nations sharply devalued their currencies, China "held the line" by not devaluing its currency (which might have prompted a new round of destructive devaluations across Asia). This policy was highly praised by U.S. officials, including President Clinton.

[17] Prior 1994, China maintained a dual exchange rate system: an official exchange rate of about 5.8 yuan to the dollar and a market swap rate (used mainly for trade transactions) of about 8.7 yuan to the dollar (at the end of 1993). The reforms in 1994 unified the two rates. Since Hong Kong also fixes its exchange rate to the dollar, China in effect also maintains a fixed exchange rate with Hong Kong.

[18] Year-end values.

[19] Only data on overall Chinese foreign reserves are publicly available. Data are not available to determine the value of assets by country held by China. Treasury Department data indicate that the total level of long-term securities (including stock, other equity, Treasury debt, agency debt, and corporate debt) held by China at the end of June 2006 was $682 billion. China's foreign exchange reserves at the end of June 2006 was $941 billion, indicating that at least 72% of China's reserves may be in U.S. assets (assuming that most of these assets are in the hands of a Chinese government entity). Source: U.S. Treasury "Report on Foreign Portfolio Holdings of U.S. Securities," May 2007; U.S. Treasury International Capital System.

[20] If the demand for yuan relative to dollars were to decline, the central bank would face the opposite situation. It would need to buy yuan from the public in exchange for U.S. dollars to maintain the peg. This strategy could only be continued until the central bank's dollar reserves were exhausted, at which point the peg would have to be abandoned.

[21] In March 2007, the Chinese finance minister announced that it would shift a small portion of the foreign reserves into higher yielding assets. Presumably, these reserves would remain invested in foreign assets; otherwise, the portfolio shift would alter the

currency's value. See Jim Yardley and David Barboza, "China to Open Fund to Invest Currency Reserves," *New York Times*, March 9, 2007.

[22] By June 14, 2007, it had appreciated by a total of 5.9%.

[23] Officially, China fixed its exchange rate to a currency basket in July 2005, which is similar to fixing the yuan to one currency except the yuan is now theoretically fixed against the (weighted) average value of the currencies in its "basket": primarily the dollar, euro, yen, and Korean won. The exact weights of the currencies in the basket has not been announced. Theoretically, this means that the yuan would no longer be fixed to the dollar, since every time the other exchange rates in the basket appreciate or depreciate against the dollar, so will the yuan, but to a lesser extent. Thus, fixing the yuan to a basket of currencies does not rule out the possibility that the yuan could appreciate against the dollar (anytime the other currencies in the basket appreciate against the dollar). In practice, the yuan has changed in value very little against the dollar when the other currencies in the basket have changed in value vis-a-vis the dollar since July 2005, which casts doubt on China's claim that it has fixed the yuan to a basket — unless it is a basket that is overwhelmingly weighted to the dollar.

[24] 2004 and 2005 data are estimates. Private portfolio capital flows are measured as portfolio investment, short-term capital, valuation changes, exceptional financing, and net errors and omissions. Some analysts have argued that some speculative flows are likely to be recorded in errors and omissions since capital controls require them to be made covertly. For more information, see Eswar Prasad and Shang-Jin Wei, "The Chinese Approach to Capital Inflows: Patterns and Possible Explanations," IMF working paper 05/79, April 2005.

[25] Some commentators have suggested that the extent of yuan undervaluation can be estimated from inflation differentials. In other words, although the nominal exchange rate has been constant, adjusting for inflation can determine how much the real rate has depreciated, and proves that the yuan is undervalued. The problem with this approach is that the estimate will be highly sensitive to the selection of the base year. For example, if the base year was 1996, the yuan would have been undervalued by 14% in 2002, but if the base year was 1994, the yuan would have been *overvalued* by 5% in 2002. The current account balance was close to zero (one definition of equilibrium) in both years.

[26] The Chinese can try to offset the upward pressure on prices by selling Chinese government securities to take the additional yuan out of circulation (called "sterilized intervention"). But this will push interest rates back up, attracting more foreign capital to China, causing the central bank's dollar reserves and the supply of yuan to expand again. It is difficult to tell whether the Chinese have sterilized their foreign reserve accumulation in recent years. All else equal, if China sterilized its intervention, the growth rate of the money supply and the inflation rate would not rise. The growth rate of one measure of the Chinese money supply, M2, accelerated in both 2001 and 2002. The growth rate of another measure, M1, decelerated in 2001 but accelerated in 2002. Inflation was very low through 2003, but rose to 3.9% in 2004. However, inflation and money growth could have been affected by factors other than reserve accumulation in recent years. It has been argued that sterilization is an "unfair" practice to use with a peg, since it is meant to prevent the price adjustment that brings trade between the two countries back into equilibrium.

[27] Ernest H. Preeg, "Exchange Rate Manipulation to Gain an Unfair Competitive Advantage: The Case against Japan and China," in C. Fred Bergsten and John Williamson, eds., *Dollar Overvaluation and the World Economy* (Washington, DC: Institute for International Economics, 2003).

[28] In addition to the general criticisms of all studies below, there some specific criticisms of the Preeg estimate. First, Preeg's conversion of the rule of thumb from dollar terms to percentage of the total trade deficit is without justification. His conversion implies that if the U.S. trade deficit were $1, a 40% decline in the dollar would lower the deficit by $1. By that logic, if the trade deficit were $1 trillion, a 40% decline in the dollar would lower the deficit by $1 trillion. Clearly, a 40% decline in the dollar cannot have such different effects on the trade deficit simply because the dollar value of the trade deficit has changed. Second, Preeg applies his estimate based on U.S. data to the Chinese trade surplus without any supporting evidence. Since the United States and China have different economies, trading patterns, trade balances, and exchange rate regimes, there is no reason to think the estimate would be the same for both countries. He also uses overall and bilateral trade balances interchangeably. There is no reason to think that a 40% decline in the dollar would have the same effect on a $400 billion U.S. overall trade deficit (from which he does not subtract FDI) as a 40% decline in the yuan would have on a $60 billion bilateral Chinese trade surplus less FDI.

[29] According to the data cited elsewhere in this report, the actual surplus in 2002 was 2.9% of GDP and 2.2% in 2003.

[30] Morris Goldstein, testimony before the Subcommittee on Domestic and International Monetary Policy, Committee on Financial Services, U.S. House of Representatives, October 1, 2003.

[31] Jim O'Neill and Dominic Wilson, *How China Can Help the World,* Goldman Sachs Global Economics Paper 97, September 17, 2003.

[32] Virginie Coudert and Cecile Couharde, "Real Equilibrium Exchange Rate in China," Centre d'Etudes Prospectives et d'Informations Internationales, working paper 2005-01, January 2005.

[33] A thorough attempt to estimate exchange rates using this method can be found in John Williamson, ed., *Estimating Equilibrium Exchange Rates* (Washington, DC: Institute for International Economics, 1994).

[34] Steven Dunaway et al., "How Robust are Estimates of Equilibrium Real Exchange Rates: The Case of China," IMF working paper 06/220, October 2006.

[35] Barry Bosworth, "Valuing the Renminbi," paper presented at Tokyo Club Research Meeting, February 9-10, 2004.

[36] Tao Wang, "Exchange Rate Dynamics," in Eswar Prasad, ed., "China's Growth and Integration into the World Economy," International Monetary Fund, Occasional Paper 232, 2004, Ch. 4.

[37] Sensible rules of thumb for long-term sustainability, such as estimating the current account deficit that would keep U.S. assets a constant share of foreign investment portfolios, need not hold in the short run. For instance, after a change in fundamentals, current account deficits may persist for several years as the United States transitions to a new steady state.

[38] "The Big Mac Index," *Economist*, February 1, 2007.

[39] Li Ong, "Burgernomics: The Economics of the Big Mac Standard," *Journal of International Money and Finance*, vol. 16, no. 6 (December 1997), p. 865.

[40] Bosworth points out that, by this measure, the Indian rupee is even more undervalued, yet few people make that argument. Bosworth, *Op Cit.*

[41] Coudert and Couharde, Op. Cit.

[42] Jeffrey Frankel, "On the Renminbi: The Choice Between Adjustment Under a Fixed Exchange Rate and Adjustment Under a Flexible Exchange Rate," National Bureau of Economic Research, working paper 11274, April 2005, p. 3.

[43] A. Benassy-Quere et al., "Burden Sharing and Exchange-Rate Misalignments with the Group of 20," Centre d'Etudes Prospectives et d'Informations Internationales, working paper 2004-13, September 2004. They find the dollar to be overvalued by 14% overall in 2001.

[44] Wang, Op. Cit.

[45] For a survey of valuation estimates and an overview of methodological considerations, see Steven Dunaway and Xiangming Li, "Estimating China's "Equilibrium" Real Exchange Rate," International Monetary Fund, working paper 05/202, October 2005.

[46] Yin-Wong Cheung, Menzie Chinn, and Eiji Fujii, "The Overvaluation of Renminbi Undervaluation," National Bureau of Economic Research, working paper 12850, January 2007.

[47] Steven Dunaway et al, "How Robust are Estimates of Equilibrium Real Exchange Rates: The Case of China," IMF working paper 06/220, October 2006.

[48] U.S. Treasury Department, *Report on International Economic and Exchange Rate Policies*, December 2006, Appendix II.

[49] U.S. and Chinese data on their bilateral trade differ substantially, due mainly to how each side counts Chinese exports and imports that are transshipped through Hong Kong. China counts most of its exports that go to Hong Kong but are later re-exported to the United States as Chinese exports to Hong Kong. As a result, Chinese statistics state that it had a $144.3 billion trade surplus with the United States in 2006. The United States counts imports from Hong Kong that originated from China as imports from China, but it often fails to attribute exports to China that pass through Hong Kong as exports to China. As a result, the United States and China cannot agree on the actual size of the U.S.-China trade imbalance. See Robert Feenstra et al., "The U.S.-China Bilateral Trade Balance: Its Size and Determinants," NBER Working Paper 6598 (June 1998).

[50] One analyst has estimated that the domestic value-added content of Chinese exports to the United States by foreign-invested firms in China to be about 20%, while 80% comes from the value of imported parts that come into China for assembly. As a result, an appreciation of China's currency would likely have only a minor effect on China's exports to the United States (since the cost of imported inputs would fall as a result). See Testimony of Professor Lawrence J. Lau before the Congressional-Executive Commission on China, *Is China Playing by the Rules? Free Trade, Fair Trade, and WTO Compliance*, hearing, September 24, 2003.

[51] For the most part, the Chinese government has tried to use administrative action to slow credit and investment growth with mixed success.

[52] This generally refers to those reserves that are sterilized (such as through the issuance of government bonds and the expansion of bank reserve requirements). According to

the IMF, in 2005, about half of China's new foreign exchange reserves were sterilized, while the rest were added to the money supply.

[53] Putting exchange rate issues aside, most economists maintain that trade is a win-win situation for the economy as a whole, but produces losers within the economy. This view derives from the principle of comparative advantage, which states that trade shifts production to the goods a country is relatively talented at producing from goods it is relatively less talented at producing. As trade expands, production of goods with a comparative disadvantage will decline in the United States, to the detriment of workers and investors in those sectors (offset by higher employment and profits in sectors with a comparative advantage). Economists generally argue that free trade should be pursued because the gains from trade are large enough that the losers from trade can be compensated by the winners, and the winners will still be better off. Critics argue that the losses from free trade are not acceptable as long as the political system fails to compensate the losers fairly. See CRS Report RL32059, *Trade, Trade Barriers, and Trade Deficits: Implications for U.S. Economic Welfare*, by Craig K. Elwell.

[54] Testimony of Franklin J. Vargo, National Association of Manufacturers, before the House Committee on Financial Services, Subcommittee on Domestic and International Monetary, Trade, and Technology Policy hearing, *China's Exchange Rate Regime and Its Effects on the U.S. Economy*, October 1, 2003.

[55] Chinese Treasury security holdings constitute about 19.1% of total foreign holdings of such securities.

[56] Some commentators have compared the undervalued exchange rate to a Chinese tariff on U.S. imports. One major difference between a tariff and the peg is that a tariff does not result in any benefit to U.S. consumers, as the peg does. A more appropriate comparison might be an export subsidy, which benefits consumers who purchase the subsidized product at a lower cost, but may harm some domestic firms that must compete against the subsidized product.

[57] See CRS Report RL32350, *Deindustrialization of the U.S. Economy*, by Craig Elwell. A thorough analysis of the trend can also be found in Robert Rowthorn and Ramana Rasmaswamy, *Deindustrialization: Its Causes and Implications*, Economic Issues 10 (Washington, DC: International Monetary Fund, 1997).

[58] Council of Economic Advisers, *2007 Economic Report of the President.*

[59] Lower wages alone do not give China a price advantage relative to the United States. U.S. workers are much more productive than Chinese workers, and this primarily accounts for their higher wages. Lower unit labor costs (wages divided by productivity) determine which country has a price advantage. In labor-intensive industries, China is likely to have lower unit labor costs; in knowledge-intensive industries, the United States is likely to have lower unit labor costs.

[60] Alliance Capital, Management L.P., Alliance Bernstein, U.S. Weekly Economic Update, *Manufacturing Payrolls Declining Globally: The Untold Story*, by Joseph Carson, October 10, 2003. Note that the study attributes most of the job reductions in China in the manufacturing sector to increased productivity in China. However, it is likely that the Chinese government's restructuring of inefficient state-owned enterprises, and consequent large-scale layoffs by such firms, was also a major factor.

[61] Alliance Capital, Management L.P., Alliance Bernstein, U.S. Weekly Economic Update, *Manufacturing Jobs Still Declining in Industrialized Economies*, by Joseph Carson, February 18, 2005.

[62] Testimony of Chairman Alan Greenspan before the Senate Finance Committee, June 23, 2005.

[63] Federal Reserve Bank of Chicago, *Chicago Fed Letter*, November 2003.

[64] According to the study, U.S. manufactured domestic exports declined by 7.5% in 2001 and by 5.6% in 2002.

[65] See Congressional Budget Office, *Causes and Consequences of the Trade Deficit*, March 2000.

[66] Nations that fail to save enough to meet their investment needs must obtain savings from other countries with high savings rates. By obtaining resources from foreign investors for its investment needs, the United States is able to enjoy a higher rate of consumption than it would if investment were funded by domestic savings alone (although many analysts warn that America's low savings rate could be risky to the U.S. economy in the long run). The inflow of foreign capital to the United States is equivalent to the United States borrowing from the rest of the world. The only way the United States can borrow from the rest of the world is by importing more than it exports (running a trade deficit).

[67] The rate of U.S. saving is among the lowest by industrialized nations. China on the other hand has one of the world's highest saving rates. China's extraordinarily high saving rate is largely the result of China's undeveloped health care system, pension system, and social safety net. For example, many Chinese individuals believe they will need to draw on personal savings to pay for health care if they or a family member had a serious illness. In addition, an underdeveloped financial system prevents most people from being able to borrow money for large purchases (such as a car or home), forcing people to rely on savings.

[68] From a foreign policy perspective, some U.S. policymakers have expressed concern over the high level of U.S. government debt owed to the Chinese government.

[69] For more information, see CRS Report RL30534, *America's Growing Current Account Deficit: Its Cause and What It Means for the Economy*, by Marc Labonte and Gail Makinen.

[70] Morris Goldstein and Nicholas Lardy (Institute for International Economics) have proposed a two-stage solution. During the first stage, the yuan would be appreciated by 15%-25%, the currency band expanded to between 5% and 7%, and the yuan would be pegged to a basket of major foreign currencies (the dollar, the yen, and the euro). In the second stage, China would, once it reformed its financial sector, adopt a managed floating exchange system. See "Two-Stage Currency Reform for China," *Wall Street Journal*, September 12, 2003.

[71] From a practical perspective, such a designation would require Treasury to negotiate with China to end such practices, something Treasury is already doing.

[72] Treasury appears to believe that under current U.S. law, there has to be *intent* to prevent an effective balance of payments or to seek an unfair competitive advantage, before a country can be designated as a currency manipulator. Sponsors of legislation to replace the term currency manipulation with fundamental currency misalignment appear to be attempting to force Treasury to make a designation when countries with large trade

surpluses make large scale interventions in currency markets to keep the value of their currencies low, regardless of whether or not they do so for balance of payments or competitive reasons.

[73] G-7 members include the United States, Japan, Canada, the United Kingdom, France, Germany, and Italy. China has also participated in G-8 meetings, which includes G-7 members plus Russia.

[74] Treasury Department Press Release, February 10, 2007.

[75] Press reports indicate that Japan has been reluctant to put pressure on China over its currency system in the G-7, in part because of criticism Japan has received over its own currency policies.

[76] Some analysts argue that China's currency policy has induced other East Asian economies, particularly Japan, Taiwan, and South Korea to intervene in currency markets to keep their currencies weak (in order to compete with Chinese exports). Thus, the United States could seek to reach a broad consensus with all the major economies in East Asia to halt or limit currency interventions.

[77] For more information on this option, see CRS Report RL33322, *China, the United States, and the IMF: Negotiating Exchange Rate Adjustment*, by Jonathan E. Sanford.

[78] Section 301 to 309 of the 1974 Trade Act, as amended. For additional information, see CRS Report 98-454, *Section 301 of the Trade Act of 1974, as Amended: Its Operation and Issues Involving Its Use by the United States,* by Wayne Morrison.

[79] In addition, any imposed U.S. trade restrictions of Chinese goods would likely reduce overall U.S. economic welfare, because the reduction in the welfare of U.S. consumers (as import prices rise) would likely exceed the increase in welfare of U.S. producers.

[80] Note, OPIC is already barred from operating in China due to existing U.S. sanctions.

[81] For example, some analysts contend that China's currency policy violates: (1) Article XV of the General Agreement on Tariffs and Trade (GATT) agreement dealing with exchange arrangements, (2) the WTO Agreements on Subsidies and Countervailing Measures, and/or (3) GATT Article XXIII dealing with nullification or impairment of the benefits of a trade agreement.

[82] Dispute resolution in the WTO is carried out under the Dispute Resolution Understanding (DSU). See CRS Report RS20088, *Dispute Settlement in the World Trade Organization*, by Jeanne J. Grimmett.

[83] Many trade analysts argue that countries are more likely to comply with rulings by multilateral organizations to which they are parties (and whose rules they have agreed to comply with) than accede to the wishes of another country under the threat of unilateral sanctions.

[84] USTR press release, November 12, 2004.

[85] See CRS Report RS20570, *Trade Remedies and the U.S.-China Bilateral WTO Accession Agreement*, by William H. Cooper.

[86] The U.S. International Trade Commission is in charge of making market disruption determinations under the safeguard provisions for most products (with the exception of textiles and apparel, which are handled by the Committee for the Implementation of the Textile Agreements, an inter-agency committee chaired by the U.S. Commerce Department). Import relief is subject to presidential approval.

[87] It is also possible that if China made changes to its exchange rate policy (such as allowing the yuan to appreciate) in order to ease political pressure from the United

States, it would expect something in return, such as U.S. pressure on China to ease on other trade issues.

[88] The United States has pending WTO dispute resolution cases against China on IPR protection and market access, trade subsidies, and discriminatory import tariffs.

[89] Another problem for China if the yuan appreciated, whether through floating or a revaluation, is that it would reduce the value of their U.S. assets. Since China held $350 billion of U.S. Treasury securities at the end of 2006 and $190 billion of U.S. agency debt in June 2005 — much of it in the central bank — these capital losses could potentially be very large. Unlike a private bank, a central bank does not have to worry about insolvency as a result of capital losses since they control their liabilities (currency), but it could potentially have negative fiscal or inflationary ramifications. See "A License to Lose Money," *The Economist*, April 30, 2005, p. 74.

[90] Some economists argue that short-term movements in floating exchange rates cannot always be explained by economic fundamentals. If this were the case, then the floating exchange rate could become inexplicably overvalued (undervalued) at times, reducing (increasing) the output of U.S. exporters and U.S. firms that compete with Chinese imports. These economists often favor fixed or managed exchange rates to prevent these unexplainable fluctuations, which they argue are detrimental to U.S. economic well-being. Other economists argue that movements in floating exchange rates are rational, and therefore lead to economically efficient outcomes. They doubt that governments are better equipped to identify currency imbalances than market professionals.

[91] This argument is made in Morris Goldstein and Nicholas Lardy, "A Modest Proposal for China's Renminbi,"*Financial Times*, August 26, 2003. Alternatively, if Chinese citizens proved unconcerned about keeping their wealth in Chinese assets, the removal of capital controls could lead to a greater inflow of foreign capital since foreigners would be less concerned about being unable to access their Chinese investments. This would cause the exchange rate to appreciate.

[92] Even in cases where jobs have shifted from the United States to China, there are still questions as to the net impact to the United States. If the United States is no longer internationally competitive in certain industries, it may be more economically efficient to allow market forces to direct resources away from those industries and toward economic activities where the United States has a greater comparative advantage. The challenge for policymakers is how to help displaced workers get the training they need to find well-paying jobs that are comparable to or better than the jobs they lost.

[93] A designation would occur based on such factors as protracted large-scale currency intervention, excessive reserve accumulation, restrictions on capital flows, or any other policy the Treasury Department determines that would warrant such a designation.

[94] OPIC has been banned from operating in China since 1989 under U.S. sanctions.

In: Currency Interventions, Fluctuations...
Editor: L. C. Hilbert, pp. 49-69
ISBN: 978-1-60456-078-7

Chapter 2

JAPAN'S CURRENCY INTERVENTION: POLICY ISSUES*

Dick K. Nanto
Specialist in Industry and Trade Foreign Affairs, Defense, and Trade Division

ABSTRACT

Japan's intervention to slow the upward appreciation of the yen has raised concerns in the United States and brought charges that Tokyo is manipulating its exchange rate in order to gain unfair advantage in world trade. This coincides with similar charges being made with respect to the currencies of the People's Republic of China and South Korea. In the 110th Congress, H.R. 2886 (Knollenberg)/S. 1021(Stabenow) (Japan Currency Manipulation Act), H.R. 782 (Tim Ryan)/S. 796 (Bunning) (Fair Currency Act of 2007), S. 1677 (Dodd) (Currency Reform and Financial Markets Access Act of 2007), and S. 1607 (Baucus) (Currency Exchange Rate Oversight Reform Act of 2007) address currency misalignment in general or by Japan in particular.

In the past, Japan has intervened (bought dollars and sold yen) extensively to counter the yen's appreciation, but since March 2004, the Japanese government has not intervened significantly, although some claim that Tokyo continues to "talk down the value of the yen." This heavy buying of dollars has resulted in an accumulation of official foreign exchange reserves that exceeded a record $893 billion (June 2007) by Japan. The intervention, however, seems to have had little lasting effect. It may only have slowed the rise in value of the yen rather than reverse its direction of change. For the past few years, the yen has been depreciating and is now at a 20-year low. Estimates on the cumulative effect of the interventions range from an undervaluation of the yen of about 3 or 4 yen to as much as 20 yen per dollar. Private company estimates of the misalignment of the yen range from an overvaluation of 1.8% to an underevaluation of 29%. The median value of these estimates is that the yen is about 15% undervalued, but it is not known how much of the undervaluation resulted from market forces and how much from intervention.

In 2006, the U.S. Secretary of the Treasury indicated that it had not found currency manipulation by any country, including by Japan. An April 2005 report by the Government Accountability Office reported that Treasury had not found currency manipulation because it viewed "Japan's exchange rate interventions as part of a macroeconomic policy aimed at combating deflation..." In its May 2006 report on

* Excerpted from CRS Report RL33178, dated July 13, 2007.

consultations with Japan, the International Monetary Fund (IMF), likewise, did not find currency manipulation by Japan. The criteria for finding currency manipulation, however, allows for considerable leeway by Treasury and the IMF.

One problem with the focus on currency intervention to correct balance of trade deficits is that only about half of the increase in the value of a foreign currency is reflected in prices of imports into the United States. Periods of heaviest intervention also coincided with slower (not faster) economic growth rates for Japan.

Major policy options for Congress include (1) let the market adjust ; (2) clarify the definition of currency manipulation; (3) require negotiations and reports; (4) require the President to certify which countries are manipulating their currencies and take remedial action if the manipulation is not halted; (5) take the case to the World Trade Organization or appeal to the IMF; or (6) oppose any change in governance in the IMF benefitting Japan. This report will be updated as circumstances require.

Japan's intervention to slow the upward revaluation of the yen has raised concerns in the United States and brought charges that Tokyo is manipulating its exchange rate in order to gain unfair advantage in world trade. This coincides with similar charges being made with respect to the currency of China. This report provides an overview and analysis of Japan's official intervention into currency markets, reviews various studies on the probable effect of that intervention, examines the charge that Japan has manipulated its exchange rate as defined by the International Monetary Fund (IMF), and reviews legislation and policy options.

Foreign governments intervene into currency markets by buying foreign exchange — usually dollars, Euros, or British pounds — in order to increase demand for dollars and support its value relative to the intervening government's own currency. Likewise, they can sell foreign exchange in order to decrease demand for dollars and increase the value of the country's own currency. In Japan's case, it has usually bought dollars from its domestic exporters in exchange for yen and used those dollars to buy U.S. Treasury securities or other liquid dollar assets.

In the 110th Congress, H.2886 (Knollenberg)/S. 1021 (Stabenow) (Japan Currency Manipulation Act) would require negotiation, reports, and other action with respect to Japan's currency actions. This bill states in its findings that Japan's exchange rate provides a subsidy to Japanese exporters and an unfair competitive advantage for Japanese automobile manufacturers. H.R. 782 (Ryan)/S. 796 (Bunning) (Fair Currency Act of 2007) would provide that exchange-rate misalignment byan foreign nation is a countervailable export subsidy and also would clarify the definition of manipulation with respect to currency.

S. 1607 (Baucus) (Currency Exchange Rate Oversight Reform Act of 2007) would require the Treasury Department to identify currencies that are fundamentally misaligned and would require action to correct the misalignment. S. 1677 (Dodd), Currency Reform and Financial Markets Access Act of 2007, would require the Treasury Department to identify countries that manipulate their currencies regardless of their intent and to submit an action plan for ending the manipulation, and gives Treasury the authority to file a case in the WTO.

Concern over currency manipulation, intervention, and misalignment stems from the basic U.S. interest in American national prosperity. Manipulation of exchange rates to undervalue foreign currencies potentially can increase the U.S. trade deficit,[1] increase U.S. dependency on foreign investors to finance U.S. budget deficits, affect the level of U.S. interest rates, and negatively affect U.S. businesses competing with imports or exporting.

In Japan's case, the Bank of Japan (in consultation with the Ministry of Finance) has bought U.S. Treasury securities and other liquid dollar assets at times when the value of the dollar relative to the yen was declining. The intended result was to keep the value of the yen from appreciating too quickly in order to keep the price of Japanese exports from rising in markets such as those in the United States and to maintain the profitability of those exports.

Some experts argue that the yen is undervalued by 10% to 29% or more. If so, this would give manyJapanese manufacturers a significant price advantage over U.S. competitors. The U.S.-headquartered automobile industry, for example, claims that the undervalued yen generates a price advantage of about $4,000 per car to vehicles made in Japan and a resultant surge in sales of such vehicles in the United States.[2] As shown in figure 1, the real effective value of the yen has reached a 20-year low, but it is not clear whether this undervaluation has resulted from government intervention and manipulation or from private market forces.[3]

Most economic studies indicate that currency intervention for large countries with floating exchange rates, such as Japan, merely slows the rate of currency appreciation or depreciation over the short run (less than 30 days) and has little effect over the long term. Whether Japan has manipulated its exchange rate under criteria set by the International Monetary Fund (IMF) is open to debate. The IMF and the Secretary of the Treasury have not found such manipulation in recent years,[4] but others charge that such manipulation has taken place. Japan claims that it has not intervened in foreign exchange markets since March 2004, although some claim that Japan still "talks down the value of the yen."

Even without official intervention, Japan's holdings of foreign exchange continue to increase because of interest Japan earns by investing that foreign exchange in U.S. Treasury bills and other securities. In 2006, Japan earned $40.3 billion more on its investments (including business direct investments) in the United States than Americans earned on their investments in Japan.[5]

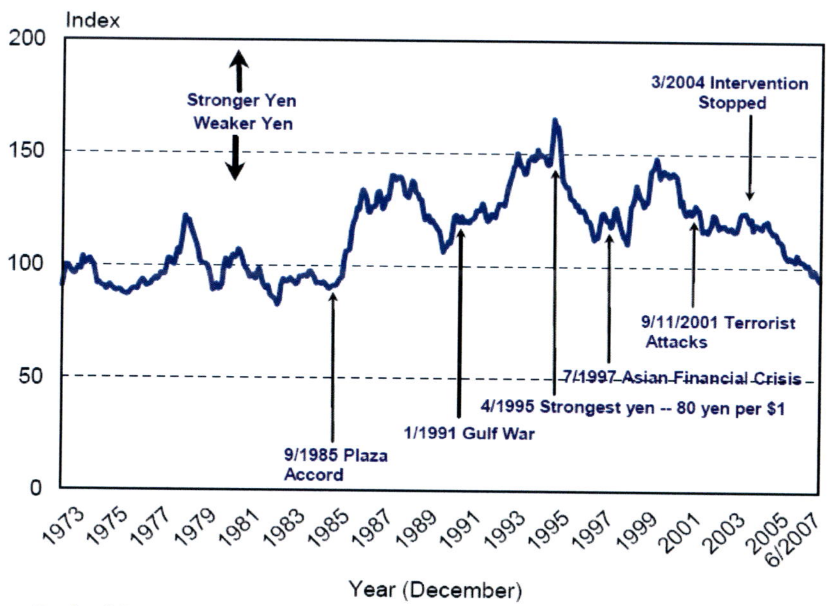

Data Source: Bank of Japan.

Figure 1. Japan's Real Effective Exchange Rate (March 1973=100).

THE INTERVENTIONS

In 1971, when the link between the U.S. dollar and gold was severed and the dollar was allowed to float within certain bands, the yen began to appreciate in value. The yen/dollar exchange rate, established during the U.S. occupation of Japan in 1949, had been held at 360 yen per dollar for 22 years. Since then, it appreciated to around 105 yen per dollar in early 2005, but in late 2005 it had depreciated to around 120 yen per dollar before rising slightly to about 119 yen per dollar in March 2007.

Japan's government has intervened in currency markets to buy dollars or other foreign exchange at times when the yen was appreciating at a pace considered to be too rapid. Japan also has intervened by selling dollars at times when the yen was depreciating too rapidly. The net result of this intervention is that Japan's holdings of foreign exchange reserves have risen to about $888 billion in March 2007.[6]

As can be seen in figure 2, the most significant of Japan's interventions to counter the yen's appreciation took place in 1976-1978, 1985-1988, 1992-1996, and 1998-2004. Since March 2004, the Japanese government has not intervened significantly in currency markets to support the value of the dollar.[7] Figure 2 also shows that despite heavy buying (or selling) of dollars during certain periods of time, the intervention seems to have had little lasting effect. It might have slowed the change in value of the yen, but the appreciation (or depreciation) occurred anyway. This is called "leaning against the wind" in economic parlance or intervening to oppose strong short-term trends rather than to reverse the direction of change. In most cases, Japan's intervention resulted in the "smoothing" of fluctuations in exchange rates rather changing the direction of movement. As one author put it, Japan seems to have won many daily battles with the foreign exchange market, yet it lost the war.[8]

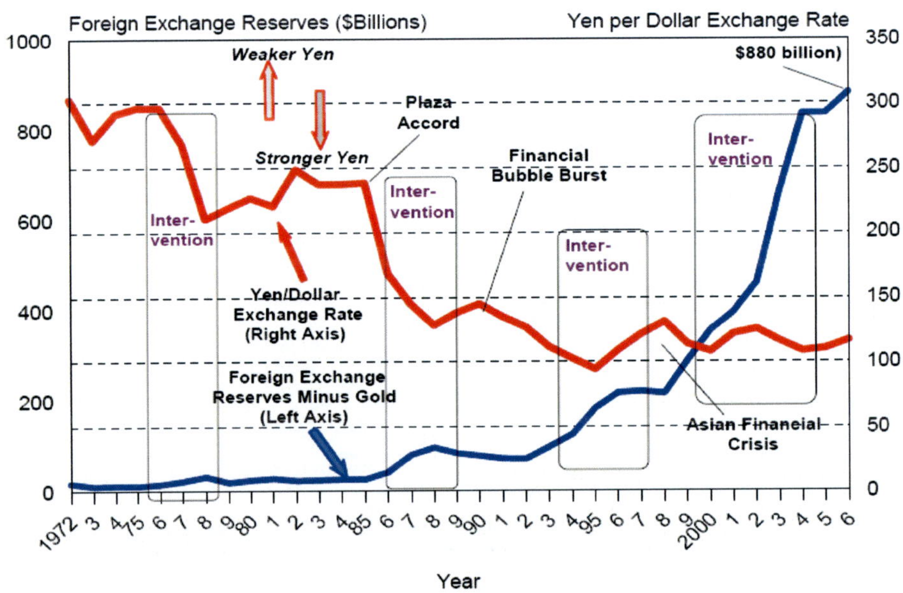

Source: Data from World Bank. World Development Indicators.

Figure 2. Japan's Exchange Rate and Foreign Exchange Reserves 1972-2006.

Even though Japan has invested hundreds of billions of dollars in buying dollar assets that are then held as foreign exchange reserves, many observers point out that such transactions are small when compared with the average daily turnover of $1.9 trillion in traditional foreign exchange markets and $2.4 trillion in over-the-counter currency and interest rate derivatives markets.[9] Currency transactions in support of imports and exports, investments, remittances, and other purposes dwarf interventions by central banks. Still, it is the effect of central government intervention on net — rather than gross — flows that make the difference (since imports and exports tend to balance on a global basis). Government purchases and sales constitute a net addition to or subtraction from global demand and supply. Also government interventions can have a powerful signaling effect on market participants who may prudently reduce their speculative buying should it be in a contrary direction to what the government is doing. Central banks also often coordinate intervention (intervening in the same direction the same day). This multiplies the effect of the intervention.

ECONOMIC STUDIES

Academic studies of intervention generally conclude that interventions did increase exchange rate volatility (moved the market), were a good indicator that the magnitude of the change in exchange value on subsequent days would decrease, and that much of it amounted to "leaning against the wind."[10] A recent study of the 19912002 period of Japanese intervention concluded that "prior to June 1995, Japanese interventions only had value as a forecast that the previous day's yen appreciation or depreciation would moderate during the current day. After June 1995, Japanese purchases of dollars had value as a forecast that the yen would depreciate" in the very short run. This analysis also confirmed that large, infrequent interventions, which characterized the latter period, had a higher likelihood of success than small, frequent interventions. For 2003 and 2004, despite the record size and frequency of the intervention by Japan, the authors found it difficult to statistically distinguish the pattern of exchange rate movements on intervention days from that of all the days in that particular subperiod. This showed little effectiveness in the interventions for that subperiod and only modest effectiveness overall.[11]

Another study examining data from 1991 to 2000 found strong evidence that "sterilized" intervention (buying of dollars offset by domestic selling of yen-denominated bonds to keep Japan's money supply unchanged) systemically affected the exchange rate in the short-run (less than one month). Large-scale intervention (amounts over $1 billion) — coordinated between the Bank of Japan and the U.S. Federal Reserve — gave the highest success rates. Of the 12 "large scale coordinated" interventions studied, 11 achieved the desired effect: they moved the yen either up or down in accordance with the policy goal of the moment, although the effects were short-lived.[12]

The estimate that the yen is 10% to 20% undervalued is emphasized heavily by U.S. automaker interests. In 2003, General Motors claimed that the yen should be trading at about 100, rather than at 110 yen per dollar.[13] In late 2005, as the dollar strengthened, General Motors claimed that the relatively weak yen (111 per dollar at the time) was providing a significant cost advantage (about $3,000 per vehicle) to Japanese automakers. GM also raised the issue of "jawboning" and verbal currency intervention (talking the yen down) by high-ranking Japanese officials.[14] In a meeting between President Bush and the Big Three U.S. automakers, General Motors Chairman Rick Wagoner indicated there is still a chasm between the auto industry and President Bush on foreign exchange issues. Wagoner said the yen, in particular, was "systematically undervalued" with the car companies estimating that Japanese competitors gain a $3,000 to $9,000 cost advantage per vehicle over U.S. auto makers thanks to what is seen as an unfair currency advantage.[15] In April 2007, the Automotive Trade Policy Council (with membership by Daimler Chrysler, Ford, and GM) claimed that Japan's weak yen policy had forced U.S. automakers to contend with a $4,000 subsidy on vehicles that their Japanese competitors export from Japan to the United States.[16]

A leading proponent of the position that Japan has manipulated its exchange rate is Ernest Preeg.[17] In one study, he concluded that Japan had manipulated its exchange rate and that the yen in 2002 was about 20% undervalued and should have been around 100 yen per dollar.[18] His analysis is based on the observation that Japan's intervention has been large, protracted, and one-sided, but the 20% figure is a rough estimate based primarily on the extent of the intervention, not on a rigorous economic model.

The International Monetary Fund also conducts surveillance over the exchange rates of its member countries. In the IMF's August 2005 report on consultations with Japan, the Fund noted that compared to the United States and the Euro Area, Japan stands out for its active use of foreign exchange market intervention as a policy instrument. The IMF reported that since 1991, the Bank of Japan had intervened on 340 days, the European Central Bank on four days (since its inception in 1998), and the U.S. Federal Reserve on 22 days. The IMF further stated that "there is some evidence that intervention has had some impact on yen movements." It then quoted Takatoshi Ito, a Japanese economist, who found that intervention of about ¥2.5 trillion (about $250 billion) on average moved the exchange rate by ¥1 per dollar or about 1%.[19] The IMF's May 2006 report on consultations with Japan did not discuss exchange rate intervention.[20]

A fundamental problem with exchange rates is that no commonly accepted method exists to estimate the effectiveness of official intervention into foreign exchange markets. Many interrelated factors affect the exchange rate at any given time, and no quantitative model exists that is able to provide the magnitude of any causal relationship between intervention and an exchange rate when so many interdependent variables are acting simultaneously.[21]

A 2007 Occasional Paper No. 7 by economists at the U.S. Treasury surveyed exchange rate models and misalignments in currencies. The authors concluded that currencies cannot be said to be misaligned without estimating what the exchange rate should be. Economists use various models to estimate such hypothetical exchange rates and then compare the modeled rates to the actual ones. The study notes that the models produce widely divergent results and depend heavily on their assumptions, methodologies, and mathematical structure in trying to capture all the relevant features of an economy, particularly the behavior of financial markets. For Japan, the authors note that according to the purchasing power parity approach, Japan's currency in 2003 was overvalued (not undervalued) by 21%. According to a Big Mac index of the cost of this hamburger across countries, in May 2006, the yen at 112 yen per dollar was 28% undervalued. Using relative labor costs to calculate real effective exchange rates, in 2004, Japan's yen was undervalued by 6.3%, but was overvalued by 2.2% using relative consumer prices in the calculation. Private sector estimates likewise varywidely. Using various methods, the Hong Kongand Shanghai Banking Corporation (HSBC) estimated the yen to have been 1.8% overvalued at the end of 2005, while Goldman Sachs estimated that it was 6.9% undervalued, while J.P. Morgan Stanley came up with the figure of 14% undervalued.[22] In 2007, Morgan Stanley reported that the thirteen models it uses to value currencies provided estimates of the exchange value of the yen being between 18% overvalued and 29% undervalued with the median at 15% undervaluation.[23] These models do not, however, differentiate between undervaluation caused by intervention and that caused by market forces.

Setting aside the problems with statistical estimates, what can be said is that the Japanese economy has generated a surplus in its trade accounts for much of recent history. Without an offsetting deficit in its capital account, market forces would have forced an appreciation of the yen that would have worked to eliminate the trade surplus. From 1977 to 2004, Japan's cumulative surplus on current account (net trade in goods and services plus remittances) totaled $2,077 billion. Offsetting Japan's surplus on current account was its net capital outflow and net official purchases of foreign exchange reserves (intervention). From 1977 to 2004, Japan recorded a deficit in its capital flows (investments in foreign securities, buying foreign companies, deposits in foreign bank accounts, etc.) of $1,314 billion. In other words, Japan's private investors sent $1,314 billion more abroad than foreigners invested in Japan. The remaining $763 billion outflow ($2,077 billion minus $1,314 billion) of dollars was primarily from official currency intervention that added to Japan's foreign exchange reserves. This net buying of $763 billion[24] in dollars — over the 1977-2004 period provided more than a third (37%) of the total capital outflow from Japan to offset the country's surplus in trade. If Japan had not intervened to this extent, the yen likely would have appreciated more than it did.

Taking the estimate by Takatoshi Ito that $250 billion in intervention moved the exchange rate by about 1% or ¥1, the net effect of the direct intervention that ended in 2004 would have been around ¥3 or ¥4 per dollar. Taking the estimates by Preeg and General Motors, the upper bound on the effect of the intervention would be around 20% or about ¥20 per dollar. The range, therefore, for the effect of exchange rate undervaluation because of Japanese intervention would be from ¥3 to ¥20 per dollar with the statistical likelihood more toward the lower end of the range.

THE LINK BETWEEN EXCHANGE VALUE AND TRADE

Setting aside the question of the efficacy of Japan's intervention into exchange markets to weaken the yen, a second question is whether changes in the yen-dollar exchange rate actually affect imports and exports. In theory, Japan's intervention by buying dollars and selling yen induces a cheaper yen which then assists Japan's exporters by allowing them either to lower their export price or to maintain their export price while increasing profits. It also makes imports relatively more expensive in Japan. Lowered export prices and higher import prices will tend to increase Japan's trade surplus which then contributes to a higher growth rate. The Bank of Japan may or may not sterilize the currency operation by selling Japanese bonds locally to keep the domestic money supply constant. In an economic sense, if the intervention is not sterilized, buying dollars is equivalent to increasing the Japanese money supply, since the Finance Ministry purchases the dollars from Japanese exporters with yen which then enters the Japanese money supply.

In actual practice, the operation of currency markets often deviates from that represented in economic theory and in models. In particular, the long-term link between intervention and the foreign exchange rate is difficult to show empirically. While the intervention has short-term effects, the long-term effects on exchange rates and trade flows are much less apparent — especially considering that most of the time, the intervention leans against the wind rather than reversing the direction of change.

A second problem is that, in practice, Japan's automakers and other exporters to U.S. markets usually do not make short-run adjustments to prices in response to exchange rate fluctuations. Unlike generic commodities (such as crude oil or wheat that have standardized commodity markets), Japan's exports tend to be brand-named products for which the sellers have some control over prices. When selling in the United States, dealers and retailers of products from Japan tend to "price to market" or set prices according market conditions.[25]

For instance, between January 5, 1994, and April 19, 1995, the Japanese yen appreciated by 34% against the dollar (it rose from 113 to 80 yen per dollar). Prices for exported products from Japan to the United States should have risen significantly, but, for example, the U.S. sticker price of a Toyota Celica ST Coup rose by only 2% (it went from $16,968 to $17,285), while the suggested retail price of a large-screen Sony Trinitron television receiver actually fell by 15%. Japanese exporters simply absorbed exchange rate changes into their costs. They tended to gain or lose profits — rather than market share — because of exchange rate changes. In the case of Toyota Motors, it is estimated that the company's profit increases by ¥25 billion ($227 million) a year for every ¥1 the currency depreciates against the dollar.[26] For shipments to the United States, economic studies have found that, on average, an exchange rate change induces a price response equal to one-half the amount, although it varies by industry.[27] An implication of this lack of a complete response of domestic prices to exchange rate changes is that a currency depreciation will not necessarily eliminate — or even reduce significantly — a nation's trade deficit.

Empirical studies indicate, however, that for most countries over the long run, a real depreciation (adjusting for domestic inflation) is likely to improve a nation's current account balance while a real appreciation is likely to worsen it. In the short-run, however, the opposite is likely to occur. This is called the J-curve effect. As the value of the yen rises, for example, some Japanese exporters do increase their prices, and U.S. importers end up paying more for the quantity of goods they need. This worsens the balance of trade before U.S. importers can switch to other suppliers.[28]

Still, Japan's balance of trade does respond somewhat in the long run to a large appreciation of the yen. Japanese exporters ultimately have to either raise prices or decrease costs of production, and importers of commodities in Japan face lower international prices. This works to reduce Japan's surplus in trade (exports fall while imports rise).

One economic study indicated that, in 2002, a 1% appreciation of the yen induced a 2.2% decrease in Japan's current account surplus (balance of trade with the world in goods and services plus unilateral transfers).[29] At that time, Japan's current account surplus was about $110 billion. Therefore, a 1% yen appreciation was estimated to decrease Japan's current account balance by about $2.4 billion. Another study for 1985-1991 found that a 10% sustained appreciation of the yen would reduce Japan's trade surplus by 0.7% of gross national product (GNP).[30] At that time, Japan's GNP was around $3,000 billion. A 1% appreciation of the yen, therefore, would have reduced Japan's trade surplus by about $2.1 billion.

In actuality, from 2002 to 2004, the yen appreciated from ¥120 to ¥104 per dollar (up by 13%), but Japan's current account surplus rose (not fell) from $113 billion to $172 billion (up by 52%).[31] Part of this rise in Japan's current account surplus may have been the J-curve effect, but in this case the yen appreciation was overshadowed by other variables. Yen appreciation may have slowed the rise in Japan's current account surplus, but it did not stop it. Other factors also came into play. These included growth in the American and other major markets, relative savings and inflation rates, the level of interest rates in various markets, earnings from investments, the competitiveness of Japanese products, the price of petroleum, competition from China, and intra-firm trade by multinational corporations.

Another question is whether Japan's intervention into foreign exchange markets raised its rate of growth. Figure 3 shows Japan's currency intervention in terms of annual rates of change in its foreign exchange reserves and the yen/dollar exchange rate. It also shows Japan's economic growth rate (in real gross domestic product). The chart indicates that many of the periods of yen appreciation and intervention into foreign exchange markets to buy dollars also were periods of relatively slower — not faster — economic growth rates. Except in the late 1970s, Japan's growth performance during periods of intervention was rather lackluster. Growth tended to be higher during periods without intervention, although it can be argued that the intervention may have helped to keep economic conditions from becoming worse than they actually were.

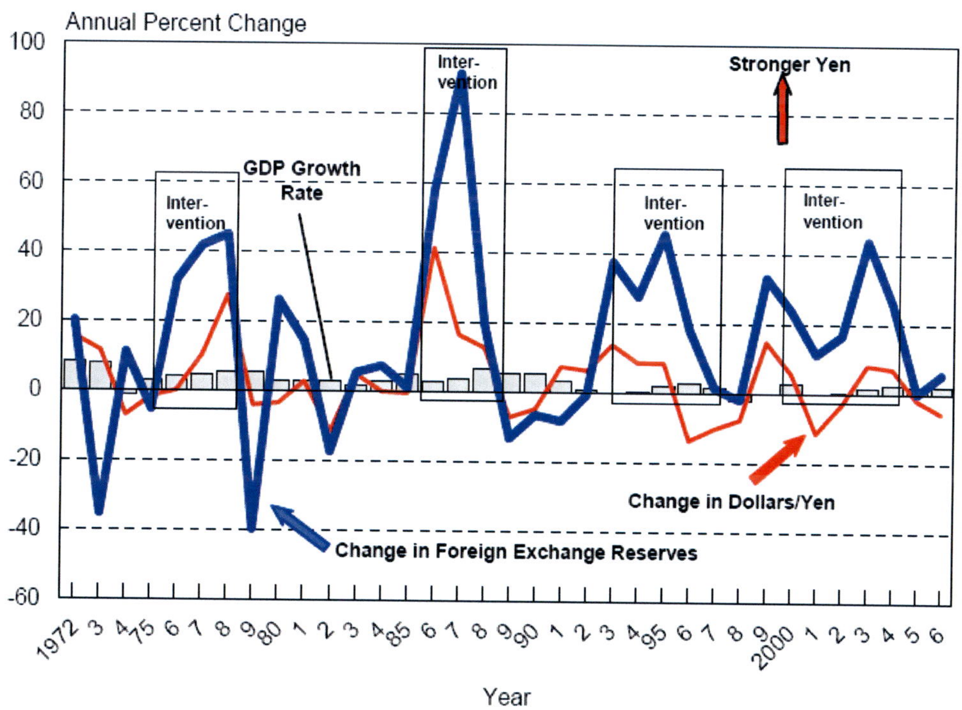

Source: Underlying data from World Bank. World Development Indicators.

Figure 3. Changes in Japan's Foreign Exchange Reserves and in the Yen/Dollar Exchange rate with Interventions and GDP Growth Rates, 1972-2006.

INTERVENTION OR MANIPULATION?

A question for U.S. policy is whether Japan's intervention into currency markets constituted manipulation of its exchange rate. Under U.S. law,[32] the Secretary of the Treasury is required to analyze the exchange rate policies of foreign countries annually (in consultation with the International Monetary Fund) and consider whether countries manipulate their exchange rate for purposes of preventing effective balance of payments adjustment or gaining unfair competitive advantage in international trade. If the Secretary considers that such manipulation is occurring with respect to countries that (1) have material global current account surpluses; and (2) have significant bilateral trade surpluses with the United States, the Secretary of the Treasury shall take action to initiate negotiations with such foreign countries on an expedited basis, in the International Monetary Fund or bilaterally, for the purpose of ensuring that such countries regularly and promptly adjust the rate of exchange between their currencies and the United States dollar to permit effective balance of payment adjustments and to eliminate the unfair advantage. The Secretary of the Treasury also is to provide reports on exchange rate policy that contain the results of exchange rate negotiations conducted pursuant to this law.

At various periods from 1988 through 1994, Treasury found that China, Taiwan, and South Korea were each considered to have manipulated their currencies.[33] In the March and November 2005 and May 2006 reports to Congress as required by the Omnibus Trade and Competitiveness Act of 1988, Treasury indicated that it had reviewed the exchange rates, external balances, foreign exchange reserve accumulation, macroeconomic trends, monetary and financial developments, state of institutional development, and financial and exchange restrictions for U.S. trading partners. In both reports, Treasury did not find currency manipulation by any country, including by Japan.[34] Likewise, in Treasury's December 2006 report to Congress, the Secretary stated that persistent Japanese deflation since 1998 has led to a substantial depreciation of the yen in real terms. Bank of Japan data indicate that the yen was at its weakest level in real trade-weighted terms in more than 20 years, even though Japanese authorities had not intervened in the foreign exchange market since March 2004.[35]

In April 2005, the Government Accountability Office examined Treasury's assessments of whether countries were manipulating their currencies and concluded that "although China and Japan have engaged in economic activities that have led to concerns about currency manipulation," Treasury "did not find that Japan met the Trade Act's definition for currency manipulation in 2003 and 2004." GAO reported that Treasury viewed "Japan's exchange rate interventions as part of a macroeconomic policy aimed at combating deflation...."[36]

In September 2005 testimony before the House Ways and Means Committee, Deputy Assistant Secretary of the Treasury David Loevinge stated that Treasury had discussed foreign exchange market issues with Japanese officials. He stated that Japan has supported the G-7 position on exchange rates, expressed in a series of G-7 Communiqués, calling for greater exchange rate flexibility. Japan also has worked with the United States to bring about greater exchange rate flexibility in China and in other large economies in East Asia.[37]

The International Monetary Fund also conducts surveillance over the exchange rates of its member countries. A 1977 decision by the Fund (as amended), a principle for guidance of member's exchange rate policies states, "A member shall avoid manipulating exchange rates or the international monetary system in order to prevent effective balance of payments adjustment or to gain unfair competitive advantage over other members." The decision, does allow, however, for governments to intervene in the exchange market if necessary to counter disorderly conditions (disruptive short-term movements in the exchange value of its currency).[38] In the IMF's August 2005 report on consultations with Japan, the Fund did not find currency manipulation, but noted that compared to the United States and the Euro Area, Japan stands out for its active use of foreign exchange market intervention as a policy instrument.[39]

As a comparison, one can compare the movement of the exchange rate between the German mark and the dollar with that for the yen and the dollar. Figure 4 shows the movement of indexes (1972 = 100) for the value of the two exchange rates. From 1972 to 2005, the yen has appreciated more than the mark, and they generally have moved together. The correlation coefficient between the two indexes is 0.82 (they move together 82% of the time). This indicates that most of the time both currencies are responding to the same outside influences.

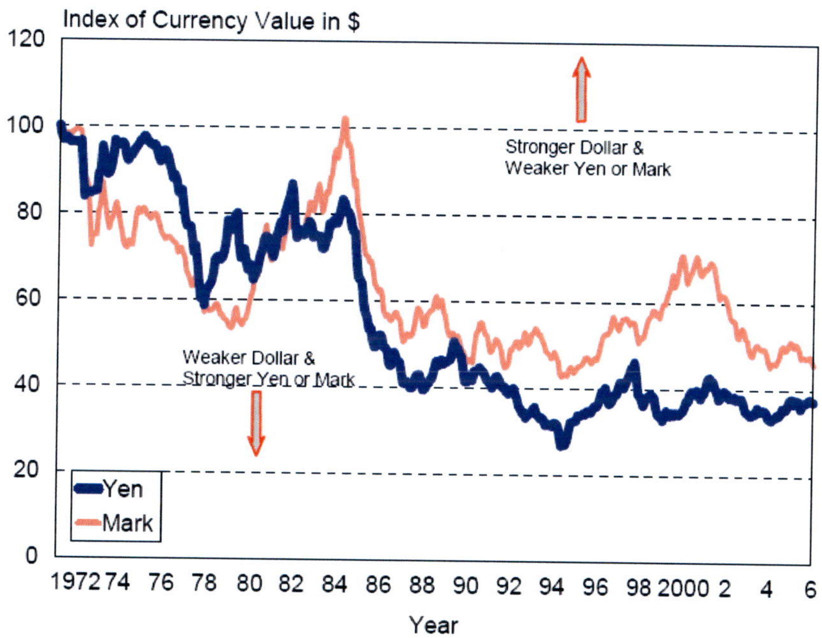

Note: 1972 = 100. Underlying exchange rates from PACIFIC Exchange Rate Service.

Figure 4. Indexes of the Value of the Japanese Yen and German Mark per U.S. Dollar.

POLICY ISSUES

Even though Japan claims that it has not intervened into currency markets since March 2004, this issue still is a U.S. policy concern because of Tokyo's past intervention and the possibility that it could resume intervening should the yen strengthen too rapidly or excessively against the dollar. Japan also may use other methods to alter the expectations of currency traders and "talk down" the yen through various statements or other "jawboning." Japan also could be caught up in the concern over China's currency policy. Policies aimed at China also could affect Japan. Currently, Tokyo seems content to abstain from active intervention into international currency markets. At some point, however, Japan may want to decrease its $830 billion in foreign exchange holdings. It would likely do this by selling dollar-denominated assets, an action that would weaken the dollar and strengthen the yen. Depending on how this potential divestiture is conducted, it could be viewed as intervention into foreign exchange markets (albeit in the opposite direction of concern).

A question remains, however, of whether the United States should take measures to compensate for past intervention by Japan. Setting aside the issue of how much past intervention actually moved the exchange rate and whether any exchange rate change affected actual market transactions, if U.S. industries were significantly impacted negatively, should remedial action be taken now? If, for example, the U.S. automobile industry lost market share because of past Japanese government attempts to reduce the value of the yen, is there action that should be taken now to remedy the lost market share?

The major policy options for Congress include the following:

- let the market adjust (do nothing);
- clarify the definition of currency manipulation;
- require reports and negotiations;
- require the President to certify which countries are manipulating their currencies and take remedial action if the manipulation is not halted; and
- convene a special meeting of the International Monetary Fund to reach an agreement on the misalignment of the yen, oppose increased voting shares or representation in international financial organizations for any country that has a currency that is manipulated or in fundamental misalignment, initiate a dispute settlement case with the World Trade Organization (WTO), or block the Overseas Private Investment Corporation from providing services to Japan.

Let the Market Adjust (Do Nothing)

Most economists argue that currency markets are so large that only extensive and coordinated intervention has any lasting effects. Countries that do intervene often find themselves "leaning against the wind" and not materially altering either the direction of or the extent of change. Also, intervention is expensive. It is not clear that Japan could afford to invest another $800 billion in U.S. Treasury securities and other liquid dollar assets. Allowing market forces to determine exchange rates while permitting central banks to intervene only to counter abnormal market shifts is the policy pursued for most major currencies of the world.

In terms of foreign exchange intervention, Japan differs from China in two important respects. First, Japan does not peg its exchange rate to any basket of currency. It generally intervenes to slow down rates of change not to maintain a certain exchange rate. It also does not require citizens to sell foreign exchange to the central bank at an official rate of exchange. Second, Japan allows for free flows of capital into and out of the country. This makes currency manipulation much more difficult in Japan, since speculators and investors can offset official buying and selling of foreign financial assets.

A currency peg without capital controls is expensive and difficult to maintain during a financial crisis. During the 1997-1998 Asian financial crisis, for example, Hong Kong maintained its pegged exchange rate partly by raising domestic interest rates to attract foreign capital and to retard capital flight by local investors (to reduce the incentive to convert Hong Kong dollars to U.S. dollars in anticipation of a drop in the value of the Hong Kong dollar). On October 23, 1997, the overnight rate of interest in Hong Kong jumped from 6.25% to 100.0% as the monetary authorities tried to stem the capital outflow. Even though Hong Kong was able to maintain its exchange rate peg, the high interest rates caused a near collapse of real estate markets there. This is one reason China still maintains some capital controls.[40] Since the Asian financial crisis, Japan and other Asian nations have negotiated currency swap agreements to provide short-term sources of foreign exchange in times of crisis.[41] This obviates, somewhat, the need to rely on interest rates to attract foreign capital.

Under a policy of allowing market forces to determine exchange rates, some intervention still may be necessary to calm excessive volatility in markets or to counter trends that overshoot because of herd mentality and other effects. In the past, the more successful of such interventions were coordinated among the large, industrialized nations.

Clarify the Definition of Currency Manipulation

A major provision of various currency bills in Congress has been to clarify the definition of currency manipulation. While this legislation apparently has been aimed primarily at China's currency policy, in cases, the bills also have cited Japan (and South Korea) in the findings.

Currently, the Department of the Treasury, in consultation with the International Monetary Fund, determines each year whether countries are manipulating their exchange rate for purposes of gaining an unfair trade advantage or preventing effective balance of payments adjustments and also have a material global current account surplus and a significant bilateral trade surplus with the United States.[42]

H.R. 1498 (Ryan)/S. 796 (Bunning) and H.R. 2886 (Knollenberg)/S. 1021(Stabenow) define exchange-rate misalignment as an undervaluation of a foreign currency (yen) as a result of protracted large-scale intervention by or at the direction of a governmental authority in the exchange market. Such undervaluation shall be found when the observed exchange rate for a foreign currency (yen) is below the exchange rate that could reasonably be expected for that foreign currency absent the intervention. In determining whether exchange-rate misalignment is occurring and a benefit thereby is conferred, the administering authority in each case would consider the exporting country:

- bilateral balance of trade surplus or deficit with the United States,
- balance of trade surplus or deficit with other trading partners,
- foreign direct investment in its territory,
- currency specific and aggregate amounts of foreign currency reserves,
- mechanisms employed to maintain its currency at a fixed exchange rate and the nature, duration, and monetary expenditures of those mechanisms, and
- may consider such other economic factors as are relevant. S. 1607 (Baucus) would define a currency for priority action if the country that issues such currency is:

- engaging in protracted large-scale intervention in one direction in the currency exchange market;
- engaging in excessive reserve accumulation;
- introducing or substantially modifying for balance of payments purposes a restriction on, or incentive for, the inflow or outflow of capital, that is inconsistent with the goal of achieving full currency convertibility; or
- pursuing any other policy or action that, in the view of the Secretary of the Treasury warrants designation for priority action.

The bills also specify that trade data are to be those of the United States and other trading partners of the exporting country, unless such trade data are not available or are demonstrably inaccurate, in which case the exporting country's trade data may be relied upon if shown to be sufficiently accurate and trustworthy.

The issue of which data to use applies primarily to China, mainly because of imports and exports that flow through, but do not originate in, Hong Kong and the general lack of confidence in China's system for compiling statistics and reporting them. The data problem, however, also arises with Japan. In 2004 for Japan, Japanese data (as accessed through the IMF or Global Trade Atlas[43]) reported a merchandise trade surplus of $110 billion (2.4% of GDP), but a compilation of partner country data (statistics from countries that export to and import from Japan) showed a surplus for that year of $208 billion (4.5% of GDP).[44]

Each bill placed more emphasis on large-scale intervention by a country into currency markets — particularly when evidenced by large accumulations of foreign exchange. Such accumulations of dollars, do not constitute *prima facie* evidence of currency manipulation, but they would be used along with other criteria to determine whether a country has been engaged in it.

The bills have not addressed the issue of sterilization in currency intervention.[45] In 2003 and 2004, Treasury found that Japan did not meet the criteria for currency manipulation in part because its exchange rate interventions were considered to be part of a macroeconomic policy to combat deflation.[46] (It was considered to be unsterilized intervention to increase the money supply.) A policy question is whether large-scale interventions are justified when part of macroeconomic policy even though they may have adverse affects on exchange markets.

Require Negotiations and Reports

Current trade law requires the President to seek to confer and negotiate with other countries to achieve:

- more appropriate and sustainable levels of trade and current account balances and exchange rates of the dollar and other currencies consistent with such balances; and
- improvement in the functioning of the exchange rate system to provide for long-term exchange rate stability consistent with more appropriate and sustainable current account balances.[47]

The United States and Japan also conduct regular cabinet and sub-cabinet meetings that provide a venue to discuss exchange rates. In addition, the two countries meet in G-7 summits and at the APEC (Asia Pacific economic cooperation) meetings where currency and exchange rate policy is discussed.[48] In a 2000 G-7 meeting, for example, the communique stated that the group had discussed developments in exchange and financial markets and said that they welcomed the reaffirmation by the Japanese monetary authorities that exchange rate policies would be conducted appropriately in view of their potential impact and that they would continue to monitor developments in exchange markets and cooperate as appropriate.[49]

Current bills related to Japan's currency in the 110th Congress would require Treasury to submit a semi-annual report to Congress on currency intervention by Japan to include any effort by Japan to create an exchange-rate misalignment (including intervention and statements by Japanese government officials). The bills also would require Treasury to submit to Congress a proposal for a comprehensive joint U.S.-European Union plan to address the exchange-rate misalignment of the Japanese yen. It also would require the U.S. government to initiate consultations with Japan for the purpose of decreasing the foreign currency holdings of the government of Japan.

Certify Currency Manipulation and Take Remedial Action

In the 110th Congress, H.R. 782 (Tim Ryan)/S. 796 (Bunning) would make exchange rate "misalignment" actionable under U.S. countervailing duty laws, require the Treasury Department to determine whether a currency is misaligned in its semi-annual reports to Congress on exchange rates.[50] This certification could then trigger certain remedial actions under U.S. trade law. S. 1677 (Dodd) would require the Treasury Department to identifycountries that manipulate their currencies regardless of their intent and to submit an action plan for ending the manipulation. It also would give Treasury the authority to file a case in the WTO.

Actions with the IMF, World Bank, WTO, and OPIC

The currency bills in the 110th Congress also would require the Secretary of the Treasury to oppose any change in the governance arrangements in International Financial Institutions (such as the International Monetary Fund or World Bank) in the form of increased voting shares or representation if the beneficiary country has a currency that is manipulated or in fundamental misalignment.

S. 1677 (Dodd) would give the Treasury Department the authority to take a currency manipulation case to the World Trade Organization through its dispute settlement mechanism or to the International Monetary Fund.

S. 1607 (Baucus) would require the United States to inform the International Monetary Fund of the failure of a country to adopt appropriate policies to eliminate the fundamental misalignment in its currency and request a consultation by the IMF with that country. The United States also would not approve any new financing by the U.S. Overseas Private Investment Corporation (including insurance, reinsurance, or guarantee) and oppose any loan to the country from a multilateral bank. In the case of a persistent failure to adopt appropriate policies to correct the misalignment, the U.S. Trade Representative would request dispute settlement consultations at the WTO.

With respect to the WTO dispute settlement mechanism, an agreement between the IMF and WTO requires the WTO to refer exchange rate disputes to the IMF and accept the IMF's findings as conclusive. If the IMF finds currency manipulation, it is not clear how a WTO dispute settlement panel would rule. There is no precedent for a case in which currency manipulation is considered to have the effect of an export subsidy and allows for direct retaliation against the exports of the offending country.

Even though the IMF has not found that Japan was manipulating its currency during its Article IV consultations, the United States could inform the IMF that it believes Japan is not complying with the requirements of Article IV. This would trigger consultations with Tokyo and a report by the Managing Director to the IMF's executive board.[51] While the IMF still might not find Japan guilty of currency manipulation, it would put pressure on the Bank of Japan not to intervene in currency markets in the future.

LEGISLATION

Legislation in the 110th Congress related to Japan's[52] currency include the following:

H.R. 782 (Ryan)/S. 796 (Bunning). Fair Currency Act of 2007. Would provide that exchange-rate misalignment by any foreign nation is a countervailable export subsidy and clarify the definition of manipulation with respect to currency.

H.R. 2886 (Knollenberg)/S. 1021 (Stabenow). Japan Currency Manipulation Act. Would address the exchange-rate misalignment of the Japanese yen with respect to the United States dollar.

S. 1607 (Baucus). Currency Exchange Rate Oversight Reform Act of 2007. Would require the Treasury Department to identify currencies that are fundamentally misaligned and would require action to correct the misalignment. Such action would include factoring currency undervaluation in U.S. anti-dumping cases, banning federal procurement of products or services from the designated country, and filing a case against in the WTO.

S. 1677 (Dodd). Currency Reform and Financial Markets Access Act of 2007. Would require the Treasury Department to identify countries that manipulate their currencies regardless of their intent and to submit an action plan for ending the manipulation, and would give Treasury the authority to file a case in the WTO.

APPENDIX

Japan's GDP Growth Rate, Yen/Dollar Exchange Rate, and Foreign Exchange Reserves, 1970-2007

Year	GDP Growth Rate (%)	Exchange Rate	Foreign Exchange Reserves (US$)
1970	10.7	360.0	4,307,530,000
1971	4.7	350.7	14,621,900,000
1972	8.4	303.2	17,563,610,000
1973	8.0	271.7	11,354,560,000
1974	-1.2	292.1	12,614,290,000
1975	3.1	296.8	11,950,210,000
1976	4.0	296.6	15,746,250,000
1977	4.4	268.5	22,340,960,000
1978	5.3	210.4	32,407,240,000
1979	5.5	219.1	19,521,520,000
1980	2.8	226.7	24,636,450,000
1981	2.9	220.5	28,208,420,000
1982	2.8	249.1	23,333,970,000
1983	1.6	237.5	24,601,580,000
1984	3.1	237.5	26,429,150,000
1985	5.1	238.5	26,718,650,000
1986	3.0	168.5	42,256,600,000
1987	3.8	144.6	80,972,870,000
1988	6.8	128.2	96,728,190,000
1989	5.3	138.0	83,957,350,000
1990	5.2	144.8	78,500,590,000
1991	3.4	134.7	72,058,840,000
1992	1.0	126.7	71,622,670,000
1993	0.2	111.2	98,524,340,000
1994	1.1	102.2	125,860,200,000
1995	1.9	94.1	183,249,800,000
1996	3.4	108.8	216,648,000,000
1997	1.9	121.0	219,648,300,000
1998	-1.1	130.9	215,470,700,000
1999	0.1	113.9	286,916,100,000
2000	2.8	107.8	354,902,100,000
2001	0.4	121.5	395,155,000,000
2002	-0.4	125.4	461,185,600,000
2003	1.4	115.9	663,289,100,000
2004	2.7	103.8	833,891,000,000
2005	1.9	118.5	834,275,000,000
2006	2.2	116.3	874,596,000,000
June 2007	2.8	around 123.0	892,761,000,000

Source: World Bank. World Development Indicators. Global Insight. Japan Ministry of Finance.

Note: The growth rate is the annual change in real gross domestic product. The exchange rate is yen per U.S. dollar, period average. Foreign exchange Reserves are official reserves excluding gold.

REFERENCES

[1] The overall size of a nation's current account balance (trade in goods and services plus unilateral transfers) is determined mainly by rates of savings and investment, interest rates, and other factors, but the foreign exchange rate plays a key role in adjusting for imbalances.

[2] Collins, Stephen. How the Misaligned Yen Hurts U.S. Automakers, *Real Clear Politics.com*. March 8, 2007.

[3] The real effective value of the yen is an index of the exchange rate adjusted to account for differing rates of inflation among Japan's trading partners and for the share of trade with each major trading partner in Japan's total trade. It is calculated by the Bank of Japan.

[4] U.S. Treasury. Report to Congress on International Economic and Exchange Rate Policies. May 2006. International Monetary Fund. Japan — 2006 Article IV Consultation Concluding Statement of the IMF Mission, May 24, 2006 (contains no mention of exchange rate manipulation).

[5] U.S. Bureau of Economic Analysis. U.S. International Transactions, by Area -Japan. Accessed April 12, 2006, on Internet at [http://www.bea.gov/international/bp_web/simple.cfm?anon=71 and table_id=10 and area_id=11].

[6] Japan. Ministry of Finance at [http://www.mof.go.jp/english/e1c006.htm].

[7] For data on intervention, see Japan. Ministry of Finance. International Reserves/Foreign Currency Liquidity. Issued monthly. Also see Foreign Exchange Intervention Operations. Issued periodically. See [http://www.mof.go.jp/english/files.htm].

[8] Dominguez, Kathryn M. "Foreign Exchange Intervention: Did It Work in the 1990s?," In *Dollar Overvaluation and the World Economy*, edited by Fred Bergsten and John Williamson, Washington, Institute for International Economics, 2003. pp. 217-245.

[9] Bank for International Settlements. Triennial Central Bank Survey of Foreign Exchange and Derivatives Market Activity 2004 - Final Results. March 17, 2005. p. 1.

[10] Neely, Christopher J. An Analysis of Recent Studies of the Effect of Foreign Exchange Intervention. The Federal Reserve Bank of St. Louis Working Paper 205-030B, Revised June 2005. p. 3, 8ff.

[11] Chaboud, Alain P. and Owen F. Humpage. "An Assessment of the Impact of Japanese Foreign Exchange Intervention: 1991-2004." Board of Governors of the Federal Reserve System, International Finance Discussion Papers, No. 824, January 2005. p. 1-5.

[12] Faum, Rasmus and Michael M. Hutchinson. "Effectiveness of Official Daily Foreign Exchange Market Intervention Operations in Japan." National Bureau of Economic Research Working Paper 9648, April 2003. p. 1-5.

[13] Meredith, Robyn. GM: Weak Yen Hurts U.S. Automakers. *Forbes*, October 21, 2003.

[14] Mohatarem, Mustafa. Statement before the House Committee on Ways and Means, Hearing on United States-Japan Economic and Trade Relations, September 28, 2005.

[15] Auto Makers Cite Open Dialogue With Bush Administration. Dow Jones News Service, November 14, 2006.

[16] Automotive Trade Policy Council. U.S. Automakers Call on G7 to Address Imbalanced Japanese Yen at Finance Ministers Meeting in Washington, News Release, April 12, 2007.

[17] Ernest H. Preeg is a Senior Fellow in Trade and Productivity at the Manufacturers Alliance/MAPI.

[18] Preeg, Ernest H. "Exchange Rate Manipulation to Gain an Unfair Competitive Advantage: The Case Against Japan and China," in C. Fred Bergsten and John Williamson, *Dollar Overvaluation and the World Economy*, Washington, Institute for International Economics, 2003. p. 273.

[19] International Monetary Fund. *IMF Country Report No. 05/273*, Japan: 2005 Article IV Consultation — Staff Report; Staff Supplement; and Public Information Notice on the Executive Board Discussion. August 2005. Ito, Takatoshi. Interventions and the Japanese Economic Recovery, paper presented at the University of Michigan Conference on Policy Options for Japan and the United States. October 2004.

[20] International Monetary Fund. Japan — 2006 Article IV Consultation, Concluding Statement of the IMF Mission, May 24, 2006.

[21] See, for example, International Monetary Fund. *IMF Country Report No. 05/273*, Japan: 2005 Article IV Consultation — Staff Report; Staff Supplement; and Public Information Notice on the Executive Board Discussion. August 2005. p. 7.

[22] McCown, T. Ashby, Patricia Pollard, and John Weeks. Equilibrium Exchange Rate Models and Misalignments. Department of the Treasury, Office of International Affairs, Occasional Paper No. 7, March 2007.

[23] Finance and Economics: Misleading Misalignments; Economics Focus. *The Economist*, June 23, 2007. P. 100.

[24] Japan's holdings of foreign exchange reserves actually rose by $811 billion over this period. Some of this may have been interest earned on its holdings.

[25] Goldberg, Pinelopi Koujianou and Michael M. Knetter. Goods Prices and Exchange Rates: What Have We Learned? *Journal of Economic Literature*, vol. 35, September 1997. pp. 1244, 1270.

[26] "Toyota Hits Year's High on Robust Car Sales, Weak Yen." *Nikkei Weekly*, August 22, 2005. p. 27.

[27] Goldberg, Pinelopi Koujianou and Michael M. Knetter. "Goods Prices and Exchange Rates: What Have We Learned?" *Journal of Economic Literature*, vol. 35, September 1997. pp. 1244, 1270.

[28] In order for a real depreciation to improve the current account, exports and imports must be sufficiently elastic respect to the real exchange rate. This condition holds for most industrialized countries for trade in manufactured goods in the long run but not in the short run. Krugman and Obstfeld, *International Economics*, pp. 450, 468.

[29] Cline, William R. The Impact of US External Adjustment on Japan. In *Dollar Overvaluation and the World Economy*, edited by C. Fred Bergsten and John Williamson. Institute for International Economics, Washington, DC, 2003. pp. 190-91.

[30] Yoshitomi, Masaru. Surprises and Lessons from Japanese External Adjustment in 1985 91. In *International Adjustment and Financing: The Lessons of 1985-1991*, edited by C. Fred Bergsten, Institute for International Economics, Washington, DC, 1991. pp. 128-29.

[31] Over the 2002-2004 period, differences in rates of inflation would have changed the real exchange rate and real current account balance somewhat.

[32] 22 U.S.C. §5304-5305.

[33] Treasury considered the following countries to be manipulating their exchange rates under 22 U.S.C. 5304: Oct 1988 Report — Korea and Taiwan; April 1989 Report — Korea and Taiwan; October 1989 Report — Korea, May 1992 Report — China and Taiwan; December 1992 Report — China and Taiwan; May 1993 Report — China; November 1993 Report — China; July 1994 Report — China.

[34] U.S. Department of the Treasury. Report to the Committees on Appropriations on Clarification of Statutory Provisions Addressing Currency Manipulation. Press Release js2308, May 25, 2005. p. 4. Report to Congress on International Economic and Exchange Rate Policies, November 2005.

[35] U.S. Secretary of the Treasury. Report to Congress on International Economic and Exchange Rate Policies. December 2006. p. 23.

[36] United States Government Accountability Office. Treasury Assessments Have Not Found Currency Manipulation, but Concerns about Exchange Rates Continue. GAO Report GAO 05-351, April 2005. p. 4.

[37] U.S. Department of the Treasury. Testimony of Deputy Assistant Secretary of the Treasury David Loevinger before the House Ways and Means Committee, JS-2954, September 28, 2005.

[38] International Monetary Fund. Surveillance Over Exchange Rate Policies, Decision No. 5392-(77/63), April 29, 1977 as amended.

[39] International Monetary Fund. *IMF Country Report No. 05/273*, Japan: 2005 Article IV Consultation — Staff Report; Staff Supplement; and Public Information Notice on the Executive Board Discussion. August 2005.

[40] For financial data, see Global Financial Data at [http://www.globalfinancialdata.com].

[41] This is called the Chiang Mai Initiative. See Seok-Dong Wang and Lene Andersen. "Regional Financial Cooperation in East Asia: the Chiang Mai Initiative and Beyond," *UNESCAP Bulletin on Asia-Pacific Perspectives 2002/03*, Chapter 8.

[42] Omnibus Trade and Competitiveness Act of 1988, 22 U.S.C. § 5304(b), § 3004(b) . The global current account surplus is the current account surplus of merchandise, services, and transfers with all other countries, while the bilateral trade surplus is the surplus in goods and services trade with one trading partner country only.

[43] The Japanese government reports trade data in yen values. They convert those data into dollars when reporting them to the IMF. Global Trade Atlas is a propriety database of trade statistics.

[44] Data from International Monetary Fund. *Direction of Trade Statistics*. September 2005. For 2004, China reported a merchandise trade surplus of $32 billion, but the exports and imports of trading partners implied a trade surplus of $314 billion. The IMF notes that data reported by exporting and importing countries can be inconsistent because of differences in country of origin or destination classification concepts, lack of destination detail, time of recording, valuation, coverage, and processing errors.

[45] Sterilized intervention refers, in the government of Japan's case, to the buying of dollars (or other foreign exchange) from Japanese holders and using those dollars to buy dollar-denominated securities in the United States while simultaneously selling yen-denominated securities in Japan to keep the domestic money supply unchanged.

[46] United States Government Accountability Office. Treasury Assessments Have Not Found Currency Manipulation, but Concerns about Exchange Rates Continue. GAO Report GAO-05-351, April 2005. p. 4.

[47] 22 U.S.C. § 5304.

[48] See, for example: U.S. Department of the Treasury. Statement of G-7 Finance Ministers and Central Bank Governors. September 25, 1999. Washington, DC.

[49] Statement of G-7 Finance Ministers and Central Bank Governors. January 22, 2000. Tokyo, Japan.

[50] The certification also can be that a country is not engaged in currency manipulation.

[51] For detail, see CRS Report RS22658, *Currency Manipulation: The IMF and WTO*, by Jonathan E. Sanford.

[52] For analysis of policy with respect to China's exchange rate, see CRS Report RL33536, *China-U.S. Trade Issues*, by Wayne M. Morrison and CRS Report RS21625, *China's Currency Peg: A Summary of the Economic Issues*, by Wayne M. Morrison and Marc Labonte.

In: Currency Interventions, Fluctuations...
Editor: L. C. Hilbert, pp. 71-89
ISBN: 978-1-60456-078-7

Chapter 3

NORTH KOREAN COUNTERFEITING OF U.S. CURRENCY*

***Raphael F. Perl*[1] *and Dick K. Nanto*[2]**
[1] Specialist in International Affairs Foreign Affairs, Defense, and Trade Division
[2] Specialist in Industry and Trade Foreign Affairs, Defense, and Trade Division

ABSTRACT

The United States has accused the Democratic People's Republic of Korea (DPRK or North Korea) of counterfeiting U.S. $100 Federal Reserve notes (supernotes) and passing them off in various countries. This is one of several illicit activities by North Korea apparently done to generate foreign exchange that is used to purchase imports or finance government activities abroad.

Although Pyongyang denies complicity in any counterfeiting operation, at least $45 million in such supernotes of North Korean origin have been detected in circulation, and estimates are that the country has earned from $15 to $25 million per year from counterfeiting. The illegal nature of any counterfeiting activity makes open-source information on the scope and scale of DPRK counterfeiting and distribution operations incomplete. South Korean intelligence has corroborated information on North Korean production of forged currency prior to 1998, and certain individuals have been indicted in U.S. courts for distributing such forged currency. Media reports in January 2006 state that Chinese investigators have independently confirmed allegations of DPRK counterfeiting.

For the United States, North Korean counterfeiting represents a direct attack on a protected national asset; might undermine confidence in the U.S. dollar and depress its value; and, if done extensively enough, potentially damage the U.S. economy. The earnings from counterfeiting also could be significant to Pyongyang and may be used to purchase weapons technology, fund travel abroad, meet "slush fund" purchases of luxury foreign goods, or even help fund the DPRK's nuclear program.

U.S. policy toward the alleged counterfeiting is split between law enforcement efforts and political and diplomatic pressures. On the law enforcement side, individuals have been indicted and the Banco Delta Asia bank in Macao (a territory of China) has

* Excerpted from CRS Report RL33324, dated January 17, 2007.

been named as a primary money laundering concern under the Patriot Act. This started a financial chain reaction under which banks, not only from the United States but from other nations, have declined to deal with even some legitimate North Korea traders. North Koreans appear to be moving their international bank accounts to Chinese and other banks. In December 2006, North Korea agreed to return to the six-party talks on its nuclear weapons program, but during the talks Pyongyang refused to discuss denuclearization officially until the Banco Delta financial sanctions were lifted. It is not known whether North Korea currently is engaged in supernote production, but such notes suspected to be from earlier production runs reportedly are readily available in a Chinese town just north of the DPRK border.

The political/security track attempts to stop the alleged counterfeiting activity though diplomatic pressures, the Illicit Activities Initiative, and direct talks with North Korea through a working group on U.S. financial sanctions that in December 2006 first met alongside the six-party talks. In these talks, the U.S. side stated that U.S. sanctions on Banco Delta could be resolved if North Korea punishes the counterfeiters and destroys their equipment. This report will be updated as circumstances warrant.

The United States has accused the Democratic People's Republic of Korea (DPRK or North Korea) of counterfeiting U.S. $100 Federal Reserve notes (supernotes) and passing them off in various countries. This is one of several illicit activities by North Korea apparently done to generate foreign exchange that is used to purchase imports or finance government activities abroad.

The purpose of this report is to provide a summary of what is known from open sources on the DPRK's alleged counterfeiting of U.S. currency, examine North Korean motives and methods, and discuss U.S. interests and policy options.

Although Pyongyang denies complicity in any counterfeiting operation, estimates are that at least $45 million in such supernotes of North Korean origin are in circulation and that the country has earned from $15 to $25 million per year from counterfeiting.[1] South Korean intelligence has corroborated information on past production of forged currency — at least until 1998 — and several U.S. court indictments indicate that certain individuals have been accused of distributing such forged currency more recently.

U.S. INTERESTS AND ACTIONS

For the United States large-scale counterfeiting of U.S. currency, whether done by North Korea or not, has a direct bearing on U.S. interests. The counterfeiting, itself, could undermine confidence in the U.S. dollar and, if done extensively enough, potentially damage the U.S. economy. It also is a direct attack on a protected asset of the United States and a violation of U.S. and other laws. If being done by the DPRK government, it violates accepted international norms. It also could affect the willingness of financial institutions in certain areas to accept legitimate U.S. currency, or it might induce them to impose surcharges when exchanging certain U.S. banknotes for their currency.

In a broader sense, the counterfeiting, to the extent that North Korea is the nation involved, arguably affects U.S. national security. North Korea is a Stalinist regime with self-announced aspirations to become a nuclear power. It is led by a communist dictator with a taste for luxury imports and need to subsidize his inner circle of supporters and broader ranks of party cadres. Yet the North Korean economy scarcely produces enough to feed its population and incurs a billion-dollar trade deficit each year. Proceeds from counterfeiting could be used to maintain the regime's power or contribute to instability in East Asia.

The United States is ratcheting up a two-pronged approach to stem the alleged North Korean counterfeiting of U.S. currency. The first is through law enforcement initiatives. The second is through political and diplomatic efforts. The immediate goal is to bring a verifiable halt to both the production and distribution of bogus U.S. currency by North Korea. In the broader perspective, curbing North Korea's illicit activities is one piece of an overall U.S. strategy to halt Pyongyang's nuclear weapons program, to defuse tensions in Northeast Asia, and to induce the DPRK to adopt policies less inimical to its own people, the region, and the world.

U.S. law enforcement actions to curb the alleged counterfeiting led to financial measures taken by the United States in September 2005 to prevent the country from laundering proceeds from its alleged illicit activities through Macao's Banco Delta Asia. As discussed below, this action froze some $24 million in North Korean accounts in that bank and caused banks in other countries also to close their North Korean accounts, even those for legitimate business. For the year following the financial restrictions, they have been Pyongyang's main complaint and the reason it had given for boycotting the six-party talks on North Korea's nuclear programs. Even after returning to the talks in December 2006, Pyongyang refused to discuss denuclearization officially until the Banco Delta financial sanctions were lifted.[2] The actions related to North Korea's counterfeiting activities, therefore, seem to be also halting progress on the larger issue of North Korea's development of nuclear weapons. (For discussion of U.S. policy, see section on "Policy Implications.")

A redesign of the U.S. $100 bill is currently in progress to include enhanced technologies to deter counterfeiters. The Department of the Treasury expects to introduce the redesigned note to the public after early 2008.[3] However, bills previously produced, are expected to remain in circulation for the foreseeable future making it possible for the DPRK to continue to circulate earlier production runs of its counterfeit supernotes.

LIMITS ON INFORMATION

Because counterfeiting is a form of clandestine criminal activity, a goal of those engaged in it is that it remain clandestine and undetected to the maximum extent possible. Thus, to the extent that the United States and other countries have information on the scope and scale of DPRK counterfeiting and distribution operations, such information is likely to be incomplete. As the DPRK is a relatively closed society, information on any production of counterfeit U.S. currency there — other than that received from defectors — is likely to be the product of intelligence sources and methods. Hence, it is unlikely that such information would be made public for fear of compromising ongoing intelligence gathering operations.

On the other hand, involvement of DPRK citizens and officials in the distribution of so called "supernotes" is more readily demonstrated once criminal investigations have been completed, arrests have been made, indictments issued, and convictions/and or confessions obtained. Indeed, a number of such indictments have been issued, and presumably a number of ongoing investigations remain in the pipeline. U.S. officials appear to be increasingly sensitive to a need to support public allegations with the weight of *de facto* legal evidence — fueling speculation that "Noreiga-type" criminal indictments[4] against the North Korean leadership may be a policy option under active consideration.

Also at issue is the credibility of information provided U.S. authorities by the South Korean government and its National Intelligence Services in matters involving Pyongyang's criminal activities. Whereas in past years Seoul's reporting on such matters was considered highly reliable, some now suggest downplaying the scope of any such activity better dovetails with the goals and objectives of Seoul's more recent conciliatory unification policy vis-a-vis the North.

The Need to Counterfeit Currency

North Korea needs to raise approximately $1 billion per year to fund its merchandise trade deficit.[5] The DPRK imports more than it exports and must generate enough foreign exchange to cover the difference through some means — either legal or illegal. Legal means include borrowing, foreign investments, foreign aid, remittances from overseas Koreans, selling military equipment not reflected in trade data, and by selling services abroad. Illegal methods include the counterfeiting of hard currency, illegal sales of military equipment or technology, sales of illegal drugs or counterfeit cigarettes and pharmaceuticals, or by shipping illegal cargo between third countries. The country also can dip into its meager foreign exchange reserves. North Korea considers the United States to be a hostile nation and often takes actions commensurate with that policy.

Alleged Areas of DPRK Criminal Activities

Allegations of North Korean drug production, trafficking, and crime- for- profit activity have become the focus of rising attention in Congress, the Administration, and the press, as well as in the diplomatic community.[6] Areas of DPRK criminal activity commonly cited include production and trafficking in: (1) heroin and methamphetamines; (2) counterfeit cigarettes; (3) counterfeit pharmaceuticals (for example "USA" manufactured Viagra); and (4) counterfeit currency (e.g., U.S. $100 bill "supernotes").[7]

DPRK production and trafficking of "supernotes" have been addressed in 2006 by both National Intelligence Director John Negroponte and President George W. Bush. In a January 26, 2006, White House Press Conference, President Bush — in commenting on the issue of income generated by North Korean criminal activity — remarked:

> When somebody is counterfeiting our money, we want to stop them from doing that. And so we are aggressively saying to the North Koreans, just — don't counterfeit our money. And we are working with others to prevent their illicit activities.[8]

Shortly thereafter, National Intelligence Director John Negroponte, in testimony before Congress, stated that North Korea "produces and smuggles abroad counterfeit U.S. currency as well as narcotics and other contraband."[9]

In a Senate Committee on Government Affairs hearing in 2003, William Bach, the Director of the Office of African, Asian and European Affairs in the Bureau for International Narcotics and Law Enforcement Affairs of the U.S. Department of State, stated:

> The U.S. Secret Service Counterfeit Division is aware of numerous cases of counterfeiting with North Korean connections. Typical of such cases was one reported in Macao in 1994, when North Korean trading company executives, who carried diplomatic passports, were arrested for depositing $250,000 in counterfeit notes in a Macao bank. There are numerous other counterfeiting incidents with links to Macao banks, North Korea, and North Korean diplomats.[10]

The State Department's 2006 *International Narcotics Control Strategy Report* released by the Bureau for International Narcotics and Law Enforcement Affairs states that, for decades, citizens of the DPRK "have been apprehended trafficking in narcotics and engaged in other forms of criminal behavior, including passing counterfeit U.S. currency." These have been carried out in league with criminal organizations around the world.[11]

Counterfeiting of foreign currency is apparently a phenomenon that is not new to the government of North Korea. Seoul's War Memorial Museum reportedly contains DPRK-manufactured South Korean currency from the 1950's, the production of which reportedly continued into the 1960's.[12] South Korean media reports cite a 1998 South Korean National Intelligence Service (NIS) Report to the effect that North Korea forges and circulates U.S. $100 banknotes worth $15 million a year. Subsequent reports to the South Korean National Assembly in the same year and in 1999 are cited in the media as stating that North Korea operates three banknote forging agencies and that more than $4.6 million in bogus dollar bills had been uncovered on thirteen occasions since 1994.[13]

Subsequent press reports (of February 2, 2006) cite a Uri Party Member of Parliament's account of a closed briefing by South Korea's National Intelligence Service to members of Korea's National Assembly to the effect that North Koreans were arrested abroad for counterfeiting offenses in the 1990's but that the Service had no evidence of the North making bogus currency after 1998.[14] Informed South Korean sources have confirmed the above stated content of the briefing, but insist that the NIS lack of hard evidence of DPRK supernote production after 1998 should not necessarily be construed to mean that such activity has ceased. Post -1998 South Korean media reports note that South Korean authorities have continued to seize bogus U.S. currency — including 1,400 counterfeit U.S. $100 bills in April 2005, but that they have not traced the source.[15] Subsequent press reports state that the United States has provided South Korea with examples of DPRK source counterfeit 2001 and 2003 series $100 notes. Moreover, the U.S. has reportedly determined that at least $140,000 worth of counterfeit notes seized by South Korean police in April 2005 was manufactured in the DPRK as part of a batch produced in 2001, and distributed by Pyongyang.[16]

On June 13, 2003, South Korea, the United States and Japan held a North Korea policy coordination group meeting and announced an agreement that reportedly stated, "The three countries' delegations express concern about the illegal activities of organizations in North Korea, including drug smuggling and money counterfeiting."[17] Moreover, media reports as recent as January 20, 2006 stated that Chinese investigators have independently confirmed allegations of DPRK counterfeiting.[18]

Arrests and indictments point to DPRK trafficking in bogus U.S. currency as recently as 2005. In August 2005, federal law enforcement authorities completed two undercover operations in New Jersey and in California which focused on the activities of members of China's Triad criminal syndicates. The operations, named Royal Charm and Smoking Dragon, reportedly netted some $4 million in supernotes believed to be of North Korean origin. Illicit narcotics, and counterfeit brand cigarettes and pharmaceuticals were seized as well. U.S. government authorities indicate there is the potential that ensuing trials and/or the plea bargaining process will reveal direct links between some of the smugglers and North Korean officials or government entities.[19]

One of the indictments issued in the above cited cases identifies Chao Tung Wu, a Taiwanese in custody for dealing in counterfeit bills, and alleges that he told undercover agents that the government of a nation — identified in the indictment as "country 2" — was producing counterfeit notes.[20] Country two has been widely cited in the media as being North Korea. Another law enforcement operation led to the arrest in Northern Ireland of Sean Garland, a leading member of an Irish Republican Army faction on charges of circulating more than $1 million of supernotes (believed to be DPRK government produced) in Britain and Eastern Europe.[21] A request for his extradition to the United States ensued in mid-October 2005.

A Stanford University Honors Thesis Researcher, Sheena Chestnut, lists thirteen reported incidents since 1994 of North Korean involvement in smuggling/distributing counterfeit U.S. currency. All of these incidents allegedly occurred in either Asia or Europe. In them, the use of DPRK diplomatic passports and the involvement of DPRK diplomats, embassy personnel, and DPRK government trading company officials connect most of these incidents to the government of North Korea in varying degrees. Taken collectively, the link is seen as being even stronger. Of these 13 incidents, 6 have occurred since 1999, the time after which the NIS reportedly is unable to conclude that the DPRK continued *producing* counterfeit notes.[22] As recently as March 2006, counterfeit supernotes were reportedly seized by police in Hong Kong from a Chinese-American man in transit from Macau.[23]

In April 2006, a Korean reporter claimed in an article in a South Korean newspaper that obtaining fake $100 bills that likely were manufactured in North Korea was a "piece of cake" in the Chinese town of Dandong just across the DPRK's northern border. According to the reporter, counterfeit bills similar to real currency fetch about 40% of their face value. Carefully manufactured $100 supernotes go for $60 to $70 each. North Koreans refer to the counterfeit dollars as "kattalio" and the business of dealing in them as "the kattalio game." After the Banco Delta financial sanctions, the article states that Pyongyang proclaimed that anyone involved in illegal drugs or fake notes would be severely punished. In March 2006, two men convicted of such activities were publicly executed. Since the Banco Delta sanctions, the number of counterfeit notes circulated through North Korea reportedly has dropped.[24] However, it may be that the number of counterfeit notes circulating within North Korea has increased since imposition of the Banco Delta sanctions.[25] Another newspaper articled reported that in the North Korean counterfeit currency market, a printed counterfeit $100 bill trades at 30% of its face value while electronically copied currency made with color copy machines trades at 10% of its face value.[26]

AMOUNT OF BOGUS U.S. CURRENCY

The amount of alleged DPRK-produced counterfeit currency in circulation is unknown. U.S. officials have been quoted citing a figure of $45 million since 1989.[27] Presumably this is the amount detected by the Federal Reserve. Officials familiar with the bogus currency in question, however, note its exceptional quality — so good that many cashier-level bank employees would likely not be able to detect the forgeries. This raises speculation that North Korea — if it is indeed producing the fakes — might need somehow to mark the currency to be able to identify its own bogus notes after production.

The amount of money that the bogus supernotes allegedly bring to the coffers of the North Korean government is unknown as well. Hence, estimates of the profit such transactions bring to the Pyongyang regime — to the extent they are based on open source material — are speculative at best. Amounts commonly cited, which take into account many factors, range from $15 million to $25 million in profit per year.[28]

DENIAL OF COUNTERFEITING BY NORTH KOREA

The DPRK has consistently denied allegations of state involvement in criminal activity, specifically in any counterfeiting activity, and it has vowed to resist U.S. pressure over the matter. A January 24, 2006 commentary carried by the state-run Korean Central News Agency reported that Pyongyang "does not allow such things as bad treatment of the people, counterfeiting, and drug trafficking."[29] In what may be an indication of DPRK willingness to curb any illicit counterfeiting activity, the DPRK Foreign Ministry announced on February 9, 2006, that "there is no evidence proving (North Korea's) issue of counterfeit notes or money laundering" but that the country "will as ever actively join the international actions against money laundering.... It is the consistent policy of the (North Korean) government to oppose all sorts of illegal acts in the financial field." The Foreign Ministry spokesman went on to say that the DPRK has "perfect legal and institutional mechanisms to combat such illegal acts as counterfeiting notes and money laundering, and any illegal acts are liable to severe punishment."[30]

STATE-SPONSORED COUNTERFEITING?

Assuming that production of bogus U.S. currency is actually taking place in North Korea, some suggest that this does not necessarily mean that such activity is being done under government sponsorship, direction, or supervision. They argue that counterfeiting is a criminal phenomenon that is widespread throughout the world, and it is rarely, if ever, state-sponsored. Others say that there may be merit to such arguments, but North Korea could be an exception to any such norms.

It can be said that it is widely acknowledged that the Pyongyang regime engages — or has engaged — in a broad range of *other* crime for profit activity. Hence, inhibitions against counterfeiting may not be strong. The sophisticated type of equipment reportedly required for the production of supernotes is generally tightly controlled and generally restricted for sale to governments. Finally, North Korea is a closed authoritarian regime, and, as such, it is unlikely that any counterfeiting activity — which requires centralized production — would not be government sponsored, or at some point, come under government control.

A Summary of Main Points

Information publically available suggests an expansion in both the scale and scope of North Korean cash-generating, criminal activity. This possibly indicates a situation in which criminal activity is playing an increasingly pivotal role in supporting North Korea's fragile economy.[31]

It is widely acknowledged that undetermined millions of dollars of so-called U.S. $100 supernotes are currently in circulation. Given the sophistication of the bills, many have concluded that they are government produced. The government of North Korea has a demonstrated history of engaging in criminal activity to raise cash.

It arguably has the disposition, opportunity, and technical means to produce forged supernotes.

Past production by North Korea of forged U.S. currency — at least until 1998 — has been reported by South Korea's National Intelligence Service. Indications of Pyongyang's more recent production of forged U.S. currency have seemingly been posited by defectors, and by Chinese investigators as well.

Many observers are convinced that the DPRK has been counterfeiting U.S. currency as matter of state policy. However, it is not fully clear from public sources whether North Korean state enterprises have continued to produce bogus dollars after 1998. At issue here is whether bills now being circulated are new or solely from stashes of earlier production runs. There appears to be a reasonable case that North Korea has continued to counterfeit U.S. currency since 1998. Also, not clear or publically announced, is the extent to which Pyongyang may have counterfeited — or may be counterfeiting — currencies other than the dollar.[32]

As North Korea is a secretive and closed society, activity taking place within the country, such as *production* of bogus foreign currencies — to the extent that such activities exist — may be difficult to demonstrate publically without compromising fragile intelligence sources and methods. In contrast, *distribution* of counterfeit U.S. currency is likely to take place in countries where the money can purchase items of value, i.e., more open and economically successful societies.[33] Numerous arrests outside the United States and recent indictments clearly involve individuals with links to the government of North Korea or its state-run enterprises.[34] This being the case, it is difficult to conclude that the government of North Korea has not been involved — at least until very recently — in distributing bogus U.S. currency.

Policy Implications

For the United States the North Korean counterfeiting of U.S. currency combined with secondary effects has a direct bearing on U.S. interests. Counterfeiting of one nation's currency by another generally is considered to be an act of economic warfare — a direct attack on the U.S. financial system.[35] There is a large difference between criminal counterfeiting by private parties and that done or sanctioned by a nation. The counterfeiting, itself, might undermine confidence in the U.S. dollar and, if done extensively enough, potentially damage the U.S. economy. If the extent of counterfeiting were in the range of $15 million to $25 million per year, however, this would represent a relatively small amount compared with the total U.S. supply of currency or the amount circulating abroad. As of February 2006, currency in circulation — that is, U.S. coins and paper currency in the hands of the public — totaled about $780 billion. Since 1994, the value of currency in circulation has risen at the rate of 6.5% per year, mostly stemming from foreign demand. The U.S. Federal Reserve estimates that between one-half and two-thirds of the value of currency in circulation is held outside the United States.[36] In the United States, most domestic transactions (by value) are done either electronically or by checks, not cash. As of December 2004, 72% of the value of currency in circulation consisted of $100 notes, the denomination allegedly counterfeited by the DPRK.[37]

Counterfeiting also can reduce the confidence by foreigners in the dollar. The dollar has become the predominant medium of exchange in international transactions. Such degraded confidence in the dollar usually can be manifested either by a surcharge on certain denominations when converting dollars to foreign exchange or in certain denominations of the dollar not being accepted at all. Currently, this affects Americans and other holders of dollar currency who rely on cash for transactions rather than credit cards, checks, or bank transfers. If the counterfeiting were to become extensive enough, however, it might depress the overall exchange value of the dollar.

Even though the suspected amount of counterfeiting by the DPRK is relatively small when compared with all U.S. currency in circulation, its importance to Pyongyang and the ruling communist party could be significant. It apparently helps fund travel abroad, meet "slush fund" purchases of foreign goods, and subsidize the lifestyles of the privileged class in Pyongyang.

Even though the macroeconomic effect of a counterfeiting operation generating around $15 million to $25 million per year is minor, counterfeiting, itself, is a violation of U.S. law. The Treasury, including the Secret Service, and the Federal Reserve have primary responsibilities for addressing the counterfeiting of U.S. currency. The Federal Reserve's role is to distribute and ensure the physical integrity, including the authenticity, of U.S. currency. The Secretary of the Treasury is responsible for issuing and protecting U.S. currency. The Bureau of Engraving and Printing produces the currency. It has announced that one of its priorities for FY2007 is to redesign the $100 note.[38] The Secret Service conducts investigations of counterfeiting activities, provides counterfeit-detection training, and is responsible for anticounterfeiting efforts abroad.[39]

So far, the United States had taken a two-pronged (but overlapping) approach toward North Korea's alleged counterfeiting activities: law enforcement and political/security pressures. The law-enforcement prong involves prosecuting or sanctioning individuals and/or institutions involved in the distribution of the bogus currency.

On September 15, 2005, the U.S. Treasury imposed USA PATRIOT Act Section 311 designations against Banco Delta Asia (BDA) in Macau. In the action, Treasury stated that the bank was a "primary money laundering concern" because, among other findings, sources indicated that "senior officials in Banco Delta Asia are working with DPRK officials to accept large deposits of cash, including counterfeit U.S. currency, and agreeing to place that currency into circulation."[40] On September 20, 2005, the Financial Crimes Enforcement Network of Treasury imposed special measures against Banco Delta Asia that prohibited U.S. institutions or agencies from opening or maintaining correspondent accounts on behalf of BDA and required covered financial institutions to exercise due diligence to ensure that no correspondent account is being used indirectly to provide services to BDA.[41]

The U.S. action against Banco Delta Asia caused an avalanche of responses both in financial and political circles. It caused such a run on accounts at the bank that the government of Macau had to take over BDA's operations and place a temporary halt on withdrawals. According to press reports, the Macau government shut down all North Korea-related accounts including those belonging to 20 DPRK banks, 11 DPRK trading companies, and 9 individuals from North Korea.[42]

The financial effects of the BDA action have been larger than expected. The crackdown also spread around the region, with Chinese, Japanese, Vietnamese, Thai, and Singaporean banks making life much tougher for North Korean account holders. In Macau, the North Korean trading firm used by Pyongyang as a de facto consulate rolled up its operations as the Macau government placed Banco Delta Asia into receivership. Not only has the action deprived major DPRK companies of an international financial base and cut into the secret personal accounts of the Pyongyang leadership, but it appears to have obstructed some legitimate North Korean trade. DPRK banks and traders reportedly are having difficulty finding other lenders to conduct their overseas business. Banks from other nations (such as the United Overseas Bank of Singapore and the Korea Exchange Bank of South Korea) have moved to sever contacts with North Korea, fearing that they, too, could face U.S. legal action.[43]

The political/security prong attempts to stop the alleged counterfeiting activity by changing the cost-benefit calculus of decision makers in Pyongyang. The strategy is to increase costs and reduce benefits in order to induce decision makers to halt the activity. The inducements used are aimed primarily at raising costs and include the Illicit Activities Initiative, the Proliferation Security Initiative, diplomatic pressures, as well as possible military threats and other policy related measures.

The Illicit Activities Initiative, coordinated by the U.S. Department of State, is aimed precisely at North Korea's alleged counterfeiting and other illicit activities. It is being developed in cooperation with other nations.[44] The Proliferation Security Initiative (PSI) is part of the larger counter proliferation effort worldwide and aimed at more countries and groups than just North Korea — but the DPRK does receive a particular focus. The PSI activity has received support from more than 60 countries and more formal participation from 11 countries, particularly Japan, Australia, the United Kingdom, France, Germany, Italy, and Spain. Under the PSI, participating countries cooperate to prevent transfers of weapons of mass destruction-related items to or from nation states and non state actors of proliferation concern. It does this through intelligence sharing, diplomatic efforts, law enforcement, and interdiction.[45]

Policymakers reportedly are divided on the ultimate goal of squeezing North Korea on its alleged illicit activities. A group of policymakers (sometimes referred to as the "hawks") favoring regime change seeks ultimately to induce a crisis within the DPRK that would lead to the downfall of Kim Jong-il. One way to achieve this is to cut off the money the DPRK generates from counterfeiting, selling illicit drugs, and exporting missiles. A second group of policymakers more in favor of engagement, seeks to resolve the North Korean problem mainly by negotiations. Its goal is to change the "bad behavior" of the DPRK by bringing the country into the circle of peaceful nations and inducing it to act in accord with international standards.[46] Each group backs initiatives to curb Pyongyang's alleged counterfeiting, but each sees the measures in a different light.

Some observers surmise that the financial action against Banco Delta Asia announced on September 15, 2005, fell too close to the September 19 joint agreement by the DPRK, the United States, and other participants in the six-party talks to be a coincidence. At the end of this fourth round of talks, the DPRK signed an agreement that set out a "visionary view of the end point of the process of the denuclearization of the Korean Peninsula."[47] These observers opine that the action was backed by so-called "hawks" in the Bush Administration to scuttle progress being made on the diplomatic front. The United States had known about the counterfeiting and money laundering activities for years. Why wait, they say, until the middle of a round of the six-party talks to take action?[48] Pyongyang has used the Banco Delta Asia action as a pretext to stay away from the six-party talks. Other observers state, however, that law enforcement efforts have a timetable of their own and that the Banco Delta Asia action occurred after a three-year investigation when the evidence gathering and other preparations were complete.

The position of the United States is that counterfeiting is an illegal activity that cannot be allowed to continue. This is a separate issue from the six-party talks. The South Korean government also has taken a firm position on this. It has clearly communicated to North Korea that such illicit activities are not acceptable and that Pyongyang should unequivocally turn away from such illicit behavior once and for all. South Korea also thinks the Banco Delta Asia issue and the nuclear negotiations should not be linked and that North Korea should return to the six-party talks.[49] Seoul reportedly has tried in vain to reach a compromise with the United States to consider Pyongyang's counterfeiting activities illegal conduct by individual North Korean firms and not by the government of the DPRK.[50] One observer stated that the bigger question being asked by China and South Korea is why is the United States chasing after North Korea's "loose change" when the country is making plutonium, the real currency of state power?[51]

On March 7, 2006, North Korea's Li Gun (head of the North America division of North Korea's Foreign Ministry) met with Assistant U.S. Treasury Secretary Daniel Glaser at the United Nations in New York as part of a back channel for communicating with each other.[52] The U.S. side spent about 20 minutes explaining its actions against Banco Delta Asia and what it expected from the DPRK. The DPRK reportedly suggested several actions to resolve the issue and for it to return to the six-party talks (including the lifting of the financial sanctions on Banco Delta Asia, forming a joint U.S.-North Korean task force to examine the counterfeiting concerns, giving North Korea access to the U.S. banking system, and providing North Korea with technical help on identifying counterfeit bills).[53] Separately, the U.S. ambassador in Seoul indicated that Washington wants Pyongyang to prove that tools used to counterfeit U.S. currency had been destroyed as evidence that North Korea had abandoned such illegal activities.[54]

In December 2006, North Korea agreed to return to the six-party talks, but during the talks Pyongyang refused to discuss denuclearization officially until the Banco Delta financial sanctions were lifted.[55] Pyongyang, however, did send the president of the Foreign Trade Bank of North Korea (Oh Gwang-chul) along with other financial experts to meet with

Deputy Assistant Treasury Secretary Daniel Glaser in the first meeting of a working group on U.S. financial sanctions that met alongside six-party talks. A second meeting is to be held in January 2007. In these talks, the U.S. side reportedly stated that the BDA issue could be resolved early if North Korea punishes the counterfeiters and destroys their equipment.[56] This is viewed by some as an easing of the U.S. position as it opens the possibility for resolving the BDA issue in order for the six-party talks to go forward.

Although South Korea has reluctantly supported the U.S. position on the counterfeiting issue, the country has different interests. While Washington is using both law enforcement and political means to place financial pressure on Pyongyang, Seoul is looking for some compromise. The basic interests of the Bush Administration lie in stopping the proliferation of weapons of mass destruction, fighting terrorism, and protecting U.S. currency. South Korea, under President Roh Moo-hyun, has placed priority on attaining regional peace, regional prosperity, engagement, and eventual long-term unification with the DPRK.[57]

Since Portugal has returned Macao to China, Beijing now has supervisory responsibility over Banco Delta Asia. China has been attempting to modernize its banking system, and for one of its banks to be accused of money laundering clearly does Beijing no good. This places pressure on China to ensure that Banco Delta Asia and other banks are clean. Immediately after the Banco Delta action, major Chinese banks dealing with foreign exchange reportedly refrained from transactions with North Korean-related firms.[58] China conducted a three-month investigation of the accusations against Banco Delta Asia that, according to South Korean diplomatic sources, confirmed the suspicions. Based on the findings, China reportedly is trying to convince North Korea that it needs to take steps in the matter.[59]

North Koreans also are reportedly attempting to circumvent the financial measures, but they have declined to disclose how they are doing it.[60] Traditionally, North Koreans have used Chinese banks for many of their international transactions, and some surmise that Kim Jong-il's trip to southern China in January 2006 may have included an attempt to move some North Korean accounts to a financial institution there. The U.S. Treasury has said that some reports suggest that North Korean agencies have been transferring assets to banks in China.[61] Others note that Austrian banks have not refrained from making transactions with North Korea.

Financial transactions with North Korea apparently still can be done through Austria and Switzerland.[62]

Japan also seeks to defuse tensions with the DPRK, but Japan has cooperated with the United States in both the Proliferation Security and Illicit Activities Initiatives. In talks in February 2006 on normalization of relations with Pyongyang, Japan announced that it intended to take up North Korea's illicit activities, including counterfeiting, in order to strengthen policy coordination with the United States and the European Union.[63]

Congress will likely continue its interest in this topic including oversight of Bush Administration actions, holding hearings to clarify U.S. policy, or using the congressional pulpit to send messages to North Korea.[64] Congress may explore possible criminal charges against Kim Jong-il in a manner similar to those against Manuel Noriega, the former leader of Panama, for drug trafficking. Other policy levers using human rights or other issues also could be employed. The United States has suggested to the DPRK that it join the Asia-Pacific Group on Money Laundering (APG), a 30 member group (including the United States, Japan, and South Korea) launched in 1997 as a sub-organization of the Organization of Economic Cooperation and Development. It is aimed at preventing illegal financial activities in the

Asia-Pacific region and would subsequently require the disclosure of all of the DPRK's illicit financial activities.[65] North Korea experts believe, however, that it will not be easy for the North to join the 30 member group.

The current strategy of the Bush Administration reportedly is to pressure North Korea but continue the diplomatic process. The fundamental issue is whether the United States should place its policy bet on the success of the six-party talks with various economic and security inducements to achieve the ultimate goals of dismantling the DPRK's nuclear weapon program or whether it should continue to administer economic and other pressures to induce Pyongyang to give up its nuclear ambitions and use the six-party talks as the vehicle to accept a possible North Korea capitulation.[66]

Since, the effect of the Banco Delta Asia action has Pyongyang scrambling, a question is whether the United States could ease its financial pressure on North Korea enough for the six-party talks to go forward or whether it should tighten the financial squeeze more — even at the risk of raising the ire of China and South Korea. Neither of these countries thinks an economic collapse or regime change in North Korea is likely to result from economic sanctions, and neither desires to deal with the economic and political effects that would follow should such a collapse occur. Yet to be determined, is the extent to which such broader strategic considerations should perhaps govern the ultimate, detailed response to the problem of North Korean counterfeiting of U.S. currency and other crime-for-profit-activity.

Currently the Bush Administration and Congress face a dilemma. The BDA action (along with the U.N. sanctions prohibiting the export of luxury goods to the DPRK) seem to be having a larger than anticipated negative effect on Pyongyang. The DPRK, however, refuses to budge in the six-party talks on its nuclear weapons program until the BDA problem is resolved and the sanctions are lifted. The question is whether the BDA and other sanctions will place enough pressure on Pyongyang to move on the nuclear weapons front or whether the sanctions merely will impose additional hardships on North Korea's general population (non-elites without close ties to the military or Communist party) and provide a pretext for Pyongyang to avoid discussing its nuclear weapons program and buy more time to develop them. The trade-off seems to be between imposing a current real financial burden on the DPRK but making no progress in halting that country's nuclear weapons program or lifting the financial sanctions in exchange for a verifiable halt to North Korea's alleged counterfeiting activities and a dim prospect that progress might be made in the six-party talks. What is clear is that the BDA sanctions have made Pyongyang more willing to meet and talk with the United States, but indications from the December 2006 six-party talks were that the DPRK was focused totally on the financial sanctions and that its negotiators had not received authority to respond to U.S. and other proposals related to their nuclear weapons program.[67]

References

[1] See section "Amount of Bogus U.S. Currency," below.

[2] Kyodo World Service. 6-way Talks' Delegates Leave Beijing After 5-Day Discussions. December 23, 2006. Note: The United States does not consider the actions to be sanctions, but North Korea has characterized them as such.

[3] Department of the Treasury. The U.S. Treasury, Federal Reserve and U.S. Secret Service Announce the Redesign of the $5 Note. News Release, Washington, June 29, 2006.

[4] Pichirallo, Joe. "Indictments Depict Noriega As Drug-Trafficking Kingpin; U.S. Had Long Backed Panamanian Leader." *The Washington Post*, February 6, 1988. pg. a.01.

[5] Note that such estimates of scale of the DPRK's foreign exchange deficit may be exaggerated as the amount may be offset by undetermined amounts of aid from the Peoples Republic of China.

[6] See generally CRS Report RL32167, Drug Trafficking and North Korea: Issues for U.S. Policy, by Raphael Perl.

[7] In July 2004, for example, the U.S. Secret Service reportedly uncovered a network selling counterfeit North Korean made cigarettes, pharmaceuticals, and $100 bills. See Frederik Balfour et. al., "Fakes," *Business Week*, February 7, 2005. Criminal indictments subsequently ensued. See generally: BBC News, "What is a superdollar?", June 20, 2004.

[8] Press conference of the President, January 26, 2006, p.9. [http://www.whitehouse.gov/news/releases/2006/01/20060126.html]

[9] See testimony of John Negroponte before the Senate Intelligence Committee on the issue of Worldwide Threats to the United States, February 2, 2005. Note that Negroponte's remarks came at a time when the six-party talks on North Korea's nuclear ambitions remained stalled over North Korea's insistence that the United States remove proposed Treasury Department sanctions against Banco Delta Asia for its alleged role in laundering proceeds of DRPK criminal activity and distributing of DPRK produced counterfeit U.S. currency. See "North Korean Counterfeiting Complicates Nuclear Crisis," by Martin Fackler, *New York Times*, January 29, 2006, p. 3.

[10] Bach, William. Hearing Testimony. Drugs, Counterfeiting, and Weapons Proliferation: The North Korean Connection. Hearing Before the Financial Management, the Budget, and International Security Subcommittee of the Committee on Governmental Affairs, United States Senate 108th Congress, First Session, S.Hrg. 108-157, May 20, 2003. p. 6.

[11] U.S. Department of State, Bureau for International Narcotics and Law Enforcement Affairs. *International Narcotics Control Strategy Report — 2006*. March 2006. Part II.

[12] See "The 'Soprano State?' North Korean Involvement in Criminal Activity and Implications for International Security," by Sheena E. Chestnut (hereinafter cited as *Chestnut*), Stanford University Honors Thesis, May 20, 2005, p.81 citing Cumings, Bruce, *Korea's Place in the Sun: A Modern History* (Norton, New York) 1997, and Michishita, Narushigwe, "Calculated Adventurism: North Korea's Military-Diplomatic Campaigns," *Korean Journal of Defense Analysis*, Vol. XVI, No.2, Fall 2004. Note that the term "Soprano State"was originally coined by *U.S. News and World Report* investigative journalist David Kaplan in 2003; see "The Far East Sopranos," by David E. Kaplan, *U.S. News and World Report*, January 27, 2003.

[13] See "Seoul's U-Turn on N. Korean Counterfeiting Could be Fatal," *Chosun Ilbo* (English Edition), December 25, 2005. The title of the 1988 report is cited as "A New Threat in the 21st Century: Realities and Responses to International Crimes."

[14] See "Korea Exchange Bank cuts ties with Macau bank accused of laundering money for North Korea," *Associated Press Report* (Seoul) Feb. 3, 2006. See also "No sign of North Korea making fake bills since 1998: spy agency," *Yonhap*, Feb. 3, 2006. Note

that media reports contain at least a handful of reports by defectors that lend credence to the notion that the DPRK produced counterfeit greenbacks under government direction prior to 1996. For a consolidated overview of such reports see Sheena Chestnut, *Soprano State*, pp. 86-89.

[15] See "Seeking international cooperation to stop manufacturing of North Korea's money," *Chosun Ilbo* (Internet Version), December 27, 2005. Media report suggestions that the DPRK may have ceased production of counterfeit greenbacks prior to the end of 1998, however, may be contradicted by at least one defector who fled the North in 2000. According to one press report, the defector, a chemist connected to the Sean Garland case, was reportedly part of a team of North Korean experts ordered to produce fake U.S. $100 bills. However, what is publically known about him, his activities, and their connection to the DPRK regime appears at this point to be anecdotal and sketchy at best. See "Counterfeiting cases point to North Korea," by Josh Meyer and Barbara Demick, *L. A. Times*, Dec. 12, 2005. Note that often statements by individuals termed "North Korean defectors," have been considered unreliable when it comes to intimate knowledge of highly secretive, closed, DPRK programs.

[16] See "U.S. says S. Korea fake notes made in North," by Jon Herskovitz and Jack Kim, Reuters, Feb. 27, 2006. Accounts in subsidiaries of the Bank of China, Hong Kong have been frozen as a result of reported links to the DPRK's trade in supernotes, and other criminal activities. See "HK link to Pyongyang 'supernotes' N Koreans have cut counterfeit deals in the city, with payments made via Bank of China subsidiary," by Greg Torode, *South China Morning Post*, February 26, 2006.

[17] See "Seeking international cooperation to stop manufacturing of North Korea's money," *Chosun Ilbo* (Internet Version), December 27, 2005.

[18] See "North Korean Counterfeiting Complicates Nuclear Crisis," by Martin Fackler, *New York Times*, January 29, 2006, p. 3.

[19] See generally, remarks of Acting Assistant Attorney General, John C. Richter of Aug.22, 2005. [http://www.usdoj.gov/criminal/press_room/speeches/2005_4193_ rmrks OprSmokngDrgnNroylChrm082405O.pdf]

[20] See "Arrest ties Pyongyang to counterfeit $100 bills," by Bill Gertz, *Washington Times*, Sept. 20, 2005, p. A1.

[21] See "North Korean Counterfeiting Complicates Nuclear Crisis" by Martin Fackler, *New York Times*, January 29, 2006, p. 3. See "Garland stands accused by US over counterfeit made in North Korea," *Irish Times*, October 17, 2005. Garland was arrested October 7, 2005, as a result of pending U.S. proceedings against him. See also Department of Justice Press Release of October 8, 2005, on Arrest of Leader of Irish Workers Party.

[22] See *Chestnut*, pp. 144-145. The South Korean media reports that authorities there had discovered 1,400 supernotes (presumed to be of DPRK origin) in April 2005, but little more is known about such reports. See "DPRK's manufacturing of counterfeit money was common sense within the National Intelligence Service," *Chosun Ilbo* (Internet Version) December 27, 2005.

[23] Torode, Greg. "Fake US Supernotes Find Their Way to HK. Pyongyang's Counterfeit Bills Are Seized from American in Transit." *South China Morning Post*, March 5, 2006, p. 3. Supernotes have reportedly shown up on 2005-2006 in Peru, Paraguay, Mongolia, Hong Kong, and Ethiopia.

[24] Kwak Tae-chung. Getting North Korean-made Counterfeit Notes is a "Piece of Cake" — Supernotes Identical to Real Ones Circulated Through the North Korea-China Border — The Powerful Economic Sanctions by the United States Has Reduced the Quantity. *Seoul Weekly Dong-A*, April 25, 2006, pp. 30-31. Original article in Korean, translated by the Open Source Center as ROK Weekly on Decreases in Circulation of DPRK-made Illegal Products in China.

[25] See Interview with Kansai University's Professor (Young Hwa?) Lee carried by Japan's TBS-TV, in an interview during a program on "Narcotics Economy in the Making of North Korea," January 16, 2007, 17:30-18:30 local time.

[26] "Smuggler's Tale: The Chinese Connection." *Dong'A Ilbo* (Internet version) January 27, 2006. Reported by Open Source Center.

[27] See Sanger, David E., "U.S. Is Shaping Plan to Pressure North Korea," *New York Times*, February 14, 2005, p. A-1. Note that this amount is more likely to be $48 million, although apparently not publically cited.

[28] See discussion in CRS Report RL32167, *Drug Trafficking and North Korea: Issues for U.S. Policy,* by Raphael Perl. See also CRS Report RL32493, *The North Korean Economy: Background and Policy Analysis*, by Dick Nanto and Emma Chanlett-Avery. For the $15 million figure on counterfeiting, see *Korea Herald*, Nov.16, 1998. See also, "Is Your Money Real?", *Newsweek*, June 10, 1996, p. 10. According to some sources, income from counterfeiting is considerably higher, i.e. $100 million. (See May 20, 2003 congressional testimony of Larry Wortzel of the Heritage Foundation.) It is said that the U.S. detects somewhere around $3-4 million per year in DPRK origin supernotes. Rough calculations of the total amount of DPRK bogus supernotes in circulation in recent years are achieved by multiplying this figure by a factor of 3 or 4 for an estimate of $9-16 million being placed in circulation per year. However, the exact amount remains elusive given the fact that much of the currency is passed in remote places and arguably banks have no financial incentive to report such forgeries if they can pass them on. Data on amounts of U.S. dollars counterfeited are not widely publicized so as not to undermine confidence in the U.S. dollar. North Korean counterfeit U.S. $100 notes have been detected in at least 14 countries including the United States since the 1970's according to media reports. On June 20, 2004, the BBC aired a "Superdollar" special which traced counterfeit $100 bills from North Korea to an official IRA source in the U.K. Reportedly millions of fake $100 bills were laundered through a *bureaux de change* in Britain. In July, 1996, a former member of the Japanese Red Army, traveling on a DPRK diplomatic passport was arrested in Thailand while trying to pass counterfeit U.S. $100 bills. See "Japanese Fake Bill Suspect Had N. Korean Passport," *Kyodo News*, July 5, 1996. For data on other forms of DPRK criminal/smuggling activity, see *Avoiding the Apocalypse: The Future of the Two Koreas*, by Marcus Noland, Institute for International Economics, Washington, D.C., June 2000, p.119. U.S. military sources reportedly estimated DPRK income from counterfeiting of U.S. currency at $15-20 million for the year 2001. See "N.K. Exported $580 Million Worth of Missiles to Middle East," *Seoul Yonhap* (English), May 13, 2003, citing Japanese *Yomiuri Shimbum* report of May 12, 2003.

[29] This is but one of a string of DPRK denials. David L. Asher, former Coordinator of the State Department's North Korea Working Group, in his February 1, 2006 remarks to

the American Enterprise Institute cited another DPRK denial: "We had neither counterfeited currency nor gotten involved in any illegal trafficking."

[30] See KCNA (official North Korean News Agency) broadcast of 1006 GMT, February 9, 2006. Reported in "North Korea vows to join international anti-money laundering drive," *MSN News*, Feb. 9, 2006, and untitled AP report from Seoul of February 9, 2006. Statements by a DPRK Foreign Ministry spokesperson are typically reserved for high level communications with the outside world. Reuters and Agence France Presse (AFP) reported on the broadcast as well.

[31] See CRS Report RL32493, *The North Korean Economy: Background and Policy Analysis*, by Dick Nanto and Emma Chanlett-Avery, January 2005. For a discussion of U.S. response options reportedly reviewed see "U.S. is Shaping Plan to Pressure North Korea," by David E. Sanger, *New York Times*, Feb. 14, 2005, A-1.

[32] Note for example, that one operation against what is believed to be North Korean linked contraband smugglers reportedly netted not only some $4 million in supernotes, but also $700 in counterfeit U.S. postage stamps. See "Crime does pay for North Korea," by Peter Brooks, *Boston Herald* (op-ed), January 17, 2006.

[33] Note that press reports indicate that the U.S. Secret Service estimates $43.4 million in counterfeit currency was circulated in the United States in 2004 alone. It is estimated that $700 billion in genuine U.S. currency exists worldwide. Generally, disclosure that large amounts of U.S. currency in use worldwide might be bogus would likely be seen not to serve the best interests of the nation. As a result, some suggest the United States may be downplaying the scale of alleged DPRK counterfeiting activity — but nevertheless according it the high policy priority the actual level of such activity warrants.

[34] See footnote number 198.

[35] Asher, David L. "The North Korean Criminal State, its Ties to Organized Crime, and the Possibility of WMD Proliferation." The Nautilus Institute. Policy Forum Online 05-92A: November 15th, 2005.

[36] The Federal Reserve Board. Currency and Coin Services. On Internet at [http://www.federalreserve.gov/paymentsystems/coin/default.htm]

[37] The Federal Reserve Board. Currency in Circulation: Value. On Internet at [http://www.federalreserve.gov/paymentsystems/coin/currcircvalue.htm].

[38] The Department of the Treasury. *Budget in Brief FY2007*. P. 87.

[39] U.S. General Accountability Office. Testimony. Counterfeit U.S. Currency Abroad: Observations on Counterfeiting and U.S. Deterrence Efforts. February 27, 1996 (GAO/T-GGD-96-82).

[40] The Department of the Treasury. Treasury Designates Banco Delta Asia as Primary Money Laundering Concern under USA Patriot Act. Press Release JS-2720. September 15, 2005. See *Federal Register*, Vol. 70 No. 181, Sept. 20, 2005 (Notices), p. 55214. The finding asserts that at least one regular North-Korean-front client of BDA was widely reported to be conducting "numerous illegal activities, including distributing counterfeit currency and smuggling counterfeit tobacco products" for over a decade. See also Department of Treasury Press Release of September 15, 2005 (JS-2720), on Treasury Designation of Banco Delta Asia as a Primary Money Laundering Concern and Treasury Dept. FINCEN Advisory of December 13, 2005, on Guidelines to Financial Institutions on the Provision of Banking Services to North Korean

Government Agencies and Associated Front Companies Engaged in Illicit Activities which encourages financial institutions worldwide to take precautions that they are not used as a conduit for the laundering of proceeds of DPRK illicit activities.

[41] See *Federal Register*, Vol. 70 No. 181, Sept. 20, 2005 (Notice of Proposed Rulemaking) p. 55217ff.

[42] See *Wall Street Journal Asia*, "North Korea's economyfeels fallout of U.S. move-Lenders sever ties after sanction threat against Macau bank," by Gordon Fairclough, Feb. 14, 2006. Note that as generally private North Korean individuals do not hold accounts outside the country, widespread speculation exists that the nine individual accounts seized belong to the upper echelons of the DPRK elite. The U.S. has accused Banco Delta Asia of accepting and circulating DPRK origin supernotes.

[43] Fairclough, Gordon. "Politics and Economics: Banks Cut Ties to North Korea — U.S. Threat Toward One Lender Has Surprisingly Big Ripple Effect." *The Wall Street Journal*, February 14, 2006. P. A6.

[44] James A. Kelly. An Overview of U.S.-East Asia Policy, Testimony before the House International Relations Committee, Washington, DC. June 2, 2004.

[45] U.S. Department of State. Bureau of Nonproliferation. The Proliferation Security Initiative (PSI) (Fact Sheet). May 26, 2005. Congressional Research Service report RS21881, *Proliferation Security Initiative (PSI)*, by Sharon Squassoni.

[46] Sanger, David. Questions Without Answers: the Korean Conundrum [Review]. *The New York Times*, January 19, 2006. Pg. E.9.

[47] U.S. Department of State. North Korea-U.S. Statement. Press Statement 2005/T13-29, September 19, 2005.

[48] See, for example: Choe, Sang-Hun. Roh Warns U.S. Over N. Korea. Blunt Speech Shows Rift Between Allies. *International Herald Tribune*, January 26, 2006, pg. 1.

[49] Ambassador Lee Tae-sik's Speech Given at the St. Regis Hotel (Washington, DC). The Korea-US Alliance - A Partnership for the Future, February 7, 2006. Korea Economic Institute. [http://www.keia.com/2-Publications/2-6-Other/LeeTSspeech.pdf]

[50] ROK Editorial Says ROK-US 'Discord' Over DPRK Counterfeiting 'Worrisome." *Dong-A Ilbo*, in Korean, January 25, 2006, p. 31. Translation by the U.S. Embassy in Seoul. Provided by Open Source Center.

[51] Hayes Says Counterfeiting Issue Sidetracks Nuclear Negotiations. *Nautilus Weekly*, February 27 - March 3, 2006 . Quote by Nautilus Institute Executive Director Peter Hayes speaking on Chicago Public Radio's Worldview Program.

[52] U.S. Department of the Treasury. Treasury Officials Brief North Koreans on Actions to Stem DPRK Illicit Financial Activity. Press Release JS-4099, March 7, 2006. "N. Korea Agrees to Discuss Counterfeit Issue with U.S." *The Chosun Ilbo*. (Digital edition) February 24, 2006.

[53] Kessler, Glenn. N. Korea Sets Terms for Return to Nuclear Talks . *The Washington Post*, March 9, 2006. P. A16. DPRK Reportedly Proposed 'Method' to Resolve Financial Dispute, Waits for US Response. Open Source Center report of Yonhap news article: N. Korea Vows Not To Join Nuclear Talks Unless U.S. Sanctions Are Lifted, March 8, 2006. Center-Left ROK Daily Carries Exclusive Interview With DPRK Delegate to New York Meeting. Open Source Center report of article in *Seoul Hankyoreh* (Internet version) in Korean. March 8, 2006.

[54] Herskovitz, Jon and Jack Kim. U.S. Says S. Korea Fake Notes Made in North. Reuters News, February 22, 2006.
[55] Kyodo World Service. 6-way Talks' Delegates Leave Beijing After 5-Day Discussions. December 23, 2006. Note: The United States does not consider the actions to be sanctions, but North Korea has characterized them as such.
[56] U.S. Offers Compromise Over N. Korea's Dollar Forgeries. *Chosun Ilbo* (Digital Chosun), December 20, 2006.
[57] Reuters. Crackdown on North Korea Strains US-South Ties. January 28, 2006.
[58] Chinese Banks Cut Transactions with North Korea-related Firms (From Kyodo News Service). BBC Monitoring Asia Pacific. March 13, 2006.
[59] ROK Daily Cites Diplomatic Source: PRC Confirms DPRK Money-Laundering in Macau Open Source Center report of article by *Chosun Ilbo* (WWW-Text in English), January 11, 2006. [*Chosun Ilbo* headline: "China Finds N.Korea Guilty of Money Laundering"]
[60] Fifield, Anna. "North Korea Is 'Looking to Beat' US Financial Sanctions." *Financial Times*, March 13, 2006. P. 1.
[61] Treasury Issues Advisory on North Korean Banking. Bulletin News Network, the White House Bulletin, March 16, 2006.
[62] Major Chinese Banks Refrain From Dealing with N. Korean Firms. Kyodo News. March 13, 2006.
[63] Japan to raise North Korea's alleged laundering, drug trafficking in talks (From Kyodo News Service), BBC Monitoring Asia Pacific, February 1, 2006. p. 1.
[64] For legislation, see; CRS Report RL33567, *Korea-U.S. Relations: Issues for Congress*, by Larry A. Niksch.
[65] U.S. asks NK to Join Int'l Group on Money Laundering. Yonhap English News. March 12, 2006.
[66] Brinkley, Joel. U.S. Squeezes North Korea's Money Flow. *The New York Times*, March 10, 2006. p. 12.
[67] Samuels International Associates, *The Nelson Report*, January 16, 2007.

In: Currency Interventions, Fluctuations...
Editor: L. C. Hilbert, pp. 91-106

ISBN: 978-1-60456-078-7

Chapter 4

FOREIGN DIRECT INVESTMENT: EFFECTS OF A "CHEAP" DOLLAR*

James K. Jackson
Specialist in International Trade and Finance Foreign Affairs, Defense, and Trade Division

ABSTRACT

Since 2002, the dollar has depreciated against a broad basket of currencies and against the euro. This depreciation has prompted some observers to question whether the "cheap" dollar is leading to a "fire sale" of U.S. firms, especially of those firms that can be identified as part of the Nation's defense industrial base. Congress has displayed a long and continuing interest in foreign direct investment and its impact on the U.S. economy. Since September 11, 2001, Congress has demonstrated a heightened level of concern about the impact of foreign direct investment in critical industries or in sectors that are vital to homeland security. In the 110th Congress, Members are considering H.R. 556, the National Security Foreign Investment Reform and Strengthened Transparency Act of 2007, which was adopted by the full House on February 28, 2007. The measure reflects a heightened level of concern about the presence of foreign investors in the economy by increasing Congressional oversight over federal reviews of foreign direct investment and by expanding the current areas of review to include homeland security and critical infrastructure.

Academic research and analysis has been relatively limited on the topic of the relationship between a depreciated dollar and any impact on foreign purchases of U.S. firms. There is also a relatively limited amount of information on this topic. Nevertheless, direct investment transactions as a whole seem to be tied more directly to the relative rates of economic growth between economies, as well as expected long-run rates of return and other economic factors, than to relatively short-term movements in the exchange rate of the dollar. Actual and expected movements in the exchange rate may influence the timing and the magnitude of foreign investors' decisions, but little research has been done on this issue.

---

* Excerpted from CRS Report RL34000, May 11, 2007.

Firms also engage in a variety of tactics to nullify or mitigate the effects of movements in the exchange rate, which would weaken the linkage between movements in the exchange rate and direct investment transactions. U.S. and foreign multinational firms have come to raise a significant part of their investment funds in the capital markets in which they are investing, which also lessens the impact of movements in the exchange rate. Furthermore, U.S. and foreign multinational firms have become skilled at using various techniques to hedge the risks of changes in exchange rates. This report assesses the current state of knowledge concerning the role of exchange rate movements in direct investment transactions, presents data on some of the major factors that influence direct investment, and provides an overview of some of the factors that influence the way in which firms finance their investments.

This report will be updated as events warrant.

Overview

The United States is unique in that it is the largest foreign direct[1] investor in the world and also the largest recipient of foreign direct investment. This dual role means that globalization, or the spread of economic activity by firms across national borders, has become a prominent feature of the U.S. economy. Through direct investment the U.S. economy has become highly enmeshed into the broader global economy. Some observers are concerned that the depreciation in the value of the dollar relative to a number of major currencies could lead to a "fire sale" of U.S. firms. Direct investment commonly refers to investment in new or established businesses and real estate, compared with portfolio investment, which refers to investment in U.S. government securities and corporate stocks and bonds. This report focuses on foreign direct investment.[2]

Foreigners invested $184 billion in U.S. businesses and real estate in 2006, according to balance of payments data published by the Department of Commerce.[3] As figure 1 shows, this represents an increase over the $104 billion invested in 2005 and compares to the sharp increase in the amount U.S. firms invested abroad in 2006 relative to the amount they invested abroad in 2005. The increase in U.S. direct investment flows mirrors a turnaround in global flows. According to the United Nation's *World Investment Report*,[4] global foreign direct investment flows increased by 29% in 2005 and 27% in 2004, after three years of declining flows.

The cumulative amount, or stock, of foreign direct investment in the United States on a historical cost basis[5] increased by $109 billion in 2005 to over $1.6 trillion. This marks a slight increase over the previous year and a significant change from the decline in foreign investment spending that had occurred since 2000.[6] The rise in the value of foreign direct investment in the United States includes an upward valuation adjustment of existing investments and increased spending that was driven by the relatively stronger growth rate of the U.S. economy, the world-wide resurgence in cross-border merger and acquisition activity, and investment in the U.S. manufacturing, information and depository institutions as overseas banks and finance and insurance companies sought access to the profitable U.S. financial market.[7]

New spending by U.S. firms on businesses and real estate abroad, or U.S. direct investment abroad, fell sharply in 2005 to $9 billion, down from the $252 billion U.S. firms invested in 2004, according to the Department of Commerce.[8] The drop in U.S. direct investment abroad reflects actions by U.S. parent firms to reduce the amount of reinvested earnings going to their foreign affiliates for distribution to the U.S. parent firms in order to take advantage of one-time tax provisions in the American Jobs Creation Act of 2004 (P.L. 108-357). Data indicate that U.S. direct investment abroad in 2006 rebounded to reach $249 billion.

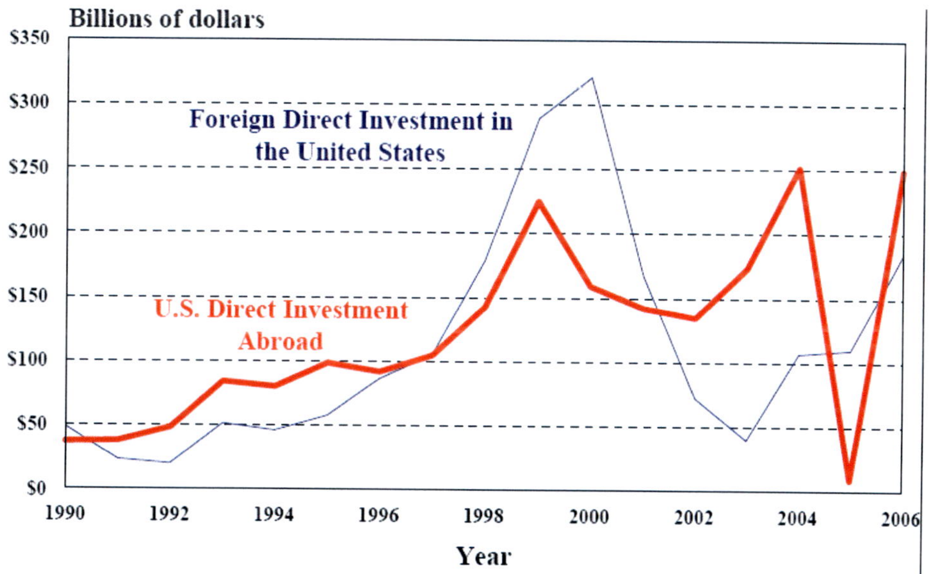

Source: CRS from U.S. Department of Commerce data

Note: the drop in U.S. direct investment abroad in 2005 reflects actions by U.S. parent companies to take advantage of a one-time tax provision.

Figure 1. Foreign Direct Investment in the United States and U.S. Direct Investment Abroad, Annual Flows, 1990-2006.

FOREIGN DIRECT INVESTMENT AND THE DOLLAR

Since 2002, the dollar has depreciated against a broad basket of currencies and against the euro. This depreciation has prompted some observers to question whether the "cheap" nominal dollar is leading to a "fire sale" of U.S. firms, especially of those firms that can be identified as part of the Nation's defense industrial base. While some aspects of foreign investment have been studied extensively by academics and others, relatively few economic studies have addressed the linkage between direct investment and movements in the exchange rate and even those studies have produced mixed results.

In general terms, most economists argue that depreciation in the exchange value of the dollar is not the key factor that drives the decision by most foreign firms to invest in the United States, although the corresponding appreciation of foreign currencies would lower the cost of assets acquired in the United States. The lower value of the dollar, however, means that the value of returns from U.S. assets are reduced as well, which would leave the overall rate of return on such investments unchanged.[9] In one study, two economists argue that an appreciation of foreign currencies relative to the dollar could boost foreign direct investment in the United States, because the appreciation leads to increased wealth for foreign firms relative to their U.S. counterparts and greater access to low-cost funds in local markets.[10] Another economist argues that appreciation of the yen in the 1980s provided some impetus for Japanese firms to increase their direct investments in the United States, because the appreciated yen lowered the price of certain firm-specific assets, such as technology and managerial skills, but that it did not necessarily improve the nominal returns to Japanese firms.[11] Actual and expected changes in the exchange rate of the dollar may well influence the timing and the magnitude of foreign investors' decisions, but little research has been done on this issue.

Foreign Direct Investment and GDP

Generally, economists argue that relative rates of growth between the U.S. and foreign economies are indicative of relative rates of return and corporate profitability and, therefore, are key factors in determining the direction and magnitude of capital flows, including direct investment flows.[12] These flows also are affected by relative rates of inflation, taxes, interest rates, and expectations about the performance of national economies, which means they can be quite volatile at times. Since the mid1990s, a combination of strong growth and low inflation in the U.S. economy likely were the main factors in attracting foreign investors. The sheer size of the U.S. economy, the vast number of investment opportunities, and the relative liquidity of the market likely also enhance the appeal of investments in the United States. From 2002 to 2005, U.S. direct investment abroad was more than twice the amount foreigners invested in the U.S. economy, reflecting the period of slower growth in the U.S. economy from 2001-2003. Both U.S. direct investment abroad and foreign direct investment in the United States increased in 2006, reflecting both the stronger rate of growth of the U.S. economy and growth in corporate earnings.

Table 1 shows annual data from 1999 to 2006 for U.S. and foreign direct investment. The data show annual inward and outward flows of direct investment and they provide some detail on the composition of the sources of those funds. The table also presents index numbers representing the nominal trade-weighted exchange rate of the dollar relative to a broad basket of currencies with the year 2000 as the base year and the annual rate of economic growth in percentage terms for thc rcal gross domestic product (GDP) of the U.S. economy. Similar sets of index numbers were constructed for the Japanese yen, Japanese direct investment in the United States, the euro, and euro-country direct investment in the United States.[13] The index numbers that represent the exchange rate between the dollar and various foreign currencies were constructed such that an increase in the value of the index means that more dollars are required to buy foreign currency, or that the dollar has depreciated relative to the value of the foreign currency. Similarly, a decline in the index means that fewer dollars are required to buy foreign currency, or that the dollar has appreciated.

Table 1. U.S. Direct Investment Abroad, Foreign Direct Investment in the United States, and Indexes of Currencies, 1999-2006

	1999	2000	2001	2002	2003	2004	2005	2006
U.S. direct investment abroad (in $billions)								
Capital	$224.9	$-59.2	$142.3	$154.5	$149.9	$244.1	$9.1	228.3
Equity capital	98.9	78.0	60.9	42.7	35.5	81.4	39.7	25.7
Reinvested earnings	64.2	93.6	69.8	85.3	121.0	157.3	-11.2	202.1
Intercompany debt	61.8	-12.4	11.6	26.5	-6.6	5.4	-19.4	0.4
Foreign direct investment in the United States (in $billions)								
Capital	$289.4	$321.3	$167.0	$84.4	$64.0	$133.2	$109.8	180.3
Equity capital	221.6	259.6	140.9	105.3	93.4	74.1	57.7	81.5
Reinvested earnings	4.1	-0.3	-33.9	1.6	14.5	55.6	58.9	101.6
Intercompany debt	63.8	61.9	60.0	-22.6	-44.0	3.5	-6.9	-2.9
Dollar index(broad, nominal)	102.9	100.0	94.8	94.2	100.1	105.2	107.7	109.5
Real GDP (% change)	4.5	3.7	0.8	1.6	2.5	3.9	3.2	3.3
Euro (index)	115.5	100.0	97.0	102.4	122.6	134.7	134.8	136.5
Euro-country investment (index)	70.5	100.0	38.8	6.7	22.7	18.8	20.8	N.A.
Pound (index)	93.7	100.0	105.3	100.9	92.7	82.7	83.3	82.3
British investment (index)	131.4	100.0	3.4	25.7	-5.3	27.7	34.9	N.A.
Japanese yen (index)	94.8	100.0	88.7	86.1	93.0	99.7	97.9	92.7
Japanese investment (index)	147.8	100.0	-40.1	83.1	109.3	228.1	179.6	N.A.

Source: Department of Commerce and Federal Reserve Board.

Note: The nominal broad dollar index is the weighted average of the foreign exchange value of the U.S. dollar against a broad group of U.S. trading partners developed by the Board of Governors of the Federal Reserve System that shows the dollar price of foreign currency; the base year of the index is 2000 with a value of 100. Real GDP is the annual growth rate in real Gross Domestic Product (GDP). Euro, pound, and yen index values represent the dollar price of the respective currencies with a base value of 100 for the year 2000. Euro-country, British, and Japanese direct investment in the United States are represented by index numbers with the base year of 2000 = 100. Index values were developed by CRS.

The index numbers in table 1 are constructed primarily as a device to facilitate the comparison of the timing and the direction of changes in the measures, not the relative magnitudes of the actual values involved. The data also show the similarity in trends between U.S. direct investment abroad and foreign direct investment in the United States. Such a similarity seems counterintuitive, since inward and outward investment flows are thought by some to be substitutes. If they are substitutes, U.S. direct investment abroad would be expected to be strongest during periods when the U.S. economy is not performing well relative to foreign economies and foreign direct investment in the United States would be expected to be weak. Instead, during periods when U.S. direct investment abroad is strong, foreign direct investment in the United States is also strong and vice versa.

U.S. direct investment abroad and foreign direct investment in the United States may follow similar investment trends over time as firms in both the United States and in foreign markets respond to increases or decreases in demand for goods and services as the U.S. economy expands or contracts, respectively. For instance, as the

U.S. rate of economic growth rises, U.S. firms would increase their investments at home in response to improved profitability and stronger sales. In addition, these firms may well increase their investments abroad as production by foreign firms increases to meet the higher level of demand in the United States. Although U.S. foreign affiliates export only about 10% of their worldwide production back to the United States, increased levels of exports by foreign firms and the correspondingly higher levels of production abroad may well stimulate production and investment abroad by the foreign affiliates of U.S. firms.

Overall, the data provide some support for the general conclusion that the inflows and outflows of direct investment are tied more directly to the overall rate of growth in the economy than they are to movements in the exchange rate of the dollar. Nevertheless, movements in the exchange rate of the dollar likely affect flows of direct investment through common linkages to the rate of growth in the economy and as firms adjust their payments of remittances in response to movements in the exchange value of the dollar.

To the extent that the rate of growth of U.S. GDP, movements in the dollar, and direct investment flows are interrelated, these interrelationships complicate efforts to separate out cause and effect chains of influence and the relative importance of any one factor. The data in table 1 generally tend to support the concept that the rate of growth in the U.S. economy, as reflected by U.S. GDP, likely has a greater influence on direct investment flows than does the exchange rate of the dollar. Data from table 1 on U.S. GDP, the nominal broad index of the dollar price of a basket of foreign currencies, and an index of foreign direct investment in the United States are shown in figure 2. Again, the index numbers for the dollar are constructed such that a rise in the value of the index indicates that it takes more dollars per unit of foreign currency, or that foreign currencies have appreciated relative to the dollar.

If movements in the exchange rate of the dollar were a key factor in driving inflows and outflows of foreign direct investment, then it would be reasonable to assume that the index for the dollar and for foreign direct investment in the United States in figure 2 would move in similar directions. In other words, a rise in the exchange rate of the dollar to foreign currencies means that it would take more dollars to buy foreign currency, or that the dollar had depreciated in value relative to the foreign currency so that it would be less costly for foreign investors. Then, an appreciation in the value of foreign currencies, and a corresponding depreciation in the value of the dollar, would be accompanied by an increase in foreign direct investment in U.S. businesses because such purchases would be cheaper in foreign currency.

Likewise a depreciation in the value of foreign currencies and an appreciation in the value of the dollar would be expected to be accompanied by a decrease in foreign direct investment in the United States. During the 2000 to 2002 period, this type of relationship seemingly held as the dollar appreciated and foreign direct investment declined. In addition, as the dollar depreciated between 2002 and 2004, foreign direct investment increased. The relationship, however, did not hold after 2004 as the dollar depreciated and as foreign direct investment declined. The similarities between the general trend in foreign direct investment in the U.S. economy and the rate of growth of the U.S. economy, as represented by the index numbers for GDP, lends some support to the conclusion that the rate of growth in the economy is likely to be a more important factor influencing the flows of direct investment than is the exchange rate of the dollar. Direct investment, movements in the exchange rate, and the relative rate of growth in U.S. GDP likely are interrelated in a number of ways that significantly complicates efforts to separate out the various chains of influence to determine direct cause-effect relationships.

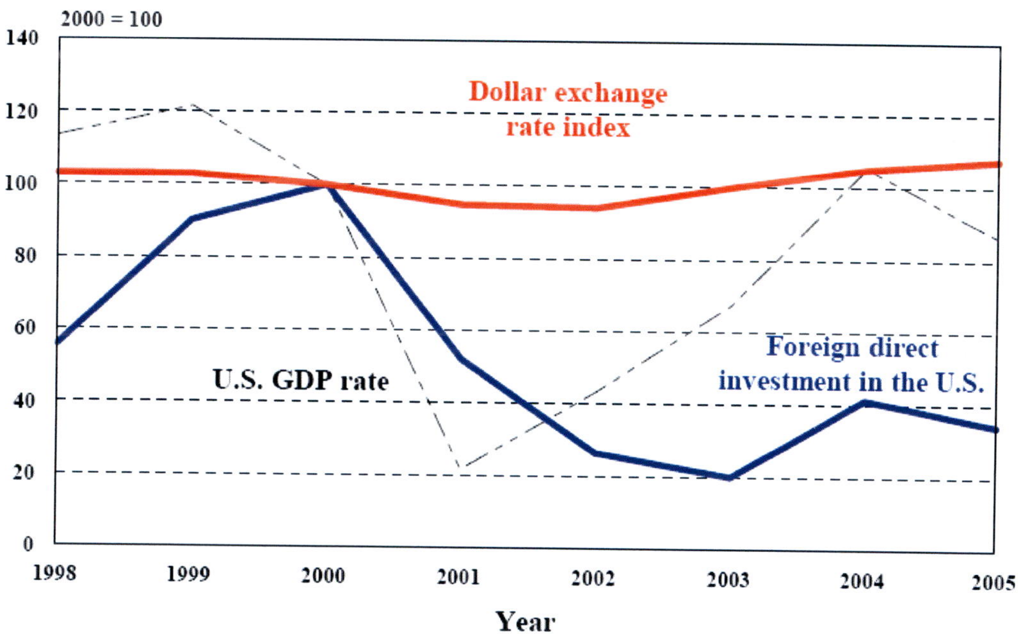

Source: U.S. Department of Commerce.

Figure 2. Foreign Direct Investment in the United States, the Dollar Price of Foreign Currency, and U.S. GDP Growth Rate.

Dollar-Euro

Figure 3 shows data for the dollar/euro exchange rate and for direct investment in the United States by euro-area countries. In this figure, a rise in the euro/dollar index indicates an appreciation of the euro relative to the dollar. The data in the figure indicate that direct investment in the United States by euro-area countries during the 1998-2005 period runs counter to the concept that movements in the exchange rate determine flows of direct investment. In fact, as the euro depreciated against the dollar in the 1998-2000 period, direct investment increased and as the euro appreciated between 2000 and 2003, direct investment fell sharply. Euro-area country direct investment in the United States has remained fairly flat since 2003, despite the stronger euro.

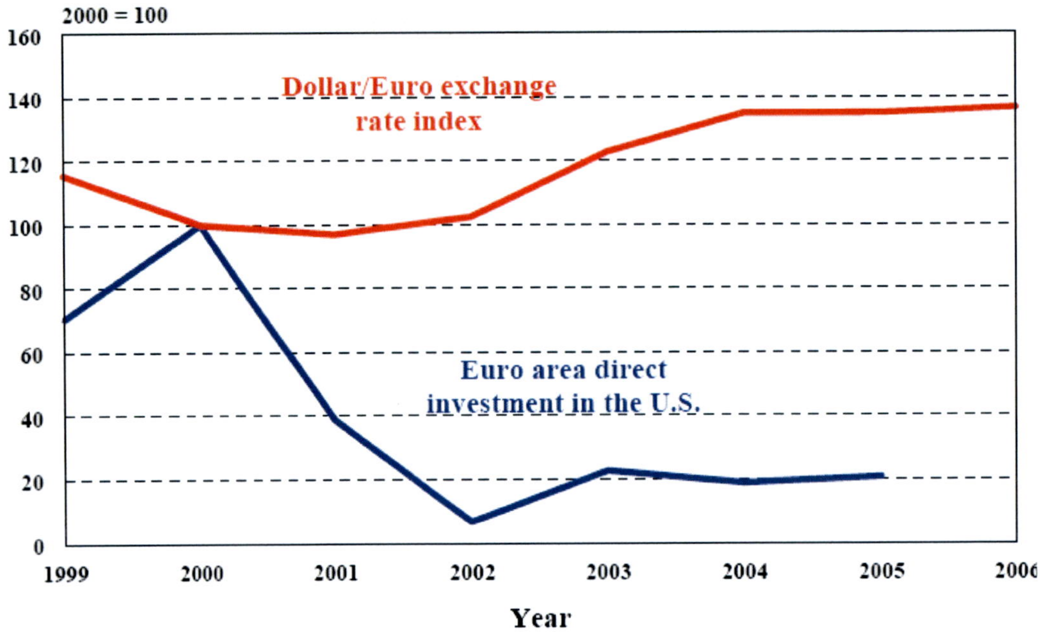

Source: U.S. Department of Commerce.

Figure 3. Foreign Direct Investment in the United States by Euro- Area Countries and the Dollar/Euro Exchange Rate Index.

Dollar-Pound

Figure 4 shows data for British direct investment in the United States and the dollar/pound exchange rate. Over the 1998-2005 period, the pound appreciated against the dollar until 2001, when it has trended down as the pound depreciated slightly through 2004. From 2004 through 2005, there was little change in the dollar/pound exchange rate. As the pound appreciated against the dollar between 1998 and 2001, British direct investment tumbled sharply in 1999 and 2000, in concert with the slowdown in the rate of growth of U.S. GDP and the height of the value of the pound against the dollar. Since 2002, British direct investment dropped again in 2003, before showing some resurgence in 2004 and 2005, even though the pound generally depreciated against the dollar.

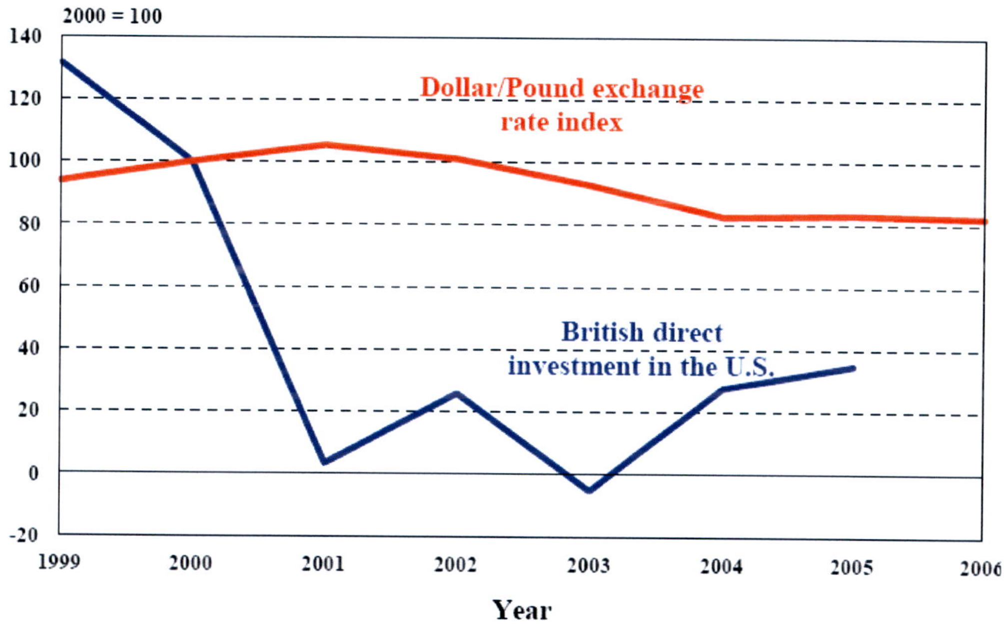

Source: U.S. Department of Commerce.

Figure 4. British Direct Investment in the United States, Dollar/Pound Exchange Rate Index.

Dollar-Yen

Similar trends are shown in figure 5, which displays the trend of Japanese direct investment in the United States and the dollar/yen exchange rate index during the 1998-2005 period. An increase in the yen/dollar index indicates an appreciation of the yen relative to the dollar. This figure indicates that Japanese direct investment in the U.S. economy did indeed follow a trend that is somewhat similar to that for the dollar/yen exchange rate, although turning points in the yen/dollar exchange rate do not correlate well with the turning points in direct investment. In fact, the turning points in Japanese direct investment spending occurred prior to changes in the dollar/yen exchange rate, which runs contrary to the concept that the exchange rate is an important factor that determines foreign direct investment. Major turning points in Japanese direct investment in the United States, however, correlate more closely with the overall patterns of U.S. GDP performance than with changes in the dollar/yen exchange rate, indicating that Japanese direct investment in the United States over the 1998-2005 period was influenced more by the relative rate of growth in U.S. GDP than by the dollar/yen exchange rate.

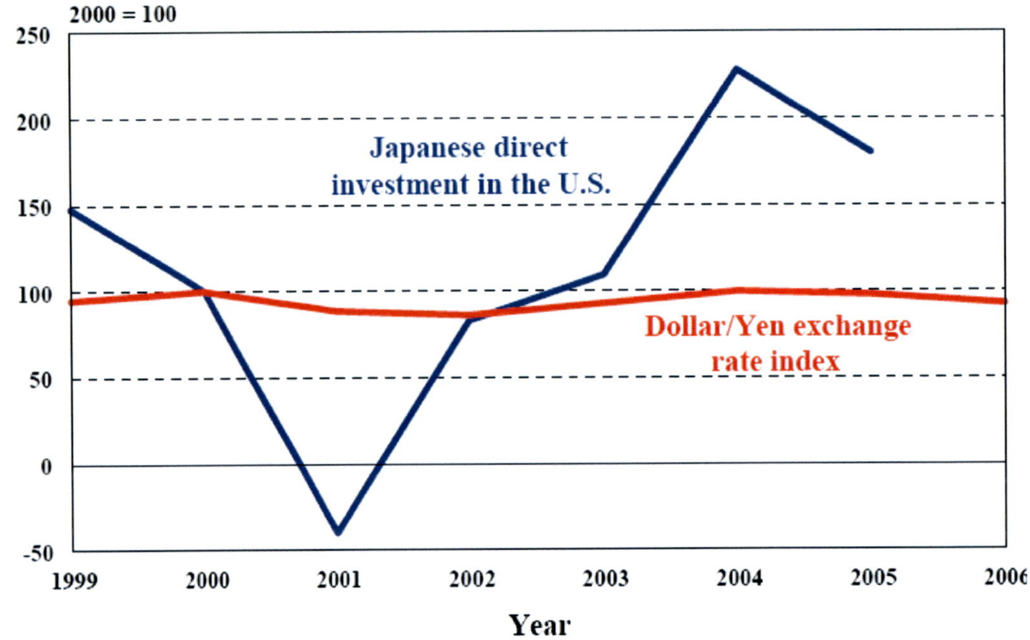

Source: U.S. Department of Commerce.

Figure 5. Japanese Direct Investment in the United States, Dollar/Yen Exchange Rate Index.

Foreign Direct Investment and Capital Markets

There are a number of factors that complicate efforts to determine a cause-effect relationship between movements in the exchange rate and direct investment. First, both direct investment and the exchange rate are closely related to the relative rate of growth of the domestic economy and it may not be possible to separate out the individual effects. Second, one characteristic of multinational firms is that they utilize foreign and international capital markets.[14] To the extent that firms can raise funds in the market in which they are investing, they can blunt exchange rate effects and weaken an expected relationship between movements in the exchange rate and direct investment. Third, multinational firms have become skilled at using specialized foreign currency markets and foreign currency derivatives that help them reduce the risk and the economic impact of changes in exchange rates. Such activities likely would lessen the impact of changes in exchange rates on direct investment transactions.

Most economists believe that the exchange rate of the dollar generally is determined by the relative long-term performance of the economy, although the exchange rate between any two particular currencies can move abruptly over the short run as a result of factors specific to individual currencies. Efforts to model and predict movements in the exchange rate of the dollar have proven to be particularly vexing because a number of factors can affect the value of the dollar and other currencies in the short run. One factor complicating efforts to determine a cause-effect relationship between movements in the exchange rate and direct investment is the apparent similarity between the inflows and outflows of direct investment, as mentioned previously.

In most cases, it would seem reasonable to assume that inward and outward direct investment generally would move in opposite directions in response to movements in the exchange rate and act somewhat as substitutes for one another. In fact, inward and outward flows of direct investment have tended to trend in the same direction over time. One possible explanation for this similarity is that the inward and outward flows of direct investment are affected by the same underlying forces, principally the relative rate of growth of the U.S. economy compared to other economies. The difficulties involved in unraveling the interrelationships between direct investment flows, the relative rate of growth of various economies, and movements in the exchange rate significantly complicate any efforts to isolate the relationship between direct investment and the exchange rate.

During periods when the U.S. economy is growing at a relatively more rapid pace than are other developed economies, foreign firms are encouraged to invest in U.S. businesses, since profits in those firms would be expected to be strong. At the same time, rising corporate earnings associated with a growing economy would encourage U.S. firms to step up their investment spending both domestically and abroad since the commanding role of the U.S. economy in the global economy means that the performance of the U.S. economy would tend to have a positive effect on economic performance abroad. The advanced development of U.S. and global financial markets and the rapid pace of globalization in trade and investment activities likely means that the U.S. and global economies are becoming increasingly intertwined, which would increase the prospect that economic events would be transmitted more rapidly between the U.S. and other economies.

Strong performance in the U.S. economy also tends to draw in foreign capital in various forms that adds to upward pressure on the dollar, so that the exchange rate of the dollar and the rate of growth in the economy would experience any number of direct, indirect (second-hand), and cross effects (third-hand). Both the rate of growth of U.S. GDP and the exchange rate of the dollar increased through the 1998 to 2000 period. As the rate of growth of the economy slowed in the 2000 to 2002 period, however, the dollar continued to appreciate due in part to the mix of macroeconomic policies in the United States that attracted inflows of capital. Since 2002, however, the exchange rate of the dollar has depreciated against the euro and a broad basket of currencies despite a general improvement in the rate of growth of U.S. GDP.

Sources of Direct Investment Funds

The data in table 1 also indicate that there are differences between U.S. and foreign firms in the sources of their funds, which likely lessens the impact of movements of the dollar on both U.S. and foreign direct investment. Both U.S. and foreign firms make little use of intercompany debt to finance their investments. Instead, multinational firms raise the bulk of their funds internally or in the particular foreign markets in which they are operating, especially if those markets are in advanced developed economies. As a result, this apparent preference for host-country sources of financing would reduce the impact of movements in the exchange rate on cross-border flows of direct investment.[15] Since nearly three-fourths of U.S. direct investment abroad is in highly developed economies with well-developed capital and equity markets similar to those in the United States, U.S. firms generally raise the funds they need in those markets.

In 1998 and 1999 as the U.S. economy was growing at a rapid rate, U.S. multinational firms financed their investments abroad with a combination of equity capital, reinvested earnings, and intercompany debt as the U.S. parent companies loaned funds to their foreign affiliates. Since 1999, intercompany debt has played a smaller role in financing overseas investments. Instead, equity capital and reinvested earnings have accounted for over 90% of the source of funds to the foreign affiliates of U.S. parent companies, with reinvested earnings accounting for about 60% of the funds the foreign affiliates of U.S. firms invested over the 2000-2005 period.

In contrast, the affiliates of foreign firms operating in the United States relied heavily on U.S. equity markets to finance over 80% of their investments during the 1999-2006 period. Reinvested earnings played a significant role in financing the investments of foreign firms only in 2004 and 2005, when the declining value of the dollar combined with the increased rate of growth of the U.S. economy to encourage foreign firms to reinvest the profits they raised in the United States back into their U.S. affiliates. This reliance on domestic sources of capital means that the relative importance of the exchange rate as a factor that affects the investment decisions of firms likely varies over time depending on other economic factors, especially the overall performance of the economy; taxes; and the performance of corporate earnings.

International Role of the Dollar and Derivatives

Volatility in the exchange value of the dollar has spurred many multinational firms to act to protect themselves against such fluctuations. As a result, firms and other enterprises that deal in foreign currencies have become accustomed to participating in what is termed "over the counter" currency transactions that are aimed at reducing the risks and mitigating the effects of changes in the exchange value of the dollar. The growth in the U.S. economy and the growth in the international role of the dollar means that the dollar is now heavily traded in financial markets around the globe and, at times, plays the role of a global currency.

The prominent international role of the dollar means that the exchange value of the dollar often acts as a mechanism for transmitting economic and political news and events across national borders. While such a role helps facilitate a broad range of international economic and financial activities, it also means that the dollar's exchange value can vary greatly on a daily or weekly basis as it is buffeted by international events.[16] A recent survey by the world's leading central banks indicate that the *daily* trading of foreign currencies totals more than $1.9 trillion, or more than the *annual* amount of U.S. exports of goods and services. The data also indicate that 90% of the global foreign exchange turnover is in U.S. dollars, substantially the same as the share reported in a similar survey conducted in 2001.[17]

In the U.S. foreign exchange market, the value of the dollar is followed closely by multinational firms, international banks, and investors who are attempting to offset some of the inherent risks involved with foreign exchange trading. On a daily basis, turnover in the U.S. foreign exchange market[18] averages $461 billion; similar transactions in the U.S. foreign exchange derivative markets[19] averages $355 billion, nearly double the amount reported in a similar survey conducted in 2001.[20] Foreigners also buy and sell U.S.

corporate bonds and stocks and U.S. Treasury securities. Foreigners now own about 54% of the total amount of outstanding U.S. Treasury securities that are publicly held and traded.[21]

The data in table 2 provide some selected indicators on the relative sizes of the various capital markets in various countries and regions and the importance of international foreign exchange markets. Worldwide, foreign exchange and interest rate derivatives, the most widely used hedges against movements in currencies, were valued at $243 trillion in 2005, nearly 60% larger than the combined total of all public and private bonds, equities, and bank assets. For the United States, such derivatives total twice as much as all U.S. bonds, equities, and bank assets.

CONCLUSIONS

The depreciation of the dollar has raised concerns that the lowered value dollar would lead to a "fire sale" of U.S. firms. Such an increase of foreign direct investment would be of concern to Congress, which has shown a heightened level of interest in the role and presence of foreign-owned firms in the economy since September 11, 2001. There is little academic research and much still to be learned about the role of the exchange rate in the decision-making process of U.S. and foreign multinational firms, but movements in the exchange rate do not appear to be a major factor in driving those investment decisions. While U.S. and foreign direct investment were both higher in 2006 than they were in 2005, neither U.S. direct investment abroad nor foreign direct investment in the United States seems to be tied too strongly to the depreciation of the dollar. There does appear to be a complex set of relationships that connect direct investment, the relative rate of growth in the economy, and movements in the exchange rate, but it is difficult to unwind these relationships to determine the relative importance of each factor. A cursory examination of the available data seems to indicate that the relative rates of growth between the U.S. and foreign economies likely is the most important factor in driving direct investment transactions.

As U.S. and foreign firms become more adept at utilizing foreign capital markets and foreign currency derivatives, they likely are reducing the importance of fluctuations in currencies as a major factor in some of their investment decisions. Nevertheless, firms likely do consider the movements in currencies and the relative values of currencies as they determine the disposition of corporate earnings. In some cases, the depreciation of the dollar relative to the euro caused foreign firms operating in the United States to retain the earnings from those operations to invest in the United States rather than to return those profits to the parent company at a depreciated value. Over the near term, more developing countries are expected to reduce national restrictions to foreign direct investment and more firms from both developed and developing countries are expected to engage in the direct investment process. As a result, these firms likely will participate more extensively in international capital markets and place added pressure on global and local capital markets as sources of funds andlikely act as agents of reform in the capital markets of developing countries. In addition, the proliferation of financial techniques, communications technology, and currency hedging strategies means that it will become even more challenging to untangle the direct and indirect factors that might determine specific cause-effect linkages between direct investment and movements in exchange rates.

Table 2. Selected Indicators of the Size of Various Capital Markets, 2005
(in trillions of U.S. dollars)

	Bonds, Equities, and Bank Assets	Stock Market Capitalization	Debt Securities			Bank Assets	Derivatives		
			Public	Private	Total		Total	OTC Foreign Exchange Derivatives	OTC Interest Rate Derivatives
World	$151.8	$37.2	$23.1	$35.9	$59.0	$55.7	$243.3	$31.4	$212.0
European Union	55.5	9.6	6.7	12.0	18.7	27.3	N.A.	N.A.	N.A.
Euro Area	40.8	6.0	5.7	9.4	15.2	18.5	94.3	12.9	81.4
United States	50.2	17.0	5.9	17.9	23.8	9.3	100.7	26.3	74.4
Japan	20.6	7.5	6.6	2.0	8.7	4.4	33.2	7.6	25.6

Source: Bank for International Settlements, *Quarterly Review*, March 2007. Total derivatives does not include equity- and commodity-linked derivatives.

REFERENCES

[1] The United States defines direct investment abroad as the ownership or control, directly or indirectly, by one "legal person" (individual, corporation, branch, partnership, association, government, etc.) of 10% or more of the voting securities of an incorporated business enterprise or an equivalent interest in an unincorporated business enterprise. 15 C.F.R § 806.15 (a)(1).

[2] For information about foreign portfolio investment in the United States, see CRS Report RL32462, *Foreign Investment in U.S. Securities*, by James K. Jackson.

[3] Bach, Christopher L., "U.S. International Transactions in 2006." *Survey of Current Business*, April 2007, p. 46. Direct investment data reported in the balance of payments differ from capital flow data reported elsewhere, because the balance of payments data have not been adjusted for current cost adjustments to earnings.

[4] United Nations Conference on Trade and Development, *World Investment Report 2006*, United Nations, 2006, p. 3.

[5] The position, or stock, is the net book value of foreign direct investors' equity in, and outstanding loans to, their affiliates in the United States. A change in the position in a given year consists of three components: equity and intercompany inflows, reinvested earnings of incorporated affiliates, and valuation adjustments to account for changes in the value of financial assets. The Commerce Department also publishes data on the foreign direct investment position valued on a current-cost and market value bases. These estimates indicate that foreign direct investment increased by $147 billion and $93 billion in 2005, respectively, to $1.9 and $2.8 trillion.

[6] Koncz, Jennifer L. and Daniel R. Yorgason, "Direct Investment Positions for 2005:" Country and Industry Detail," *Survey of Current Business*, July 2006, p. 20.

[7] McNeil, Lawrence R., "Foreign Direct Investment in the United States: New Investment in 2005," *Survey of Current Business*, June 2005, pp. 32-33.

[8] Weinberg, Douglas B., Kelly K. Pierce, and Erin M. Whitaker, "U.S. International Transactions, Second Quarter of 2006," *Survey of Current Business*, October 2006, p. 85. Direct investment data reported in the balance of payments differ from capital flow data reported elsewhere, because the balance of payments data have not been adjusted for current cost adjustments to earnings.

[9] Bloningen, Bruce A., *A Review of the Empirical Literature on FDI Determinants*, NBER Working Paper Series #11299, April 2005.

[10] Froot, Kenneth A. and Jeremy C. Stein, "Exchange Rates and Foreign Direct Investment: An Imperfect Capital Markets Approach." *The Quarterly Journal of Economics*, November 1991, pp. 1191-1217.

[11] Bloningen, Bruce A., "Firm-Specific Assets and the Link Between Exchange Rates and Foreign Direct Investment." *The American Economic Review*, June 1997, pp. 447-465.

[12] Lipsey, Robert E. and Irving B. Kravis, *The Competitive Position of U.S. Manufacturing Firms*. Cambridge, Mass., National Bureau of Economic Research, 1985. (Working Paper No. 1557), p. 2; and Ray, Edward John. *The Determinants of Foreign Direct Investment in the United States: 1979-1985*. Cambridge, Mass., National Bureau of Economic Research, 1988, p. 2

[13] For the purposes of this analysis, Chinese direct investment in the United States is not included, since the Chinese yuan is effectively pegged against the value of the dollar.

[14] Desai, Mihir A., C. Fritz Foley, and Kristin J. Forbes, *Financial Constraints and Growth: Multinational and Local Firm Responses to Currency Crises*. NBER Working Paper 10545, June 2004; Desai, Mihir A., C. Fritz Foley, and James R. Hines, Jr., *A Multinational Perspective on Capital Structure Choice and Internal Capital Markets*. NBER Working Paper #9715, May 2003.

[15] Bobillo, Alfredo Martinez, Pablo de Andres Alonso, and Fernando Tejerina Gaite, "Internal Funds, Corporate Investment and Corporate Governance: International Evidence," *Multinational Business Review*, Fall 2002, pp. 151-162. There are other factors that also may cause firms to prefer internal sources of funds over external sources, see Hubbard, R. Glenn, "Capital-Market Imperfections and Investment," *Journal of Economic Literature*, March 1998, pp. 193-225.

[16] Samuelson, Robert J., "Dangers in a Dollar on the Edge," *The Washington Post*, December 8, 2006, p. A39.

[17] *Triennial Central Bank Survey: Foreign Exchange and Derivatives Market Activity in 2004*. Bank for International Settlement, March 2005, pp. 1-2. A copy of the report is available at [http://www.bis.org/publ/rpfx05t.pdf]. The 2001 survey is: *Central Bank Survey of Foreign Exchange and Derivatives Market Activity in April 2001: Preliminary Global Dat*a. Bank for International Settlement, October 2001.

[18] Defined as foreign exchange transactions in the spot and forward exchange markets and foreign exchange swaps.

[19] Defined as transactions in foreign reserve accounts, interest rate swaps, cross currency interest rate swaps, and foreign exchange and interest rate options.

[20] *The Foreign Exchange and Interest Rate Derivatives Markets Survey: Turnover in the United States*. The Federal Reserve Bank of New York, April 2004, p. 1-2. A copy of the report is available at [http://www.newyorkfed.org/pihome/triennial/fx_survey.pdf]

[21] *Treasury Bulletin*, March 2007. Table OFS-2, p. 48.

In: Currency Interventions, Fluctuations...
Editor: L. C. Hilbert, pp. 107-118

ISBN: 978-1-60456-078-7

Chapter 5

THE SINGLE EUROPEAN PAYMENTS AREA (SEPA): IMPLEMENTATION DELAYS AND IMPLICATIONS FOR THE UNITED STATES*

Walter W. Eubanks
Specialist in Economic Policy Government and Finance Division

ABSTRACT

The Single European Payments Area (SEPA) is a planned electronic payments system that upon completion in 2010 would allow individuals, small- and medium-sized businesses, and corporations to make electronic payments throughout the European Union as efficiently and safely as such payments are being made on the national level today. However, the implementation process has been plagued with delays. The most recent delay occurred on December 12, 2006, when a vote on the Payment Services Directive was scheduled to be taken. But unresolved regulatory policy issues among member states prevented it from happening. One reason for the delay is pressure from European bankers who are uncertain about their ability to profitably recoup their costs once the system is constructed. The legislative status of the directive is that the President of the European Council is re-drafting it and between July 12 and September 12, 2007, a vote should be taken in the Plenary Committee of the European Parliament.

Congress is interested in SEPA because it has been monitoring the European Union's effort to unify its 27 member countries' financial markets. Congress recognizes that upon implementation of these efforts, such as the EU Financial Services Action Plan (FSAP), the Financial Conglomerate Directive (FCD), and now the Payment Services Directive (PSD), American firms doing business with the European Union could be significantly impacted.

The European payments systems are extremely fragmented. There are 27 national systems governed by national and local laws and practices. On average, the cost of making payments in the EU remains relatively expensive, even though more less-expensive electronic payments are being made, replacing the more costly cash and paper-check payments. European payment services costs include the inefficiencies caused by the use of non-standard customer interface, incompatible formats between foreign and

* Excerpted from CRS Report RL33952, dated April 5, 2007.

domestic banks, and a low degree of automation in banks' internal systems. By one measure, these inefficiencies and others are estimated to cost the EU between 2% to 3% of its gross domestic product (GDP) (the EU GDP was $13.4 trillion in 2005 which would mean between $268 and $402 billion).

This report presents a brief background on the efforts to create SEPA by the European government and the banking industry. It assesses the current electronic payments systems from the wholesale (large value) level and the retail (small value) level of payments. The report then examines the attempts to develop the pan-European automated clearinghouse system (PEACH). It summarizes the provisions of the Payment Services Directive that establishes the legal and regulatory basis for SEPA. The last two sections examine the implications of SEPA for U.S. international banks and conclude with an outline of the potential advantages and disadvantages of SEPA for European and American financial services providers.

This report will be updated as developments warrant.

INTRODUCTION

The European Union (EU)[1] is developing an electronic payments system to allow national financial services providers to offer Eurozone-wide electronic payment services. SEPA is expected to allow individuals, small- and medium-sized enterprises (SMEs), and corporations to make electronic payments throughout the Eurozone as efficiently and as safely as such payments are being made domestically today. SEPA is to bring about similar economically unifying effects in electronic payments as the Euro (€) banknotes and coins brought about since their January 2002 introduction. Because of that introduction, businesses and individuals in the Eurozone are able to make cash payments within and across 13 countries using a single purse of currency. SEPA has been a work in progress since its conception in 2002. Numerous delays and lack of regulatory agreements have frustrated the European Commission in Brussel, its main advocate,[2] even though the private European banking industry is expected to pay for SEPA. The lack of progress could be explained by the European bankers' uncertainty about their ability to profitably recoup their costs once the system is constructed in 2010.[3]

SEPA is of interest to Congress because it continues to monitor the European Union's efforts to unify its financial services markets. Congress recognizes that, upon completion of SEPA, American firms, customers, and investors could be significantly impacted by such efforts as the financial services action plan (FSAP), the Financial Conglomerate Directive (PSD), and the Payments Services Directive. Congress is also committed to working with U.S. and EU financial regulators to ensure U.S. financial services providers fair access to European and American financial markets.

A major recent development in the European efforts to unify its markets was that the European Parliament failed to take a scheduled December 12, 2006 vote on the Payment Services Directive that the European Commission published in 2005.[4] One reason for not having a vote is disagreement on legal and regulatory changes which are necessary to make SEPA operational. The PSD is aimed at removing most of the legal and regulatory barriers to market competition in the European Union, particularly the Eurozone and overcoming the regulatory obstacles to inter-Eurozone payments. The directive, for example, addresses fundamental questions raised regarding liability and burden of proof in cases of credit card fraud, execution time, and value date of transactions and treatment of nonmember countries' banks doing business in the Eurozone.

This report presents a brief background of the European Commission and the European banking industry efforts to create a single European payments area. It examines the current electronic payments system as it stands from both the wholesale (large value) and retail (small value) levels transactions. The next part of the report assesses the attempt to develop the pan-European automated clearinghouse system (PEACH). Then, it outlines the provisions of the Payment Services Directive that establish the legal and regulatory basis for SEPA. Thc final two sections of the report examine some of the implications of SEPA for U.S. international banks and outline some potential advantageous and disadvantageous effects of SEPA.

SEPA Background

To plan SEPA, the European Commission gave the preparatory work to the European Payments Council (EPC), which is a coalition founded by 65 banks and three European credit sector associations. The European Commission sees the creation of an integrated payments system as a logical follow-up to the introduction of the Euro and expects big savings and greater efficiencies for consumers and businesses from SEPA. However, SEPA is likely to impose some significant costs on the European banking industry in the process of its development, including increased spending on advanced technology in software and hardware infrastructure. As one European Central Bank publication states, "This restructuring [for SEPA] will, in the short term, generate considerable costs; however, in the medium to long term, the European banking industry will benefit from cost savings regarding euro area payments, and also from potential new revenue streams."[5] The European banking industry does not seem to be convinced about the future benefits. Consequently, it has been slow in developing SEPA. The slowness of the creation of SEPA has brought criticisms of the EPC and the banking industry, including a threat of possible regulatory intervention unless efforts to create SEPA are sped up.[6] The EPC response was that SEPA is on schedule in accordance with the revised December 2004 roadmap. The revisions clearly overlooked the benchmarks set in the earlier roadmap of 2002-2010.[7]

On the government side, concerns were expressed by the European Commission, and the European Central Bank because the EPC has missed critical points on its own roadmap. One argument the European Commission put forth is that EPC's efforts so far would not remove the fragmentation of the Eurozone payments system because the needed massive irreversible migration of users from the current dominant national systems to SEPA may not come about. Some in the European Central Bank argue that the banking industry should speed up the SEPA implementation process.[8] In defense of the EPC, Gerard Harsink, its chairman, responded that the council was responsible only for drawing up the rules and standards for the payment products and for implementing them.[9] The implementation is being held up by lack of approval of the PSD, which is aimed at integrating the existing national payment systems into a pan-European system.

The EU Payments System

If SEPA is developed, it would be one of the world's largest electronic payments system. In 2004, the then 25-member payments system made an estimated 231 billion transactions (cash and non-cash) with a total value of € 52 trillion or $63 trillion.[10] But there was a relatively small volume of cross-border transactions (97% of the payments were within member states, with only 7 billion cross-border transactions).[11] Even so, seven billion is a significant number of transactions. The process of switching from paper checks, notes, and coins to electronic payments has already begun. Non-cash payment transactions in 2004 amounted to 65.3 billion transactions in the European Union.[12] The number of electronic payments (card payments, credit transfers, and direct debits) has been steadily climbing, replacing payments that were made with checks and cash. Total check payments declined from 8.9 billion in 2000 to 7.5 billion in 2004. Figure 1 shows that the total number of electronic payments increased from 37.9 billion in 2000 to 57 billion in 2004. Using data from the Commission's retail banking study and the European Central Bank, there were an estimated 166 billion cash transactions in the EU in 2004.[13]

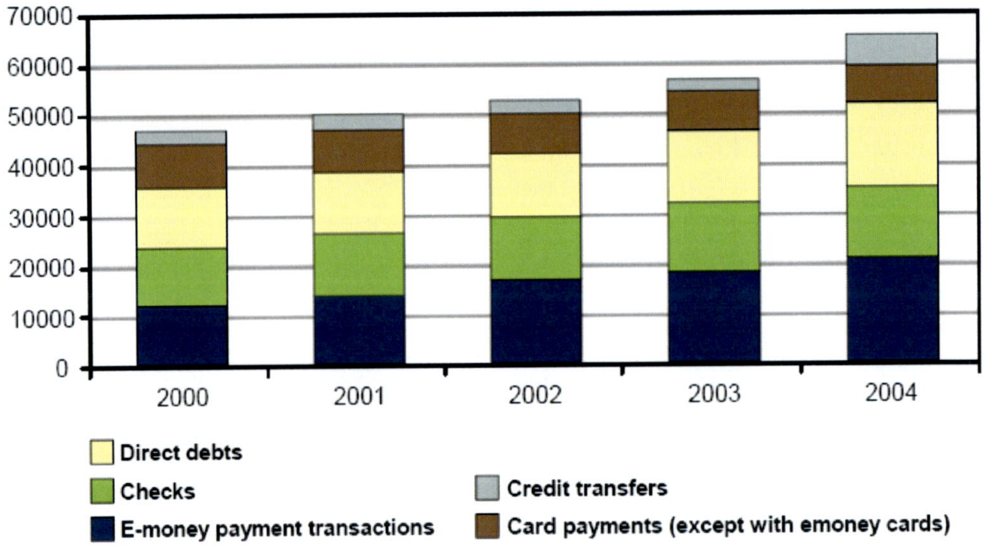

Source: Commission Services Retail Banking Sector Inquiry, 2005-2006.

Figure 1. Number of Non-Cash Payments in the EU (millions).

The estimated aggregate cost of the existing payments system ranges from 2% to 3% of gross domestic product (GDP) (the EU GDP was € 10.4 trillion or $13.4 trillion in 2005,[14] which makes the estimated cost between $268 and $402 billion). However, the cost of the payments systems of Belgium, the Netherlands and Sweden are between 0.3-0.5% of GDP. Switching to more electronic payments would lower these costs; the use of cash alone accounts for 60% to 70% of the total inefficiency of the system.[15] A major reason for the high cost is that the European payments systems are made up of many separate systems. There are 27 national systems governed by national and local laws and practices. Stakeholders who have profited from the existing systems are not likely to readily change to

SEPA. The prices for payment services take into account the inefficiencies caused by the use of nonstandard customer interfaces, incompatible formats between foreign and domestic banks, and a low degree of automation in banks' internal systems.[16] The EU's main argument for SEPA is that it would lead to a less fragmented payments system that would benefit from economies of scale and reduced transaction costs.

The European banking industry's concern about SEPA is partly that it will have to restructure its currently profitable wholesale and retail payments system to accommodate SEPA. SEPA is expected to have the greatest impact on retail transactions (small value transactions). The wholesale (large value transactions) electronic payments system, which handles most of the cross-border transactions, is functioning well, but it too must be restructured. In support of the argument for SEPA, the EU Commission found huge price differences in providing payment services among member nations. The difference was as high as eight times. In addition, in some countries, the standard execution time for cross-border payments is one day, while in others it takes up to three days.[17]

The Wholesale Electronic Payments System

Most wholesale transactions are made through major banks with corresponding banking relationships with local banks in most important foreign cities. At least 80% of bank-to-bank cross-border payments are made through corresponding banking arrangements or via intra-bank transactions (the same banks with offices in other countries).[18] In addition, there are governments and private wholesale payments systems. Fedwire is Federal Reserve Wire Network for American bank transactions. The European Union has TARGET, which is the Trans-European Automated Real-time Gross Settlement Express Transfer, consisting of the European Central Bank (ECB) and 16 member countries' central banks systems. TARGET and TARGET 2 are also critical tools for the implementation of monetary policyfor the EuroSystem through the European System of Central Banks. Another EU-wide wholesale electronic payment mechanism is the EURO1 system of the Euro banking association. EURO1 processes interbank payments. There are also three other smaller large-value systems located in France, Finland, and Spain.[19]

The Retail Electronic Payments System

On the retail side, the construction of SEPA began in February 2004, but soon ran into difficulties. In assessing the different EU-infrastructures in place for processing payments, the European banking industry opted for the creation of a pan-European Automated Clearing House (PEACH). ACH systems are large volume electronic payment processing systems. The system usually enables corporations and consumers to make routine payments more efficiently than cash or checks. Payrolls, recurring bill payments, and government payments to individuals and agencies such as Social Security benefits are examples of typical ACH payments. ACHs are broadcasters of payments to many payees or receivers of payments from many payees for a single ACH customer.

PEACH would be able to make these payments throughout the Europan Union, but would have required banks to either close their systems and move to another infrastructure, or transform proven and efficient national ACHs into PEACHs. In 2005, a number of existing automated clearinghouses declared their intention to become SEPA-compliant without necessarily transforming their systems into PEACHs. Indications are that the EuroSystem would accept this approach. It encourages both the migration of national to SEPA-compliant infrastructures and the establishment of additional PEACH providers to encourage the necessary competition in the market.[20] The banking industry's effort to minimize costs has been a contributing factor in the slowness of implementing the PEACH process.[21]

Furthermore, there is little confidence among financial analysts that these systems will work efficiently together. While the openness to a variety of SEPA-compliant infrastructures facilitates agreements among the EU-member countries, it undercuts capturing the cost savings from economies of scale. It is essential that a critical mass of payment instruments is processed in the PEACH infrasture, including local volumes, in order to be competitive with the lower unit costs of the large national ACHs. A major reason for the resistance to SEPA is that the bulk of the costs of processing intra-EU payments lies within the financial institutions (client order/reporting automation, back office automation). A critical mass of payments is needed to significantly reduce the unit cost of this processing.

Excess Profits in the Retail Electronic Payments Systems

The fragmentation in EU financial markets with 27 national regulators and local laws and practices could lead to excess profits for lack of competition. Figure 2 shows the profitability of credit cards issuing at the country level, using 2004 data (specific countries were not identified). While there is some controversy about the way costs were calculated in these estimates,[22] the data shows that the income generated from issuing credit cards was higher than the associated cost of issuing credit cards in all 25 member states. The weighted average profit ratio varied from 3% to 147% with an average of 65%, suggesting strongly that there are excess profits in the EU credit card market.

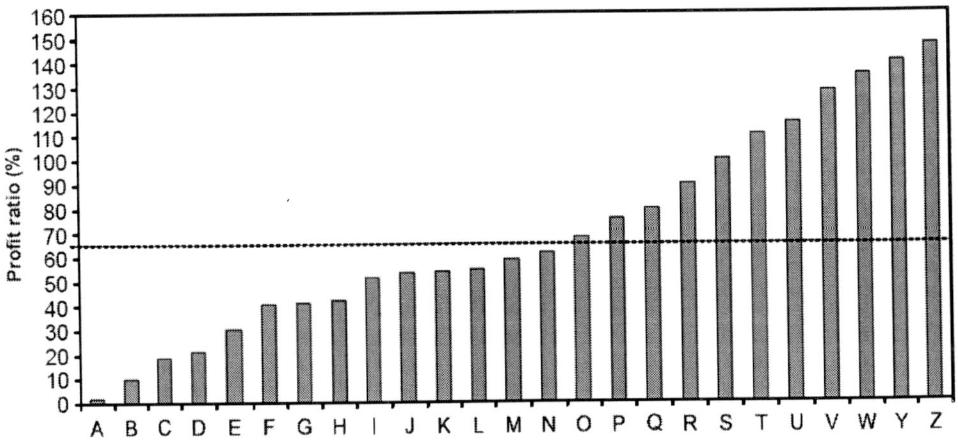

Source: Commission services retail banking sector inquiry, 2005-2006.

Figure 2. Profit Ratio Differentials in Credit Card Issuing, 2004.

Furthermore, the fragmentation and the lack of competition were evident in the variation in fees for ATM withdrawals and credit transfers (not shown) between banks and across member states. For example, some banks charge a fixed amount per transaction and others levy a percentage of the transaction amount. Others apply a mixed structure, combining methods of determining the charges. In the European Commission's study from which this data was obtained, the weighted average fee for a € 100 ATM withdrawal on another bank with a debit card is € 1.14. However, the fee charged ranged from pennies to € 8. Greater variability was found for credit transfers. Credit transfers are payments that are made between bank accounts at the instruction of the payer. For the same €100 credit transfer, the weighted average fee in the 12 EU member states was € 2. However, the weighted average fee ranged from € 0 to € 10. The study concludes that the characteristics of the retail banking industry make it difficult to compare similar products. But, the pricing behavior of banks provides some initial indications on the degree of competition in the market.[23]

PROVISIONS OF THE PAYMENTS SERVICES DIRECTIVE

In September 2005, the European Payments Council adopted the SEPA Direct Debit Rulebook for national consultation. What the member nations had to consider in this Rulebook was a complete set of business rules, practices, and standards which govern the direct debit scheme in SEPA. The Rulebook includes the roles and responsibilities of the participants, business and operational rules, and legal and contractual frameworks. A major unresolved issue for the EPC is the way debts are issued, amended, and cancelled. But this could be overcome by the passage of the Payment Services Directive. The Payment Services Directive could resolve issues such as whether the debtors can give the mandates to debit their accounts directly to the creditors, or whether the debtors should give the mandates to their banks, either directly or through the creditors.[24] Currently in some countries, debtors give the mandates to the creditors; in other countries, the debtors give the mandates to their banks.

The directive being considered for approval by the European Parliament contains the regulatory provisions of the Rulebook. These provisions affect the following institutions: credit institutions, e-money issuers, money transfer companies, automated teller machine (ATM) providers, companies offering bill payment services, mobile phone operators, digital payment service providers, credit unions, and central banks in supervising proportioning of risk in four-party payment schemes.[25] Upon implementation these legal requirements would allow these institutions to operate in SEPA.

The Payments Services Directive's structure consists of six titles:

- Title I sets out the subject matter, scope, and definitions. It excludes central banks and public authorities and specifies the financial institutions and services that are covered by the directive. It covers electronic payments in the EU and between EU and non-member countries
- Title II establishes the regulatory regime for payment institutions covered by the directive. It provides the general rules that apply to payment institutions. It also covers rules governing agents of payment institutions.
- Title III establishes the transparency of conditions for payment services. It provides the consumer protection provisions to be carried out mainly through disclosure

requirements for transparency. It also covers disclosure requirements concerning currency exchanges.

- Title IV sets out the rights and obligations of participants using the payment system services. It covers the authorization of payments including what constitutes authorization and what happens when an unauthorized payment is being made and establishes the refunding mechanisms for different types of payments.
- Title V establishes the payments committee and provides the schedule of directive updates.
- Title VI contains the provisions specifying the transposition requirements that member states would have to make to harmonize the payments systems. Should the directive pass the European Parliament with agreed-to national amendments, it would then go on to the member states for implementation.[26]

The legislative status of the directive is that the President of the European Council is re-drafting the directive. The European Parliament's economic lead committee expects to get the President's re-draft on May 30, 2007. June 10, 2007 is the deadline for amendments in the Economy Committee. On July 11, 2007, a vote is to take place in the Economy Committee. Between July 12 and September 12, 2007, a vote should be taken in the Plenary Committee of the European Parliament.[27]

SEPA's Implications for the United States

The single European payments area could have some significant implications for U.S. international financial services providers. However, until the system is operational, the actual extent of SEPA's impact on the United States remains speculation. SEPA is not likely to significantly change the wholesale-side electronic payments, which rely heavily on corresponding banking relationships and government-operated payments systems. Where the impact of SEPA is likely to be felt is on the retail side of the payments business. Even if the system only partially reaches its optimal efficiency goals in retail payments, there is no assurance that these benefits will be fully shared with U.S. financial services providers. The main reason is that common legal and regulatory standards that are being negotiated naturally exclude the United States, which is mainly on the sidelines. It is possible that the outcome of these negotiations could make it more difficult for U.S. institutions to compete in Europe. For example, under SEPA, U.S. financial services providers could be relatively disadvantaged by additional regulatory requirements or denied benefits made possible by SEPA. In short, U.S. institutions' customers may have to pay additional fees or meet specific requirements to make electronic payments within the Eurozone.

U.S. financial institutions could be placed under special regulations under SEPA, as the EU has done in the past. Such regulation could limit the type of services U.S. providers offer and the price they charge for those services. The EU 2002 Visa Decision is an example. Interchange fees are interbank fees paid between the card payer's bank and the payee's bank for the card issuance and the electronic clearing and settlement of the card's transactions. To lower the cost of credit cards for European merchants, the European Commission pressured Visa Europe to apply a fixed fee per transaction in determining its interchange fees.

MasterCard, on the other hand, was allowed to base its interchange fee on a percentage of the transaction value. The Commission reported that the decision had the effect of reducing Visa cross-border interchange fees, while MasterCard enjoyed higher revenues from its cross-border interchange fees.

The European Commission complained to the European banking industry about interchange fees. It argued that these fees are higher than they should be in the EU. However, the Commission has not mandated how EU member states determine interchange fees as it did for MasterCard and Visa. The most recent Commission study shows that interchange fees remain excessive in many member countries that are using one or both methods to determine their fees.[28] Because U.S. financial institutions are outside these negotiations but are subject to their decisions, member states could gain an advantage on U.S. institutions by negotiating exemptions and/or amendments in favor of their countries' financial institutions.

A further possible concern is that the European Commission plans to build SEPA using Europeans enterprises exclusively. Because SEPA is European built, U.S. institutions' access to SEPA doesn't necessarily have to be a concern. However, the lack of U.S. presence in the rules' negotiations as well as the physical construction could later create problems in terms of software and hardware compatibility and protocol for U.S. institutions' access. Visa Europe, the card payment organization with vast experience in developing electronic payments exchanges for credit and debit cards as well as other methods of electronic payments, is expected to play a significant role in building SEPA.[29] However, to get this business Visa Europe had to separate from the Visa umbrella organization. Visa Europe is now a not-for-profit enterprise owned by 6,000 European member banks.

The newly incorporated Visa Europe has the opportunity to bid for new business as well as more flexibility to deal with the changing European payments system.[30]

The United States is excluded because the European banking association, whose members make up the majority of the European Payments Council that are responsible for planning SEPA, has made it clear that only European-owned and controlled organizations can bid for non-card processing work in constructing the pan-European Automated Clearing Houses (PEACHs) for debit and credit transactions.[31] According to the chief executive of Visa Europe, "building this single market, which we wholeheartedly support, is very unique and will require investment in infrastructures and — most importantly — very close co-operation between European banks. We believe the association's structure is the best way to facilitate this."[32]

CONCLUSION

On most fronts, SEPA's potential impact is largely uncertain. The objectives of the Payment Services Directive are critical hurdles for the European Union to overcome. Like most government-led initiatives SEPA is focused on the reduction of costs to end users — individuals, SMEs, and corporations. Initially, however, the SEPA effort translates into higher cost for European financial services providers that supply these electronic payment services domestically and across borders. The European banking industry is resisting SEPA because they are reluctant to invest in a more efficient payment system from which there is little or no assurance that they will be able to profitably recover the cost of their investments.

Despite the heated debates in the European Parliament, it is very likely that the Payment Services Directive will be approved. However, like other directives, it is likely to be loaded with amendments, which could reduce SEPA's effectiveness in lowering end users' costs for payments transactions.

If U.S. financial services institutions are forced to adapt to regulatory modifications of each national system that is permitted under the Payment Services Directive negotiations, U.S. financial services providers could lose their competitive advantage. On the other hand, if the directive is effectively implemented, harmonizing member states' laws and regulations, and eliminating regulatory fragmentation, U.S. international institutions could benefit from dealing with one set of regulations instead of dealing with financial regulatory subtleties of 27 member states. U.S. providers in many areas of financial services are already technologically competitive in the European Union, which makes them capable of exploiting the new opportunities that SEPA might create more quickly than some of their European competitors.

REFERENCES

[1] The European Union's member countries have expanded to 27. Only 12 members were in the Eurozone until recently. Slovenia joined the Eurozone January 1, 2007, increasing the zone's membership to 13. Countries in the Eurozone are Austria, Belgium, Finland, France, Germany, Greece, Ireland, Italy, Luxembourg, Netherlands, Portugal, and Spain. Denmark, Sweden, and the United Kingdom have retained their national currencies. The extension included Bulgaria, Cyprus, Czech Republic, Estonia, Hungary, Latvia, Lithuania, Malta, Poland, Romania, Slovakia, and Slovenia for a total membership of 27.

[2] The European Commission is the executive body of the European Union. Its primary role is to propose and implement legislation similar to the executive branch of most national governments.

[3] For more details about this explanation, see the Federal Reserve System, Staff Study 175, *The future of Retail Electronic Payments Systems: Industry Interview and Analysis,* Dec. 2002, p. 18.

[4] For an updated version of this legislation, visit [http://www.europarl.europa.eu/omk/sipade3?PUBREF=-//EP//NONSGML+REPORT+A6-2006-0298+0+DOC+PDF+V0//EN and L=EN and LEVEL=2 and NAV=S and LSTDOC=Y].

[5] European Central Bank, The Single Euro Payments Area (SEPA):An Integrated Retail Payments Market, Nov., 2006, p.8.

[6] Tobias Buck, Brussels accuses banking industry of stalling on single euro payments area, *Financial Times,* Feb. 9, 2006, p. 1.

[7] For more details, see the European Payments Council's roadmap for the SEPA at [http://www.europeanpaymentscouncil.org/documents/Roadmap%20public%20version% 204th%20April.pdf], 16 p.

[8] ECB Tells European Banks to Get Moving on Plans for Single European Payments Areas, *BNA Banking Report,* Mar. 6, 2006, p.1, [http://ippubs.bna.com/NWSSTND /IP/BNA/bar.nsf/SearchAllView/52EA66EFFDFDCD6A85257127000E92DD?Open and highlight=S EPA].

[9] Tobias Buck, Brussels accuses banking industry of stalling on single euro payments area, p. 2.

[10] While there are no official estimates of the number of cash transactions for the United States, non-cash transactions in 2004 were estimated to number around 100 billion. See Table 2 in CRS Report RS22525, *Electronic Banking: The Post-Check 21 Payments System*, by Walter W. Eubanks.

[11] HM Treasury, Payment Services in the EU, *Payment Services Directive: a consultative document*, July 2006, p 2.1.

[12] See ECB 2006 Blue Book: Payment and Securities Settlement Systems in the European Union and in the Acceding Countries — Addendum Incorporating 2004 data. Available at [http://www.ecb.int/pub/pdf/other/bluebook2006addendem.pdf].

[13] See HM Treasury, Payment Services in the EU, *Payment Services Directive: a consultative document*, July 2006, p 2.1, and European Commission, *Report on the Retail Banking Sector Inquiry*, Jan. 31, 2007, p. 81, [http://ec.europa.eu/comm/ competition/ antitrust/others/sector_inquiries/financial_services/sec_2007_106.pdf].

[14] European Commission, Europe in figures — Eurostat yearbook 2006-2007, Feb. 20, 2007, p. 153.

[15] HM Treasury, Payment Services in the EU, Payment Services Directive: a consultative document, July 2006, p. 2.10.

[16] European Central Bank, Improving Cross-Border Retail Payment Services: The Eurosystem's View, Sept. 1999, p. 10.

[17] HM Treasury, Payment Services in the EU, Payment Services Directive: a consultative document, July 2006, p. 2.7.

[18] Yoon S. Park, The Inefficiencies of Cross-Border Payment: How Current Forces are Shaping the Future, Visa International Service Association, Jan. 17, 2007. p. 2.

[19] Bank for International Settlements, *Payment Systems in the euro Area,* the CPSS Red Book 2003, p. 75, [http://www.bis.org/cpss/paysys/ECBComp.pdf].

[20] European Central Bank, Towards a Single EURO Payments Areas — Objectives and Deadlines, Feb. 2006, pp.16-20.

[21] A network of automated clearing houses processes small-value electronic payments and retail electronic transfers. Electronic payments are frequently facilitated by a private electronic message transfer system. One of the largest and widely known electronic messaging systems is the Society for Worldwide Interbank Financial Telecommunications (SWIFT).

[22] European Commission, *Report on the Retail banking Sector Inquiry,* Jan. 31, 2007, p. 169, http://ec.europa.eu/comm/competition/antitrust/others/ sector_inquiries/ financial_ service s/sec_2007_106.pdf].

[23] European Commission, *Report on the Retail banking Sector Inquiry,* Jan. 31, 2007, pp. 62-63.

[24] Ibid., p. 14.

[25] An example of the four parties is the cardholder, the cardholder's bank, the merchant, and the merchant's bank.

[26] HM Treasury, *Payment Services Directive: a consultative Document,* July 2006, p. 3.113.17, [http://www.hm-treasury.gov.uk/media/39B/0A/ payments_ condoc 040706. pdf].

[27] Shona Ferrier, *APACS and the Payment Services Directive,*APACS the UK Payments association. Available at [http://www.earthport.com/Downloads/ EU_Payments DirectiveOverview.pdf]
[28] European Commission, *Report on the Retail banking Sector Inquiry,* Jan.31, 2007, pp. 114-116.
[29] Tobias Buck, "Visa to focus on developing Sepa Regime," *Financial Times,* Oct. 11, 2006, p. 1.
[30] Ibid.
[31] Jane Croft, "Visa to Spin off European division," *Financial Times,* Jun. 29, 2004, p.1.
[32] Peter Thai Larsen, "Visa to go public in radical shake-up," *Financial Times*, Oct., 11, 2006. p 1.

In: Currency Interventions, Fluctuations...
Editor: L. C. Hilbert, pp. 119-127
ISBN: 978-1-60456-078-7

Chapter 6

THE DOLLAR'S FUTURE AS THE WORLD'S RESERVE CURRENCY: THE CHALLENGE OF THE EURO*

Craig K. Elwell
Specialist in Macroeconomics Government and Finance Division

ABSTRACT

Globally, central bank holdings of reserve currency assets have risen sharply in recent years. These "official holdings" have nearly tripled since 1999 to reach $5 trillion by the end of 2006. Nearly $3 trillion has been amassed by developing Asia and Japan. China, in particular, now has official reserves that exceed $1 trillion. In addition, the oil-exporting countries have increased their official reserves by about $700 billion. The dollar's status as the dominant international currency has meant that as much 70% of this large accumulation of official reserves are of some form of dollar asset.

There are significant advantages for the United States in having the dominant reserve currency. These advantages include reduced exchange rate risk and lower borrowing costs. However, these large accumulations of dollar assets in foreign official holdings also means that foreign central banks have become important participants in and influences on U.S. financial markets and the wider U.S. economy.

Four factors — share of world output and trade, macroeconomic stability, degree of financial market development, and network externalities — combine to influence the choice of a reserve currency. The euro has improved its standing in all four areas but the dollar retains significant advantages. Available data show only modest diversification from dollar assets by foreign central banks from the time of the euro's introduction in 1999 through the end of 2006. The dollar's share of total official reserves rose through the 1990s, reaching a peak value of about 72% global reserves in 2001. By 2003 that share fell to about 66% and remained near that level through 2006. The euro's share of global official reserves rose from about 18% in 1999 to 25% in 2003, but has remained near this level through 2006.

Looking to the future, the dollar's status as the dominant reserve currency may be challenged by the euro because it increasingly offers many of the advantages of the dollar but fewer of the risks. The dollar's most important advantage is the size, quality, and stability of dollar asset markets, particularly the short-term government securities market where central banks tend to be most active. The high liquidity of these financial markets makes the dollar an excellent medium of exchange. A further advantage is the power of "incumbency" conferred by the "network-externalities" that accrue to the currency that is dominant. Together these factors make it unlikely there will be a large or abrupt change in the dollar's reserve currency status.

However, the euro is seen by some as poised to challenge the dollar in the store of value function of a reserve currency. The sheer magnitude of dollar assets in the official reserves of foreign central banks and the realistic prospect of continued, and perhaps disorderly, depreciation of the dollar against most currencies, place central banks at considerable risk of incurring large capital losses on their dollar asset holding. With more than enough dollar reserves to meet liquidity needs, prudent asset management would seem to dictate some diversification away from the dollar and toward the euro. This report will be updated as events warrant.

THE RISING INTERNATIONAL IMPORTANCE OF "OFFICIAL HOLDINGS"

Central bank holdings of reserve currency assets have risen sharply in recent years. These "official holdings" have nearly tripled since 1999 to reach $5 trillion by the end of 2006. These large accumulations of reserves have been concentrated among countries with large global current account surpluses. Nearly $3 trillion has been amassed by developing Asia and Japan. China, in particular, now has official reserves that exceed $1 trillion. In addition, the oil-exporting countries have increased their official reserves by about $700 billion.[1]

The dollar's status as the dominant international currency has meant that as much as 70% of this large accumulation of official reserves is held in some form of dollar asset. The U.S. Treasury reports that through mid-2005, 34% of the more than $3 trillion outstanding marketable Treasury securities was being held in foreign official reserves. (All foreign holdings, official and private, amount to 52% of all outstanding Treasury securities.)[2] These large accumulations of dollar assets in foreign official holdings mean that foreign central banks have become important participants in U.S. financial markets, as well as in the wider U.S. economy.[3]

For the United States, there are significant benefits to being the world's reserve currency. Central banks' demand for the reserve currency tends not to be as volatile as that of private investors. This stabilizes the demand for dollars and reduces the foreign exchange risk faced by U.S. companies in their international transactions. Exchange rate risk is also reduced because the United States borrows in its own currency so that the appreciation of foreign currencies against the dollar cannot increase debt service cost or raise default risk.

Another major benefit of being the primary international reserve currency is that it enables the United States to borrow abroad at a lower cost then it otherwise could. This cost advantage occurs because there will be a willingness of foreign central banks to pay a liquidity premium to hold dollar assets.

Also, the dollar's status as the world's reserve currency raises the likelihood of foreigners using U.S. asset markets. This added foreign involvement increases the breadth and depth of these markets, which then tends to attract even more investors, which then continually magnifies the benefits of being the reserve currency.

Since 2003, sharply rising capital inflows from foreign central banks have financed on average about 50% of the U.S. current account deficit, increasing the sustainability of the trade deficit by compensating for a sizable weakening of private capital inflows.[4] It is estimated that these recent official reserve accumulations have kept U.S. long-term interest rates from 0.5 to 1.0 percentage points lower than otherwise.[5]

Historically, a single currency has been the dominant reserve currency. In the 19th century sterling played this role, succeeded by the dollar in the 20th century. As the 21st century has begun to unfold the dollar has remained the dominant international currency. But the euro, created in 1999 as part of the European monetary union (EMU), has been seen by some economists as a potential challenger to the dollar's dominant position as an international currency in the 21st century.[6]

To the degree that the euro displaces the dollar in the official holdings of central banks, the benefits to the United States of the dollar as a reserve currency will be reduced. The viability of the euro as a substitute for the dollar will hinge on several factors that determine how well it can perform the necessary roles of a reserve currency for a central bank

The Roles of a Reserve Currency

An international currency is one used by non-residents to accomplish the three standard roles of any currency: be a medium of exchange, a unit of value, and a store of value. However, for central banks these three roles serve different needs than those of the private investor:

- The *medium of exchange* function serves the need for foreign exchange intervention as central banks attempt to counter unwelcome changes in the value of their domestic currency caused by private inflows and outflows of capital.
- The *store of value* function serves the need for reserve accumulation as self-insurance against periodic balance of payments crisis and as a public demonstration of commitment to exchange rate stability.
- The *unit of account* function serves the need of some countries for a monetary anchor to bolster domestic monetary policy in combating inflation.

Typically, the currency used as the medium of exchange will also serve as the main store of value. Also, because of the large scale of recent reserve holdings, some central banks may turn more attention to the currency's ability to also provide the store of value function of concern to private investors — steadiness of asset value and rate of return.

The already large holdings of dollar assets and the prospect of continued depreciation of the dollar's exchange rate are likely to be seen by foreign central banks as major disincentives for using dollars as their principal reserve currency. In contrast, the appreciation of the euro exchange rate and the substantial increase in the liquidity of the euro caused by the improvement in the breath and depth of euro financial markets since 1999 raises the attractiveness of the euro as a reserve currency.

Four Factors Influencing Choice of a Reserve Currency

Economists have identified four factors that will jointly influence how well a currency can serve central banks as a medium of exchange, as a store of value, and as a unit of account.

First, the larger a country's share of world output and trade the more likely it is that other countries will use it as a monetary anchor or in external transactions. This factor tends to raise the likelihood that other countries will hold liabilities denominated in its currency and therefore tends to also hold more of its assets in the same currency. The euro is probably not at any sizable disadvantage relative to the dollar in this category.

Second, macroeconomic stability, particularly price stability, is needed to establish confidence in the currency's value. Without this confidence a currency's ability to play its role as a unit of account and as a store of value is undermined. The dollar's status in this category may be eroded by the prospect of long-term exchange rate depreciation.

Third, a high degree of financial market development, offering large size and high liquidity, makes it more likely that a country's currency will be used by foreign central banks as the medium of exchange for currency intervention. Also, a broad and deep financial sector tends to reinforce overall economic stability. In this area, the dollar has been singularly attractive. But the development of euro area financial markets has advanced steadily since its 1999 introduction.

Fourth, network externalities create a self-generating demand for a dominant currency. The more often a currency is used as a medium of exchange, the more liquid it becomes and the lower are the costs of transacting in it, leading, in turn, to it becoming even more attractive to new users. Network externalities create a tendency toward having one dominant currency and confer a substantial *incumbency advantage* to the dollar over the euro.[7]

None of these influences on the choice of a reserve currency is likely to change quickly, acting to make any shift in the status of the dominant reserve currency a slow process, with substantial changes most often emerging over decades.[8]

The Current Currency Composition of Official Reserves

Data on the currency composition of official reserves is imperfect. The most comprehensive source is the International Monetary Fund's (IMF) currency composition of foreign exchange reserves (COFER) database.[9] Included in this series are monetary authorities' claims on non-residents in the form of banknotes, bank deposits, treasury bills, short-term and long-term government securities, and other claims usable to meet balance of payments needs. However, COFER data do not include the holdings of currency by the issuing country. Also, the COFER data only provides national currency specific information for about 70% of total global reserves because the reserves of many emerging economies are missing from the tally. Despite these limitations, the COFER data will most likely reveal basic trends in holdings of the dollar and euro in global official reserves.

The COFER data show only modest diversification from dollar assets by foreign central banks from the time of the euro's introduction in 1999 through the end of 2006. The dollar's share of total official reserves was at its lowest point in the early 1990s at about 45%. Through the 1990s that share rose, in large measure because of accumulation of dollar reserves by emerging economies, reaching a peak value of about 72% global reserves in 2001. By 2003, that share fell to about 66% and has remained near this level through 2006. The euro's share of global official reserves rose from about 18% in 1999 to 25% in 2003, but has remained near this level through 2006.

Again, the source of much of the change in both the level of official reserves and their distribution among currencies was central banks in developing countries, accounting for 58% of the growth of total foreign exchange holdings in this period, and also decreasing their share of dollar holdings from 70% to 60%, and increasing their share of euro holdings from 19% to 30%. In contrast, among industrial economies the dollar share of holdings held steady and the share of euro holdings increased modestly.

Another interesting change in the 1999-2006 period was a fall in the share of yen assets in official reserves (down from 6% to 3%) and a rise in the share of pounds sterling (up from 2.7% to 4.4%). This relatively small increase in the international status of the pound may be insignificant by itself, but could very significant for the status of the euro if the United Kingdom were to join the EMU.

EURO VS. DOLLAR

In the framework of the three functions of a reserve currency: being a medium of exchange, a store of value, and a unit of account, how does the euro stack-up against the dollar?[10]

As a Medium of Exchange

This is typically the most important one to be fulfilled by any well functioning currency. For central banks, this role will revolve around use of the currency for intervention in foreign exchange markets. Intervention is a task that places a premium on liquidity, the capability — on short notice, possibly in adverse conditions — of turning assets quickly into cash with little or no impact on the asset's price. The liquidity of a currency in both foreign exchange markets and asset markets is important.

In foreign exchange markets, the Bank of International Settlements' (BIS) most recent *Triennial Survey of Foreign Exchange and Derivatives Markets* shows that on April of 2004 the euro entered on one-side of 37% of all foreign exchange transactions. The dollar's share of transactions on foreign exchange markets fell from 94% in 1998 to 89% in 2004.[11]

In asset markets, central banks invest in instruments with limited risk, making conditions in the country's government security markets the most relevant for the choice of an intervention currency. The attractiveness of the euro has been increased by the formation of the EMU, creating the world's second largest government securities market. In 2005, the outstanding stock of government securities of the several euro area governments totaled $4.7 trillion. This compares to $4.2 trillion of outstanding U.S. treasury securities. Suggesting that more than size may matter, the largest government securities market is Japan, but the holding of yen-denominated reserves has declined in recent years.

Despite the greater size and rising attractiveness of the euro area's government securities market, the U.S. Treasury market has several advantages that continue to enhance its attractiveness to foreign central banks. First, the short-term segment of the U.S. Treasury market, composed of about $950 billion U.S. Treasury bills with terms of three months to one year, is about twice as large as the euro area counterpart. Treasury bills are a low risk and highly liquid instrument that are well suited to the reserve currency needs of central banks.

Second, U.S. Treasury securities have a single issuer and the euro area has twelve. The several issuers of euro assets are not of uniform credit worthiness. U.S. Treasury securities carry a AAA credit rating but some euro area economies government securities have a lower credit rating.

Third, the U.S. Treasury market appears to offer far greater liquidity than the euro area government securities markets. One indicator of this is a daily turnover in U.S. government securities markets of nearly $500 billion. Japan is second largest at $150 billion per day. Turnover is an indicator of how easily a market can absorb large transactions without changing the asset's price. The superior (small) bid-ask spreads found in the U.S. government securities market are further evidence of their very high liquidity.

As a Unit of Account

In official use this role is largely linked to the selection of an exchange rate as a monetary anchor. In recent years, the euro has increased in importance in fulfilling this role. In 2004, the IMF reported that out of 150 pegged currencies, 40 used the euro as an anchor currency. However, because of incomplete reporting, this type of tally may understate the true degree of attachment — "gravitational pull" — of one currency to another.

An alternative approach is to examine the actual co-movements of currencies to determine how closely currency's track the euro and the dollar. This currency sensitivity evidence suggests that the euro's gravitational importance is rising. European countries outside of the EMU, such as Switzerland, Sweden, Norway, as well as eastern and central Europe move very closely with the euro. In Latin America, as well, there is evidence of the increasing gravitational pull of the euro, particularly in Brazil and Chile. One other very notable change has been for the traditional dollar-influenced currencies of Australia, Canada, and New Zealand mirroring from one-half to two-thirds of the euro's movement. In contrast, the currencies of emerging economies in Asia generally follow the dollar quite closely.

Thus, while the dollar is still the most important currency as a monetary anchor, the euro has become a viable international competitor to the dollar in its role as a unit of account for central banks. However, some caution in judging the degree of convergence is called for because the depreciation of the dollar since 2002 makes it difficult to separate temporary changes from permanent changes. Have central banks moved away from the dollar as a monetary anchor only until the dollar stabilizes again or has the structure of demand for the currency changed permanently?

As a Store of Value

The critical criterion for a currency to be a good store of value is the ability to maintain real purchasing power over time. That ability will be closely tied to a country pursuing stable and sustainable macroeconomic policies. Although the United States has in recent years consistently maintained vigorous economic growth and relatively low inflation, large current account deficits and the prospect of substantial and, perhaps, disorderly depreciation of the dollar's exchange value may erode the dollar's ability to serve as an international store of value.

Since early 2002, the dollar has fallen in value by about 30% or about 5% per year. That depreciation more or less erases any positive yield on treasury securities held by foreign central banks. The bilateral comparison shows even greater depreciation against certain currencies, with the dollar down 11% against the euro in 2006 alone. The ultra-high liquidity of U.S. asset markets has perhaps provided sufficient advantage to compensate for the eroding effect of the depreciating dollar on the rate of return on dollar assets.

But, because the large scale of worldwide official holding seems to exceed the amount needed for intervention purposes, central banks may begin to focus more on expected rate of return and less on liquidity in managing their holdings. Nominal rates of return have been generally higher on dollar assets than euro assets, however, expected depreciation of the dollar relative to the euro likely erases this advantage. Therefore, with the steady growth in the depth and breadth of euro area asset markets providing investment alternatives to the dollar, there is likely to be a rising incentive for central banks to use a greater share of the more stable euro to meet their store of value objectives.

However, diversification away from the dollar by central banks may be constrained by the need to maintain a balance between the currency composition of their assets and its countries' external liabilities because many countries borrow in dollars. Asset-liability currency balance, particularly for emerging economies, tends to reduce the prospect for balance sheet mismatches in times of crisis and improves the foreign investors evaluation of the country's credit worthiness. Data for emerging market economies for the 2003-2005 period show the dollar's share of external liabilities to be about 66% and its share of reserves assets to be only 59%. In contrast, the euro's share of external liabilities was 24% and share of reserves was 31%. Therefore, by this criterion the dollar is under represented in official reserves and the euro is over represented.

In addition, it is possible to diversify across asset types within a particular currency so as to improve likely risk adjusted returns. There has been an increase in foreign official holdings of U.S. agency bonds, particularly mortgage backed securities issued by Fannie Mae and Freddie Mac, and U.S. corporate bonds, according to the New York Fed. Given the typically conservative investment behavior of most central banks, there is likely only limited scope for this type of diversification.

Conclusion

The dollar's status as the dominant reserve currency may be challenged by the euro because it increasingly offers many of the advantages of the dollar but fewer of the risks.

Nevertheless, the dollar retains significant advantages. The most important advantage is the size, quality, and stability of dollar asset markets, particularly the short-term government securities market where central banks tend to be most active. The high liquidity of these financial markets makes the dollar an excellent medium of exchange for foreign central banks.

A further advantage is the power of "incumbency" conferred by the important "network-externalities" that accrue to the currency that is currently dominant. Together these factors make it unlikely there will be a large or abrupt change in the dollar's reserve currency status.

However, the euro does seem poised to challenge the dollar in the store of value function of a reserve currency. The sheer magnitude of dollar assets in the official reserves of foreign central banks, and the prospect of continued sizable, and perhaps disorderly, depreciation of the dollar against most currencies, places central banks at considerable risk of incurring large capital losses on their dollar asset holding. With more than enough dollar reserves to meet liquidity needs, prudent asset management would seem to dictate some diversification away from the dollar and toward the euro.

Any sizable weakening in the demand for dollar assets by foreign central banks would tend to push down their price and push up U.S. interest rates. This can be expected to have a dampening effect on interest sensitive activities such as business investment, housing, and consumer durables. On the other hand, the selling off of dollar assets would tend to depreciate the dollar's exchange rate and provide a boost to exchange rate sensitive activities of exporting and import-competing industries. From the standpoint of the global economy the efficiency advantages of primarily using dollar reserves may be offset by the enhanced stability of more diversified official holdings.[12]

REFERENCES

[1] International Monetary Fund, *Global Financial Stability Report*, World Economic and Financial Surveys, April 2007, pp. 74-76.

[2] U.S. Department of the Treasury, *Treasury Bulletin* (Washington: April 2007), p. 56.

[3] See CRS Report RL32462, *Foreign Investment in U.S. Securities*, by James K. Jackson.

[4] See CRS Report RS21951, *The U.S. Trade Deficit: Role of Foreign Governments*, Marc Labonte and Gail Makinen.

[5] See Mathew Higgens and Thomas Klitgaard, "Reserve Accumulation: Implications for Global Capital Flows," Federal Reserve Bank of New York, *Current Issues in Economics and Finance*, vol. 10, no. 10, October 2004.

[6] Barry Eichengreen, *Sterling's Past, Dollar's Future: Historical Perspectives on Reserve Currency Competition*, National Bureau of Economic Research, Working Paper no. 11336, April 2005.

[7] See B.J. Cohen, *Life at the Top: International Currencies in the 21st Century*, Princeton Essays in International Finance No. 221 (Princeton: December 2000).

[8] A fuller discussion of these four considerations can be found in Barry Eichengreen and Donald Mathieson, *The Currency Composition of Foreign Exchange Reserves - Retrospect and Prospect*, IMF Working Paper no. 00/131, July 2000.

[9] IMF Statistics Department, COFER database.

[10] This discussion in this section closely follows the analysis in a recent BIS study. See Gabriele Galati and Phillip Woodbridge, *The Euro as a Reserve Currency: The Challenge to the Pre-Eminence of the U.S. Dollar*, Bank for International Settlements, BIS Working Papers no. 218, October 2006.

[11] BIS, Central Bank Survey of Foreign Exchange and Derivatives Markets Activity (Basel: March 2005)

[12] Many economists argue that it would be preferable to have one international currency rather than a national currency playing that role. Special Drawing Rights (SDR) is a currency created by the IMF in 1969 as a substitute for the dollar and gold (or any other national currency) as a reserve currency. It has never assumed a major role in international finance, however.

In: Currency Interventions, Fluctuations...
Editor: L. C. Hilbert, pp. 129-135
ISBN: 978-1-60456-078-7

Chapter 7

CURRENCY MANIPULATION: THE IMF AND WTO*

Jonathan E. Sanford
Specialist in International Political Economy Foreign Affairs,
Defense, and Trade Division

ABSTRACT

The International Monetary Fund (IMF) and World Trade Organization (WTO) approach the issue of currency manipulation differently. The IMF Articles of Agreement prohibit countries from manipulating their currency for the purpose of gaining unfair trade advantage, but the IMF lacks effective means for enforcing that rule. The WTO has rules against export subsidies, but these are very narrow and specific and do not seem to encompass currency manipulation. Several options might be considered for addressing this matter in the future, if policymakers deem this a wise course of action. This report will be updated as conditions require.

This report describes how the International Monetary Fund (IMF) and World Trade Organization (WTO) deal with the issue of currency manipulation. It identifies possible venues for the discussion of currency manipulation. It also discusses apparent discrepancies in their charters and ways those differences might be addressed.

INTERNATIONAL FINANCIAL AND TRADE ORGANIZATIONS

In the realm of international finance and trade, the IMF and WTO are the most prominent and most important multilateral institutions. They are charged with important tasks for keeping world trade and finance flowing freely.

* Excerpted from CRS Report RS22658, dated May 7, 2007.

International Monetary Fund

The IMF is the leading organization in the area of international monetary policy. With the end of the cold war, its membership is now nearly universal. Only North Korea, the Vatican, and four other mini-countries in Europe — none of which have their own currency — are not members of the Fund. The IMF makes loans to countries undergoing financial or balance of payments crises, it provides technical assistance to governments on monetary, banking and exchange rate questions, it does research and analysis on international monetary and economic issues, and it provides a forum where countries can discuss international finance issues and seek common ground on which they can address common problems.

The IMF offers its member countries at least three venues where international economic issues can be discussed. First, the IMF's International Monetary and Finance Committee (IMFC) meets twice annually to review trends in the world economy and identify issues of concern. Second, the IMF Executive Board meets weekly to discuss pending loans and policy issues affecting the Fund. Third, the members of the Fund may meet every five years to discuss whether and by much the financial resources of the IMF should be expanded through a quota increase.

The IMFC operates on a consensus basis and rarely takes formal votes. It is primarily a forum for the exploration of relevant concerns. The chairman's statement, which follows each meeting, summarizes the discussion, outlining the areas of agreement and those where further consultation among the membership is necessary. The report of the IMFC's deliberation serves to guide the Fund's Executive Board and other bodies as they address the issues considered by the IMFC. The IMFC is important because the countries that agree to proposals at those meetings also work later within the international organizations to accomplish those goals. The IMFC can be a good forum for discussing exchange rate issues in a general way, but it is not well suited either to propose changes in exchange rate procedures or to settle disputes between individual countries.

Negotiations about increases in the IMF's resources offer another opportunity where countries can raise policy or organizational issues which concern them. With 16% of the vote, the United States can block the 85% favorable vote necessary to approve any quota increase plan. Other groups of countries can also compile the 15% vote necessary to block agreement. Thus, a broad consensus is necessary for a quota increase to be approved. Generally speaking, these talks are not a good venue for resolving disputes between member countries. The only real leverage that countries have at these meetings is their willingness to withhold their consent to a final agreement. Few countries are likely to be willing to give up a position (the exchange rate value of their currency, for example) that they believe is important to their interests just to get the right to contribute more money and get a few more votes in the IMF.

The IMF Executive Board has the power to approve or deny pending loans and to make changes in the procedures and policies of the IMF. (However, things that require changes in the Articles of Agreement must be referred to the Fund's Board of Governors and approved by 85% of the IMF membership.) The Executive Board has the authority to consider disputes between member countries about interpretation of IMF rules or complaints where one country argues that another is not complying with its obligations under the Articles. If a country does not wish to change its behavior after the Executive Board has ruled against it, the Board has little power — other than the authority to expel the malefactor from membership — to enforce its views. Countries are free to continue the disputed practice, however, after they cease to be a member of the IMF.

The IMF has no authority to tell currency traders what value they should assign to particular currencies as they conduct their commercial operations. Market rates can be affected by decisions that governments make about fiscal or monetary policy or by actions governments take in foreign exchange markets. These actions are often taken with an eye to their impact on exchange markets — and the consequent impact on trade and capital flows — but they are not normally considered to be forms of currency manipulation. The IMF has no authority to tell governments that they should or should not take these actions.

World Trade Organization

The WTO is the central organization in the world trade system. When the WTO was created in 1995, countries were required to accept as a condition of WTO membership the existing set of international trade rules contained in the General Agreement on Tariffs and Trade (GATT), along with obligations that expanded on existing rules and in some cases covered new areas, such as international trade in services and trade-related international property rights.

Unique among the major international trade and finance organizations, the WTO has a rigorous dispute settlement mechanism for enforcing its rules. If a country believes another country has violated the WTO rules, to its detriment, it may request the appointment of a dispute settlement panel to hear its complaint. The other country cannot veto the establishment of a panel or block enforcement of its decision. The panel reviews the arguments in the case and renders judgment based on the facts and WTO rules. If the losing party does not comply with the ruling within a reasonable period of time, the WTO, if requested by the complaining Member, may authorize that Member to impose retaliatory measures (usually customs duties) against that country's goods or to take other appropriate retaliatory measures against that country's trade.

Whether currency issues could fall under the jurisdiction of the WTO remains a debatable proposition. The WTO rules specify that countries may not provide subsidies to help promote their national exports. Most analysts agree that an undervalued currency lowers a firm's cost of production relative to world prices and therefore helps to encourage exports. Under the WTO's strict definition, however, it would be difficult to show that this practice would be an export subsidy.[1]

This is because subsidies are defined, by the WTO, as financial contributions or other income or price support by a government that confers a benefit on the recipient. Export subsidies (i.e., subsidies "contingent on export performance") are expressly prohibited. To challenge a subsidy in the WTO, a subsidy must be specific to an industry; export subsidies, however, are considered specific per se. Government financial support can take a variety of forms, such as direct payments to the exporter, the waiver of tax payments or other revenue that would otherwise be due from the exporter, or special government purchases or the provision of low-cost goods or services (other than general infrastructure) that lowers the cost of production. Even if currency manipulation could be shown to be "financial contribution" or "other income or price support" under WTO rules, it would still have to be shown to be "contingent on export performance," which is likely not the case with respect to the practice at issue.

The guidelines regarding subsidies date from the early days of the current international trade regime. The GATT adopted in 1947 contained a subsidy article (Article XVI); a few changes were made in 1957 and 1962, and an agreement on subsidies was negotiated during the 1973-1979 Tokyo Round of trade negotiations. During most of this period, until the world financial system frayed in the 1970s, the International Monetary Fund exercised strict control over exchange rates. Countries could not change their exchange rates up or down from the level recognized by the IMF by more than 10% without the Fund's consent. Moreover, "A member shall not propose a change in the par value of its currency except to correct fundamental disequilibrium."[2] It was inconceivable during this period that a country could persistently value its currency at a level below that specified by the IMF. Consequently, GATT rules and the trade agreements negotiated during this period did not include any provisions requiring that countries refrain from manipulating their exchange rates for the purpose of stimulating exports. When the IMF's rules were changed in 1978, so that it no longer played its role governing world exchange rates, the GATT's rules were not changed to reflect the new reality of international finance. When the WTO was created in 1995, it adopted the existing GATT rules as its own.

POLICY OPTIONS IN THE MULTILATERAL SPHERE

Though their roles and responsibilities differ, the IMF and WTO were both created to facilitate sound, stable, and orderly growth in world trade for the purpose of enhancing the living standards and the development of the productive capacity of all countries that participate in it. The IMF was created in 1944, among other things, "to facilitate the expansion and balanced growth of international trade and to contribute thereby to the promotion and maintenance of high levels of employment and real employment and to the development of the productive resources of all members as primary objectives of economic policy."[3] The WTO was created in 1995 for a similar purpose. The agreement establishing the WTO also says that the members recognize "that their relations in the field of trade and economic endeavor should be conducted with a view to raising standards of living, ensuring full employment and a steady growing volume of real income and effective demand, and expanding the production of and trade in goods and services" in order to achieve sustainable development, protection and preservation of the environment and to do this in a manner "consistent with their respective needs and concerns at different levels of economic development."[4]

A number of countries have been suspected or accused in recent years of manipulating the value of their currency for the purpose of gaining unfair trade advantage. The IMF Articles of Agreement prohibit this sort of behavior, but the Fund has no capacity to enforce that prohibition. By contrast, the WTO has the capacity to adjudicate trade disputes, but to date there has not been a dispute settlement ruling or other WTO decision making clear that the WTO has responsibility or authority to address suspected issues of currency manipulation. In other words, the IMF's Article IV prohibits currency manipulation for the purpose of gaining unfair trade advantage, but it cannot stop it. WTO dispute settlement could be used as a vehicle to deter countries from engaging in impermissible trade practices, but it is far from clear that currency manipulation would be considered to be a subsidy and that the trade it generates would thus be considered to be unfairly subsidized. Should policymakers wish to address this situation, several options (discussed below) might be considered.

Amend the Articles of the IMF

One option for proponents of steps to address the issue of currency manipulation might be changes in the IMF's Articles of Agreement that would give it more authority over the international exchange rate system and more capacity to require country compliance with IMF rules. This would restore, to some degree, a large measure of the authority over exchange rates that the IMF possessed when it first came into being in 1946. Two objections might be raised, however.

First, an 85% majority vote of the IMF member countries would be required for any change in the IMF Articles of Agreement. Most countries seem to believe that the present system of floating and fixed exchange rates is working reasonably well, despite concerns about possible currency manipulation by some countries. There does not appear to be the kind of broad agreement on the need for changes — and agreement as to what those changes should be — that would be necessary to amend the IMF's basic rules.

Second, few countries want the IMF to have the kinds of power over their economies that it would need if it were able to compel countries to comply with its rules. For example, if the IMF had the power to declare China's currency to be undervalued and to require changes, it would also have a corresponding power to declare the U.S. dollar or the Euro to be overvalued and to require the United States or the Euro zone countries to make changes in their domestic policies sufficient to correct that situation.

Amend the WTO Agreements

Another possibility might be a formal change in the WTO agreements to give WTO Members an effective way to address currency manipulation with the intent or effect of gaining unfair advantages in world trade. Most effective in discouraging the practice would seem to be a change or clarification in the WTO definition of "subsidy" so that currency undervaluation constituted a subsidy and thus undervaluation that was contingent on export performance would be prohibited, just as direct payments to exporters are prohibited today. To preserve the prerogatives of the IMF, the WTO would likely need to ask the Fund's executive board to determine whether a currency is being manipulated before disputes based on that allegation could be considered by a dispute settlement panel.

It would not be easy to amend WTO agreements, however, because the amendment process is complex and in practice the unanimous consent of all WTO Members would likely be needed. Countries with undervalued currencies could easily block the adoption of the amendment. However, they would have to act in public, and they would have to argue in effect that Article IV should not be mandatory as far as their trade is concerned. It is not very likely that an amendment could be adopted by this means. Most likely, a change of this sort in WTO agreements would occur through multilateral trade negotiations, during which the

United States and like-minded countries would trade this change for some other change desired by countries with the other point of view.

Improve the IMF-WTO Agreement

An alternative approach might be efforts to strengthen the existing interagency agreement between the WTO and the IMF. The present agreement was signed in 1996 and updated in mid-2006. Among other things, it stipulates (paragraph 1) that the two organizations "shall cooperate in the discharge of their respective mandates."[5] It says (paragraph 2) the two agencies "shall consult with each other with a view to achieving greater coherence in global economic policymaking." It also says (pargraph 8) that the two agencies shall communicate with each other about "matters of mutual interest."

It is unreasonable to expect that one international organization will enforce the rules of another international organization. This is particularly the case if the one body lacks the capacity to enforce its own rules and if the activities in question are not violations of the other body's rules. On the other hand, it is reasonable to think that one might advise the other that its operations were hindering the first "in the discharge of" its assigned duties. The WTO's and IMF's different approaches to the question of exchange rate manipulation do not seem to be steps toward "greater coherence in global economic policymaking." This would seem to be the kind of situation for which a communication about "matters of mutual interest" might be appropriate. As best as can be determined, the IMF has not formally communicated views on this matter to the appropriate authorities of the WTO.

Amendments to the IMF-WTO interagency agreement might help clarify or perhaps ameliorate the situation. Any member country government may propose that changes be made in an existing agreement or that the decision-making bodies of the two organizations consider adopting new interagency agreements. The IMF's Executive Board and the WTO's Ministerial Conference and Governing Council can make ordinary decisions by majority vote. This seems to include approval of compacts with other international bodies. Neither may use such agreements to amend their basic rules or to fundamentally change their operating procedures in violation of their respective charters.

Currently, it is difficult for one WTO member country to protect itself from unfair trade from another country if that trade is generated by currency manipulation rather than by the kinds of direct subsidies prohibited by the WTO. In this case, the country that manipulates its currency in order to expand unfairly its international trade could complain that another country was violating the rules of the WTO if it took steps to protect itself from the unfair trade generated by the complaining country's currency maneuvers, for example, by placing tariff surcharges on the complaining country's imports.

There may be grounds for improving WTO-IMF collaboration in this respect. No agreement between them can change their basic rules. However, they could agree that their disparate treatment of currency manipulation is anomalous and inconsistent with their promise to "cooperate in the discharge of their respective mandates" and to promote "greater coherence in global economic policymaking." They could agree to work together to identify and to mitigate areas where their rules and procedures were not consistent or not mutually supportive and to identify areas where policy or institutional changes might be needed if their Members wish to address this problem. They could also agree that the WTO should ask the

IMF to determine whether a country were manipulating its currency for the purpose of preventing adjustment or gaining unfair trade advantage if the issue arises in the WTO. No such requirement currently exists.

REFERENCES

[1] Agreement on Subsidies and Countervailing Duties, Articles 1 to 3.

[2] This language is quoted from Section 5 of the original language of Article IV as approved by the 1944 Bretton Woods conference and confirmed by all member countries when the IMF officially came into existence in 1946.

[3] Articles of Agreement of the IMF, Article I. Six purposes for the establishment of the IMF are cited. This is the second.

[4] Agreement Establishing the World Trade Organization, 1995, preamble.

[5] Agreement Between the International Monetary Fund and the World Trade Organization, updated June 30, 2006. See [http://www.imf.org/external/pubs/ft/sd/index.asp?decision=DN26].

In: Currency Interventions, Fluctuations...
Editor: L. C. Hilbert, pp. 137-143
ISBN: 978-1-60456-078-7

Chapter 8

CHINA'S CURRENCY: A SUMMARY OF THE ECONOMIC ISSUES*

***Wayne M. Morrison*[1] *and Marc Labonte*[2]**
[1] Foreign Affairs, Defense, and Trade Division
[2] Government and Finance Division

ABSTRACT

Many Members of Congress charge that China's policy of accumulating foreign reserves (especially U.S. dollars) to influence the value of its currency constitutes a form of currency manipulation intended to make its exports cheaper and imports into China more expensive than they would be under free market conditions. They further contend that this policy has caused a surge in the U.S. trade deficit with China and has been a major factor in the loss of U.S. manufacturing jobs. Threats of possible congressional action led China to make changes to its currency policy in 2005, which has since resulted in a modest appreciation of the yuan. However, many Members have expressed dissatisfaction with the pace of China's currency reforms and have warned of potential legislative action. This report summarizes the main findings CRS Report RL32165, *China's Currency: Economic Issues and Options for U.S. Trade Policy*, by Wayne M. Morrison and Marc Labonte and will be updated as events warrant.

From 1994 until July 21, 2005, China maintained a policy of pegging its currency (the renminbi or yuan), to the U.S. dollar at an exchange rate of roughly 8.28 yuan to the dollar. The Chinese central bank maintained this peg by buying (or selling) as many dollar-denominated assets in exchange for newly printed yuan as needed to eliminate excess demand (supply) for the yuan. As a result, the exchange rate between the yuan and the dollar basically stayed the same, despite changing economic factors which could have otherwise caused the yuan to either appreciate or depreciate relative to the dollar. Under a floating exchange rate system, the relative demand for the two countries' goods and assets would determine the exchange rate of the yuan to the dollar. Many economists contend that for the first several years of the peg, the fixed value was likely close to the market value. But in the past few years, economic conditions have changed such that the yuan would likely have appreciated if it had been floating. The sharp increase in China's

* Excerpted from CRS Report RS21625, dated July 11, 2007

foreign exchange reserves (which grew from $403 billion at the end of 2003 to $1.2 trillion at the end of March 2007) and China's large merchandise trade surplus (which totaled $178 billion in 2006) are indicators that the yuan is significantly undervalued.

China Reforms the Peg

The Chinese government modified its currency policy on July 21, 2005. It announced that the yuan's exchange rate would become "adjustable, based on market supply and demand with reference to exchange rate movements of currencies in a basket," (it was later announced that the composition of the basket includes the dollar, the yen, the euro, and a few other currencies), and that the exchange rate of the U.S. dollar against the yuan would be immediately adjusted from 8.28 to 8.11, an appreciation of about 2.1%. Unlike a true floating exchange rate, the yuan would (according to the Chinese government) be allowed to fluctuate by 0.3% on a daily basis against the basket.[1] Since July 2005, China has allowed the yuan to appreciate steadily but very slowly. It has continued to accumulate foreign reserves at a rapid pace, which suggests that if the yuan were allowed to freely float it would appreciate much more rapidly. The current situation might be best described as a "managed float" — market forces are determining the general direction of the yuan's movement, but the government is retarding its rate of appreciation through market intervention.

U.S. Concerns over China's Currency Policy

Many U.S. policymakers and business and labor representatives have charged that China's currency is significantly undervalued vis-à-vis the U.S. dollar (even after the recent revaluation), making Chinese exports to the United States cheaper, and U.S. exports to China more expensive, than they would be if exchange rates were determined by market forces. They further argue that the undervalued currency has contributed to the burgeoning U.S. trade deficit with China (which hit $233 billion in 2006) and has hurt U.S. production and employment in several U.S. manufacturing sectors that are forced to compete domestically and internationally against "artificially" low-cost goods from China. Furthermore, some analysts contend that China's currency policy induces other East Asian countries to intervene in currency markets in order to keep their currencies weak against the dollar in order to compete with Chinese goods. Critics contend that, while it may have been appropriate for China during the early stages of its economic development to maintain a pegged currency, it should let the yuan freely float today, given the size of the Chinese economy and the impact its policies have on the world economy.

China's Concerns over Modifying Its Currency Policy

Chinese officials argue that its currency policy is not meant to favor exports over imports, but instead to foster economic stability through currency stability, as many other countries do. They have expressed concern that floating its currency could spark an economic crisis in

China and would especially be damaging to its export industries at a time when painful economic reforms (such as closing down inefficient state-owned enterprises) are being implemented. They further contend that the Chinese banking system is too underdeveloped and burdened with heavy debt to be able to deal effectively with possible speculative pressures that could occur with a fully convertible currency. Concerns have also been raised over the effects an appreciating yuan would have on farmers (due to lower-priced imports). Chinese officials view economic stability as critical to sustaining political stability; they fear an appreciated currency could reduce employment and lower incomes in various sectors, and thus could cause worker unrest. However, Chinese officials have indicated that their long-term goal is to adopt a more flexible exchange rate system and to seek more balanced economic growth through increased domestic consumption and the development of rural areas, but they want to proceed at a gradual pace to ensure economic stability.

Implications of China's Currency Policy for Its Economy

If the yuan is undervalued vis-a-vis the dollar (estimates rage from 15 to 40% or higher), then Chinese exports to the United States are likely cheaper than they would be if the currency were freely traded, providing a boost to China's export industries (and, to some degree, an indirect subsidy). Eliminating exchange rate risk through a managed peg also increases the attractiveness of China as a destination for foreign investment in export-oriented production facilities. However, an undervalued currency makes imports more expensive, hurting Chinese consumers and Chinese firms that import parts, machinery, and raw materials. Such a policy, in effect, benefits Chinese exporting firms (many of which are owned by foreign multinational corporations) at the expense of non-exporting Chinese firms, especially those that rely on imported goods. This may impede the most efficient allocation of resources in the Chinese economy. Another major problem is that the Chinese government must expand the money supply in order to keep purchasing dollars, which has promoted the banks to adopt easy credit policies. In addition, "hot money" has poured into China from investors speculating that China will continue to appreciate the yuan. At some point, these factors could help fuel inflation, overinvestment in various sectors, and expansion of nonperforming loans by the banks — each of which could threaten future economic growth.

Implications of China's Currency Policy for the U.S. Economy

Effect on Exporters and Import-Competitors

When exchange rate policy causes the yuan to be less expensive than it would be if it were determined by supply and demand, it causes Chinese exports to be relatively inexpensive and U.S. exports to China to be relatively expensive. As a result, U.S. exports and the production of U.S. goods and services that compete with Chinese imports fall, in the short run. (Many of the affected firms are in the manufacturing sector.)[2] This causes the trade deficit to rise and reduces aggregate demand in the short run, all else equal.[3]

Effect on U.S. Consumers and Certain Producers

A society's economic well-being is usually measured not by how much it can produce, but how much it can consume. An undervalued yuan that lowers the price of imports from China allows the United States to increase its consumption through an improvement in the terms-of-trade. Since changes in aggregate spending are only temporary, from a long-term perspective the lasting effect of an undervalued yuan is to increase the purchasing power of U.S. consumers. Imports from China are not limited to consumption goods. U.S. producers also import capital equipment and inputs to final products from China. An undervalued yuan lowers the price of these U.S. products, increasing their output.

Effect on U.S. Borrowers

An undervalued yuan also has an effect on U.S. borrowers. When the U.S. runs a current account deficit with China, an equivalent amount of capital flows from China to the United States, as can be seen in the U.S. balance of payments accounts. This occurs because the Chinese central bank or private Chinese citizens are investing in U.S. assets, which allows more U.S. capital investment in plant and equipment to take place than would otherwise occur. Capital investment increases because the greater demand for U.S. assets puts downward pressure on U.S. interest rates, and firms are now willing to make investments that were previously unprofitable. This increases aggregate spending in the short run, all else equal, and also increases the size of the economy in the long run by increasing the capital stock.

Private firms are not the only beneficiaries of the lower interest rates caused by the capital inflow (trade deficit) from China. Interest-sensitive household spending, on goods such as consumer durables and housing, is also higher than it would be if capital from China did not flow into the United States. In addition, a large proportion of the U.S. assets bought by the Chinese, particularly by the central bank, are U.S. Treasury securities, which fund U.S. federal budget deficits. According to the U.S. Treasury Department, China (as of April 2007) held $414 billion in U.S. Treasury securities, making China the second largest foreign holder of such securities, after Japan. If the U.S. trade deficit with China were eliminated, Chinese capital would no longer flow into this country on net, and the government would have to find other buyers of U.S. Treasuries. This would likely increase the government's interest payments.

Net Effect on the U.S. Economy

In the medium run, an undervalued yuan neither increases nor decreases aggregate demand in the United States. Rather, it leads to a compositional shift in U.S. production, away from U.S. exporters and import-competing firms toward the firms that benefit from Chinese capital flows. Thus, it is expected to have no medium or long run effect on aggregate U.S. employment or unemployment. As evidence, one can consider that the U.S. had a historically large and growing trade deficit throughout the 1990s at a time when unemployment reached a three-decade low. However, the gains and losses in employment and production caused by the trade deficit will not be dispersed evenly across regions and sectors of the economy: on balance, some areas will gain while others will lose. And by shifting the composition of U.S. output to a higher capital base, the size of the economy would be larger in the long run as a result of the capital inflow/trade deficit.

Although the compositional shift in output has no negative effect on aggregate U.S. output and employment in the long run, there may be adverse short-run consequences. If output in the trade sector falls more quickly than the output of U.S. recipients of Chinese capital rises, aggregate spending and employment could temporarily fall. This is more likely to be a concern if the economy is already sluggish than if it is at full employment. Otherwise, it is likely that government macroeconomic policy adjustment and market forces can quickly compensate for any decline of output in the trade sector by expanding other elements of aggregate demand. The deficit with China has not prevented the U.S. economy from registering high rates of growth since 2003.

The U.S.-China Trade Deficit in the Context of the Overall U.S. Trade Deficit

While China is a large trading partner, it accounted for only 15.4% of U.S. merchandise imports in 2006 and 26% of the sum of all U.S. bilateral trade deficits. Over a span of several years, a country with a floating exchange rate can consistently run an overall trade deficit for only one reason: a domestic imbalance between saving and investment. Over the past two decades, U.S. saving as a share of gross domestic product (GDP) has been in gradual decline. On the one hand, the U.S. has high rates of productivity growth and strong economic fundamentals that are conducive to high rates of capital investment. On the other hand, it has a chronically low household saving rate, and recently a negative government saving rate as a result of the budget deficit. As long as Americans save little, foreigners will use their saving to finance profitable investment opportunities in the United States; the trade deficit is the result.[4] The returns to foreign-owned capital will flow to foreigners instead of Americans, but the returns to U.S. labor utilizing foreign-owned capital will flow to U.S. labor.[5]

Chinese statistics indicated that more than half of its exports to the world are produced by foreign-invested firms in China, many of which have shifted production to China in order to gain access to low-cost labor. (The returns to capital of U.S. owned firms in China flow to Americans.) Such firms import raw materials and components (much of which come from East Asia) for assembly in China. As a result, China tends to run trade deficits with East Asian countries and trade surpluses with countries with high consumer demand, such as the United States. Overall, in 2006, China had a $55 billion trade deficit with the world excluding the United States. These factors imply that much of the increase in U.S. imports (and hence, the rising trade deficit with China) is largely the result of China becoming a production platform for many foreign companies, rather than unfair Chinese trade policies.

Most Recent Events

In September 2006, President Bush and President Hu agreed to establish a Strategic Economic Dialogue (SED) in order to have discussions on major economic issues at the "highest official level." China's currency policy was a major topic during the first SED meeting held in December 2006 and the second meeting held in May 2007. The two sides agreed to work to reduce global imbalances through increased savings in the United States and increased domestic consumption and exchange rate flexibility in China. However, China refused to agree to any new major changes to its currency policy. From July 21, 2005 to June 11, 2007, the dollar-yuan exchange rate went from 8.11 to 7.57, an appreciation of about 6.7%.

Congressional Legislation

Many Members contend that the pace of China's currency reforms and level of the yuan's appreciation against the dollar have been too slow, and some have introduced legislation to put further pressure on the Chinese to speed reforms or to enable U.S. producers to use U.S. trade law to address the impact of China's undervalued currency. Summaries of major provisions of these bills are listed below:

- H.R. 321 (English) would increase tariffs on imported Chinese goods if the Treasury Department determined that China manipulated its currency, and would require the United States to file a WTO case against China over its currency policy and to work within the WTO to modify and clarify rules regarding currency manipulation. H.R. 1002 (Spratt) would impose 27.5% in additional tariffs on Chinese goods unless the President certifies that China is no longer manipulating its currency.
- S. 364 (Rockefeller) would apply U.S. countervailing laws (dealing with government subsidies) to products imported from non-market economies (such as China), and would make currency manipulation actionable under this measure. H.R. 782 (Tim Ryan) and S. 796 (Bunning) would make exchange rate "misalignment" actionable under U.S. countervailing duty laws, require the Treasury Department to determine whether a currency is misaligned in its semi-annual reports to Congress on exchange rates, prohibit the Department of Defense from purchasing certain products imported from China if it is determined that China's currency misalignment has disrupted U.S. defense industries, and would include currency misalignment as a factor in determining safeguard measures on imports of Chinese products that cause market disruption.
- H.R. 2942 (Tim Ryan) would apply countervailing laws to nonmarket economies, make an undervalued currency a factor in determining antidumping duties, require Treasury to identify fundamentally misaligned currencies and to list those meeting the criteria for priority action. If consultations fail to resolve the currency issues, the USTR would be required to take action in the WTO.
- S. 1607 (Baucus) would require the Treasury Department to identify currencies that are fundamentally misaligned and to designate such currencies for "priority action" under certain circumstances. Such action would include factoring currency undervaluation in U.S. anti-dumping cases, banning federal procurement of products or services from the designated country, and filing a case against in the WTO. S. 1677 (Dodd) requires the Treasury Department to identify countries that manipulate

their currencies regardless of their intent and to submit an action plan for ending the manipulation, and gives Treasury the authority to file a case in the WTO.

REFERENCES

[1] On May 15, 2007, the Chinese government increased the daily band to 0.5%.

[2] U.S. production has moved away from manufacturing and toward the service sector over the past several years. U.S. employment in manufacturing as a share of total nonagricultural employment fell from 31.8% in 1960, to 22.4% in 1980, to 10.4% in December 2006. This trend is much larger than the Chinese currency issue, and is caused by changing technology (which requires fewer workers to produce the same number of goods) and comparative advantage.

[3] Putting exchange rate issues aside, most economists maintain that trade is a win-win situation for the economy as a whole, but produces losers within the economy. Economists generally argue that free trade should be pursued because the gains from trade are large enough that the losers from trade can be compensated by the winners, and the winners will still be better off.

[4] Most economists believe that the United States runs a trade deficit because it fails to save enough to meet its investment needs and must obtain savings from other countries with high savings rates. By obtaining foreign investment (in effect, borrowing), the United States can consume more (including more imports) than it would if investment were funded by domestic savings alone — this results in a trade deficit.

[5] China on the other hand has one of the world's largest savings rate. U.S. officials have urged China to take steps to boost domestic consumption (and hence increase imports).

INDEX

A

B

C

F

G

H

P

Q

R

S

W

Y